Mechademia : Second Arc

Mechademia (ISSN 1934-2489) is published twice a year in the summer and winter by the University of Minnesota Press, 111 Third Avenue South, Suite 290, Minneapolis, MN 55401-2520. http://www.upress.umn.edu

Postmaster: Send address changes to Mechademia, University of Minnesota Press, 111 Third Avenue South, Suite 290, Minneapolis, MN 55401-2520.

All submissions must be between 5000-7000 words. Essays that are substantially longer cannot be accepted. Citations should be given in Chicago Manual of Style 17th ed. using bibliographic endnotes rather than footnotes or in-text citations. Please see the Mechademia Style Guide (see PDF on mechademia.net) for more details on citation style and essay formatting. Submissions and editorial queries should be sent to submissions@mechademia.net.

Books for review should be addressed to

Forrest Greenwood
Indiana University Innovation Center
2719 E 10th St
Bloomington, IN 47408

Brian White
#101 Etosu O2, 26-14
Edogawa-ku, Shinozaki-machi 4-chome
Tokyo
Japan

Address subscription orders, changes of address, and business correspondence (including requests for permission and advertising orders) to Mechademia, University of Minnesota Press, 111 Third Avenue South, Suite 290, Minneapolis, MN 55401-2520.

Subscriptions: For our current subscription rates please see our website: http://www.upress.umn.edu. Digital Subscriptions for Mechademia are now available through the Project MUSE Journals Collections at https://muse.jhu.edu.

Mechademia : Second Arc

VOLUME 16, NO. 1
WINTER 2023

MEDIA MIX

Platforms, Characters, and Worlds

Terms, Histories, and Methods

Introducing the Media Mix

MARC STEINBERG

"Media mix" names the Japanese and transnational practice of creating, marketing, circulating and engaging with cultural goods serially across media types—from games and light novels to manga and anime to toys, foodstuffs and much else. In some accounts it designates something like transmedia storytelling; in others it names an ecology of practices and relations between media forms; in yet others it names the queer potentialities or community-forming properties of fan-based practices around cross-media serializations.

It is a term, a series of often lucrative media and licensing practices, and an epistemology implied by the term and formed in practice.[1] It is a set of models for how to *do* media business; how to organize media production and distribution; how to merchandise products; how to think about media conglomeration and its effects, even. It is well-worn pathways reused time and again; but it is also occasionally new experiments with emergent media forms (not to be confused, however, with "mixed media" art—a single artwork composed of different mediums). It has various histories or ways of historicizing, depending on what aspects one highlights and what story one wants to tell. The media mix is also the body of theories and theoretical works that are associated with these histories. It is a cast of characters: real life figures in the form of industry leaders or day-to-day practitioners; but also fictional characters and the media mixes built around them. It is likewise a set of techniques developed by the media industry over the past decades—the past century according to some. On a granular level it is the advertisement on a manga cover or in a train announcing the soon-to-be-released anime version of the manga and the coming media mix around it. On a macro level and in an academic context it is also a call for distinct fields of study to intersect—from medium-specific fields like animation studies to game studies to toy studies; to fields like industry studies or platform studies; and the object of various methodologies from ethnography to textual reading to historical or archival research. Media mix practices are embedded in the very term *contents* in Japan and Korea, the plural form of content that designates IP-dependent media mixes.[2] It is a field of open possibilities as much as it is entrenched commercial transactions.

This volume of *Mechademia: Second Arc* features articles that offer exciting new paths forward in media mix research. They shed new light on the media mix as practice, as theory, or as history—and quite brilliantly take media mix research in new directions. Building on the work of the past two decades on the topic, but also bringing in other distinct fields from game studies to platform studies and media historical research informed by decolonial and feminist perspectives, this special issue features exciting new work, emerging scholars, and novel interventions. The media mix itself continues not only to persist but to adapt and change; so too should scholarship. This special issue showcases cutting-edge work in the field, taking the topic in new directions that will, I hope, in turn inspire further work.

In this introduction I offer a brief and necessarily limited mapping of existing work on the topic, some significant new directions of research, and a summary of the contributions made in this volume. I take the liberty of offering extensive citations since bibliographies are sometimes the best place to learn about the richness of a field of study—with the caveat that even these are too limited to cover all the work produced and focus almost entirely on English language materials.

Media Mix Then and Now

This special issue comes out 11 years after the 2012 publication of my *Anime's Media Mix* (perhaps the first book dedicated to the topic); 14 years after Thomas Lamarre's 2009 book *The Anime Machine* that offers some crucial insights on the media mix and Tanaka Emi's 2009 media mix theorization; 17 years after Anne Allison's *Millennial Monsters*, which tracked Pokémon media mixes; two decades since Mizuko Ito's early 2000s work on the media mix and play (the first English-language work on the topic), and Azuma Hiroki's theories of otaku consumption; and more than three decades since Ōtsuka Eiji's theory of narrative consumption (1989), which has become one of the frequent reference points for media mix theory—though he does not use the term.[3] Prior work in children's literature and marketing in Japan of the 1950s and '60s equally paved the way for this research. As for the term itself? The term media mix / *media mikkusu* was first widely adopted to describe the serial franchising of media in Japan in the mid- to late-1980s. Before that there were other terms in use (including the odd but quite materialist "three-dimensionalization of mass communication" [*masukomi no rittaikai*] coined by Kan Tadamichi in the late 1950s), none sticking the way media mix did.[4]

Over the past decade there has been a wealth of research, books, articles, and analyses of the media mix, some tracing it back to Japan's wartime propaganda (Ōtsuka in particular has been at the forefront of this, in both his own work and edited work, bringing new generations of scholars to trace media mix histories to the wartime propaganda machine), others, like Sandra Annett, moving it into considerations of transcultural fandoms.[5] If my 2012 book anchored it around anime, Alexander Zahlten's work on the 1980s popular films and Kadokawa in particular and Rayna Denison's work on adaptation and more recently Ghibli production studies have been two particular sites for the close consideration of the media mix in relation to cinema.[6] Jason Karlin and Patrick Galbraith's edited volumes have put the concept to work in idol studies and in relation to the media convergence discourse more popular in North America.[7] Work in game studies since the mid-2010s has been suggesting (convincingly) the need to port the concept to game studies, from a 2015 special issue of *Kinephanos* edited by Martin Picard and Jérémie Pelletier-Gagnon, to the 2019 DiGRA conference on "Game, Play and the Emerging Ludo-Mix," to recent work by Dorothy Finan and Joleen Blom showing the productive work that can be done at this intersection.[8] Complex historical and theoretical questions have been raised about the very term media mix—what epistemologies of mixing it presumes, and whether it assumes there are media that pre-exist the mix.[9] Kathryn Hemmann has asked how to queer the media mix.[10] Akiko Sugawa and Edmond Ernest dit Alban have been advocating for a fuller consideration of women's media mixes, particular in urban environments, taking the media mix to the streets, asking how and where and in what embodied forms the media mix is lived.[11] And this overview only scratches the surface, as it does not include most of the incredible Japanese-language scholarship that has also blossomed over the past decade in particular. It also does not include the parallel fields of media franchising and transmedia that tend to focus on the US as its object of study—though as the work of Derek Johnson, Henry Jenkins, and others acknowledges, many of these works also have transpacific connections.[12] Stevie Suan's work to decenter Japan in studies of anime given its transnational production circuits could equally and effectively be taken up to focus on the inter-Asian networks of the media mix.[13] Work on boys love by scholars such as James Welker and Thomas Baudinette does just this; as does Jinying Li's writing in this issue and elsewhere.[14]

In brief, it is a good moment to revisit the media mix as a topic. What are the limits of the area as sketched and defined, where can it be pushed further, and what potentials does it have either as framing series of questions or as a springboard for cross disciplinary conversations? I open this review of literature with my own book because, for better or worse, it sometimes too narrowly set the parameters of research (around anime) or the historical lineage (post-1960s)— parameters I'm delighted to see articles in this volume challenge, destabilize, and quite profoundly transform. I am particularly thrilled to present the work in this volume since much of it features newer voices in the field, suggesting bright futures for the topic—and for Asian media studies more broadly. In addition to article-long research pieces I also solicited shorter "provocations" from a few leading voices in this field of research. Many of these articles ask crucial questions about what has been excluded from media mix research so far, or what existing research might contribute to other fields. From women's pro-wrestling to Instagram use as an extension and transformation of the print club; from the structuring role patriarchy has in pre-school media mixes to the impasses of nation-based media mix (versus transmedia) research; to the importance of considering bodies in space as key components of this research— what is included here stretches the existing contours of media mix research. Indeed, the works included here do precisely what I'd dreamed they would: expand the medium locus, gender, and time period of media mix analyses from the present, often anime-centric and presentist work, to other media, women theorists, and historically sophisticated interventions. This is certainly more than I could have hoped for in preparing the call for papers for this volume.

I suggest here, from my own perspective, some further issues for media mix or media mix-adjacent research to grapple with. The first, raised by Kimberly Hassell here, as well as in my own recent work and that of Aurélie Petit, is the relation of the media mix to platform studies and internet studies, increasingly significant (and expanding) fields of research.[15] Petit in particular explores the uglier side of anime fandom and its links with the alt-right and what she terms gender-exclusionary practices. This draws on larger questions about logics of exclusion (or alternatively what Tressie McMillan Cottom terms "predatory inclusion"[16]) on or around the Internet that upholds forms of patriarchy and white supremacy—including the complex manifestations of both in Asia and Asian studies.[17] The second is to create more fulsome conversations with adjacent fields of research such as production studies (as advocated here and elsewhere by Hartzheim), Japanese industry studies and streaming video (notably by Shinji Oyama and Yoko Nishioka), and game studies (notably Blom and Ernest dit Alban in this issue).[18] This work points to the wider industrial context for the media mix, including questions about how the shift to streaming—whether on Netflix, Crunchyroll, or bilibili—affects everything from animation production to geographies of circulation to how much the media mix remains a component of anime in the streaming context. Third, expanding the geographies of media mix analysis seems crucial too; Chinese technology giant Tencent's investment in content production and Korean tech giant Kakao's embrace of webtoons are both media mix-adjacent practices of tech-content conglomeration. Such a geographical expansion would require a reckoning with emergent formations of media power with inter-Asian regional specificities that deserve both further analysis and critique. Fourth, much can be learned from the material and elemental turns of media studies, whether via the turn to a logistical media studies, which draws attention to how media circulate in the world, or via the elemental approach to media, which asks us to consider the infrastructures, machines, and environments that make mediation possible.[19]

Finally, I continue to think—along with Seuffert's article in this volume on women's wrestling and Nan's on Imperial-era idol media mixes—about all the other non-anime/manga/game fields in which the media mix might offer a useful framework for deeply researched media historical analysis. What fields are we not paying attention to just because media mix research has historically been anchored around the study of anime-related media? Even as I continue to believe in the importance of research around "anime's media mix" I equally believe we must expand research beyond it—as so many of the contributions here so eloquently do.

Brief Overview of Articles in This Issue

This issue opens with four shorter provocations meant to suggest new pathways for research around the media mix or ask key questions relevant to its study. In the first, Bryan Hikari Hartzheim offers an overview of research on the media mix while also making a plea for an embrace of production studies approaches, reminding us that "the study of media mix is also the study of people." In his piece he focuses our attention on four crucial areas for media mix production research.

In the second intervention, Alexander Zahlten asks a key question: how do we *sense* the media mix? If the media mix is a system of connections between media, how is it we can make sense of—and research—the media mix in its totality? To frame this question he engages past work on the topic, draws on systems theory—uniquely suited to offer insights into how to study large scale systems like the media mix—and suggests pathways forward. Building on these methodological questions, Jinying Li focuses our attention on so-called *danmaku* or *danmu* in the Chinese context, the "bullet curtain" comments that float over the video image in platforms like bilibili or Niconico Video. The indistinctness between content and system that Zahlten highlights is here further developed by Li who argues that we need to *"rethink media formations as force fields."*

In the fourth provocation, Akiko Sugawa-Shimada focuses our attention on the relation between media mix and 2.5D productions, highlighting the fandoms associated with the media mix in particular. The research she and her associates have been doing in this area is significant (and an earlier issue of *Mechademia* is dedicated to introducing them).[20] Here she emphasizes how the media mix is "dynamized" through and by fan activities.

Three sections follow, with the topics bleeding one into the other. Opening the "Gender, Politics, and Power" section, Kirsten Seuffert directs us to the media landscape of women's professional wrestling in the 1970s and 1980s, a moment when women wrestlers crossed over to idol singers, and brought a distinct form of corporeality to the media mix. Contra analyses of the media mix that focus on the immateriality of the character, Seuffert shows how different media ecologies require attention to different kinds of materiality and corporeality. This article offers a close, deeply engaging account of spaces previously outside the purview of media mix analysis. It is a model article that offers both new empirical research and theoretical engagement with the media mix concept—and in doing so sets the tone for the rest of this volume. Gender and idols equally inform Nan Mei Mingxue's article "Imperial Media Mix." Moving back in time and asking questions about historization, Nan focuses on distinct media mix strategies during the wartime period, differentiating two notable models of the "imperial media mix" at work. This contributes to idol studies in resituating the history of idol groups to the wartime era—and showing the complex work of these groups to at once ideologically integrate their listeners as Imperial subjects (the goal of Japanese Empire) and make a profit (the goal of recording companies). Akiko Sano's consideration of "Anpanman and Patriarchy: Media Mix for Preschool Children in Japan" extends Nan's pairing of Empire and commerce to account for the intersection between capitalism and patriarchy that the Anpanman media mix represents.

Preschool media mixes function, Sano argues, as necessary, *infrastructural* parts of childcare for mothers expected to take on the sole duty of caring for their children. As such she focuses on the social function of the media mix. Beyond its expressive potentials the media mix functions within the current crisis of care as a means of getting by for mothers who often work and bear the duties of childcare at the same time. It is a sobering portrait indeed, and one that resituates media mix from entertainment to survival mechanism.

Opening the "Platforms, Characters, and Worlds" section, Kimberly Hassel continues this focus on gender and women's practices. In "The World as Photo Booth" Hassel combines media mix studies with platform studies to offer a longer history of Instagram practices of making the world a photobooth by taking this practice back to "purikura." This fresh take on photo-sharing apps and Instagram pushes girls' practices to the forefront of media mix research, and equally demands that Silicon's Valley's story of platforms not be the only one told. Joleen Blom's "The *Genshin Impact* Media Mix" picks up this emphasis on platform studies, here focusing on one free-to-play game to demonstrate the wider stakes of asking the fields of game studies and media mix studies to intersect—and together better account for a regional approach to the "platformization of cultural production."[21] Building on some existing work in this regard, Blom shows how the character analysis offered by media mix research could benefit game studies, while game studies' focus on mechanics, play, and monetization systems could help nuance media mix research. Both lead to larger responses to the need to analyze the "platformization of cultural production" in context-specific ways. Paul Ocone's "Contents Tourism, the Media Mix, and Setting Moé" resonates with Hassel's article in asking media mix research to consider more seriously the issue of space—of the media mix as a world. Offering a typology of several modes of fan relationships to actual space, Ocone's article asks us to consider "setting moé," where the setting (rather than characters) lead to fan pilgrimages around particular media mixes. Olga Kopylova closes this section by offering an analysis of power relations in the production of media mixes, focusing on the distinct roles taken by character designers and animators in creating (or disrupting) the homogeneity of the character image. This attention to production studies nicely echoes Hartzheim's call to better integrate production studies into research on the media mix.

The final section, "Terms, Histories and Methods" features debates around terminology and history to ask wider questions about the political consequences of method. In so doing these works implicitly build on many previous articles in this issue that challenge method (Zahlten, Seuffert, Blom, Hassel), historical trajectory (Nan), or terminology (Li, Sano, Ocone). Ōtsuka Eiji opens this section by challenging my periodization of the media mix to the 1960s, making a convincing case that the media mix must be traced back to wartime Japan and government-led media efforts. This also addresses the social function of the media mix in a manner that emphasizes Sano's point that the media mix ultimately functions as a support of patriarchy—albeit here as a support of Empire. Continuing on the thread of space, while also linking it to questions of gender and method, Edmond Ernest dit Alban's article and title ask what it means when "Disney meets Anime." What methodological issues are brought to light in the tension between the framework of transmedia (prominent in North American scholarship) and the media mix (as deployed in Japan and Japan studies)? How might these tensions allow us to go beyond the impasses Ernest dit Alban detects in the nation-focused, male-centered accounts? In posing these questions they also direct our attention to the materially situated, women-led practices of the media mix thus far too little attended to in existing studies of the media mix, building on their own earlier work, and echoing the work undertaken by Seuffert, Sano, and Hassel in the issue.[22]

Finally, "Between Media Mix and Franchising Theory: A Workshop on the Theoretical Worlds of Transmedia Production" offers a selected and well-constructed account of an academic workshop organized to stage a dialogue between theories of the media mix and theories of media franchising at the Digital Games Research Association (DiGRA) conference at Ritsumeikan University in Kyoto, Japan. This 2019 dialogue is a nice way to bring the volume to a close, reflecting on a past event and previous works from the perspective of 2023. If held again, this workshop would no doubt refer to many of the wonderful interventions showcased in this special issue.

Indeed, the articles here reinvigorate the media mix concept and demonstrate thrilling ways forward for this area of research. They suggest an exciting future and emergent formations of a field I am now convinced we can call "media mix studies."

....

Marc Steinberg is Professor of Film Studies at Concordia University, Montreal, and director of The Platform Lab. He is the author of *Anime's Media Mix: Franchising Toys and Characters in Japan* (University of Minnesota Press, 2012) and *The Platform Economy: How Japan Transformed the Commercial Internet*

(University of Minnesota Press, 2019), as well as co-author of *Media and Management* (University of Minnesota Press, 2021). He co-edited *Media Theory in Japan* (Duke University Press, 2017), as well as special issues of *Asiascape: Digital Asia* on "Regional Platforms," and *Media, Culture & Society* on "Media Power in Digital Asia: Super Apps and Megacorps."

Acknowledgments

I would like to thank the contributors for their incredible work in this volume. As I've said above, I truly believe they are opening a new chapter in the study of the media mix. I would also acknowledge the hard and time-intensive labor of the peer reviewers who worked with the contributors to refine their articles. I would, finally, like to acknowledge the incredible care and time that *Mechademia: Second Arc* co-editor-in-chief Sandra Annett put into this volume from its inception through to its final stages. The intellectual, editorial, and agenda-setting work editors put into a journal is often unseen and taken-for-granted. This special issue would not exist without Sandra Annett, and I thank her for her commitment to the field, her editorial prowess, and her time.

Notes

1. Alexander Zahlten, "Media Mix and the Metaphoric Economy of World," in *The Oxford Handbook of Japanese Cinema*, ed. Daisuke Miyao (Oxford: Oxford University Press, 2014), https://doi.org/10.1093/oxfordhb/9780199731664.013.008.
2. Marc Steinberg, *The Platform Economy: How Japan Transformed the Commercial Internet* (Minneapolis: University of Minnesota Press, 2019).
3. Marc Steinberg, *Anime's Media Mix: Franchising Toys and Characters in Japan* (Minneapolis: University of Minnesota Press, 2012); Thomas Lamarre, *The Anime Machine* (Minneapolis: University of Minnesota Press, 2009); Emi Tanaka, "Media Mikkusu No Sangyō Kōzō" (The industry structure of the media mix)," in *Kontentsu Sangyōron* (On the contents industry), ed. Deguchi Hiroshi, Tanaka Hideyuki, and Koyama Yūsuke (Tokyo: Tokyo Daigaku Shuppan, 2009), 159–88; Anne Allison, *Millennial Monsters: Japanese Toys and the Global Imagination* (Berkeley: University of California Press, 2006); Hiroki Azuma, *Otaku: Japan's Database Animals*, trans. Jonathan E. Abel and Shion Kono (Minneapolis: University of Minnesota Press, 2009); Ōtsuka Eiji, *Monogatari Shōhiron: Bikkuriman No Shinwagaku* (A theory of narrative consumption: Mythology of Bikkuriman) (Tokyo: Shin'yōsha, 1989).
4. Steinberg, *Anime's Media Mix*, 71–72.
5. Sandra Annett, *Anime Fan Communities: Transcultural Flows and Frictions* (New York: Palgrave Macmillan, 2014), https://doi.org/10.1057/9781137476104.

6. Alexander Zahlten, "The End of Japanese Cinema: Industrial Genres," *National Times, and Media Ecologies*, 2018; Rayna Denison, "Franchising and Film in Japan: Transmedia Production and the Changing Roles of Film in Contemporary Japanese Media Cultures," *Cinema Journal* 55, no. 2 (2016): 67–88; Rayna Denison, *Studio Ghibli: An Industrial History*, Palgrave Animation (Cham, Switzerland: Palgrave Macmillan, 2023), https://doi.org/10.1007/978-3-031-16844-4.

7. Patrick W. Galbraith and Jason G. Karlin, *Idols and Celebrity in Japanese Media Culture* (Basingstoke: Palgrave Macmillan, 2012); Patrick W. Galbraith and Jason G. Karlin, *Media Convergence in Japan* ([New Haven, CT]: Kinema Club, 2016).

8. Martin Picard and Jérémie Pelletier-Gagnon, "Introduction: Geemu, Media Mix, and the State of Japanese Video Game Studies," *Kinephanos* 5, no. 1 (December 2015): 1–19; Joleen Blom, "The Manifestations of Game Characters in a Media Mix Strategy," *Comics and Videogames: From Hybrid Medialities to Transmedia Expansions*, ed. Andreas Rauscher, Daniel Stein, and Jan-Noël Thon (London: Routledge, 2021), https://www.taylorfrancis.com/chapters/oa-edit/10.4324/9781003035466-15/; Dorothy Finan, "Idols You Can Make: The Player as Auteur in Japan's Media Mix," *New Media & Society* 25, no. 5 (2021): 881–97, https://doi.org/10.1177/14614448211015625.

9. Zahlten, "Media Mix"; Thomas Lamarre, *The Anime Ecology: A Genealogy of Television, Animation, and Game Media* (Minneapolis: University of Minnesota Press, 2018).

10. Kathryn Hemmann, *Manga Cultures and the Female Gaze* (Cham, Switzerland: Palgrave Macmillan, 2020).

11. Akiko Sugawa-Shimada, "Emerging '2.5-Dimensional Culture': Character-Oriented Cultural Practices and 'Community of Preferences' as a New Fandom in Japan and Beyond," *Mechademia* 12, no. 2 (2020): 124–39; Edmond Ernest dit Alban, "Pedestrian Media Mix: The Birth of Otaku Sanctuaries in Tokyo," *Mechademia* 12, no. 2 (2020): 140–63; Akiko Sugawa-Shimada and Sandra Annett, "Introduction," *Mechademia* 15, no. 2 (2023): 1–7.

12. Henry Jenkins, *Convergence Culture: Where Old and New Media Collide* (New York: New York University Press, 2006); Derek Johnson, *Media Franchising: Creative License and Collaboration in the Culture Industries* (New York: New York University Press, 2013); Akinori Nakamura and Tosca Susana, "The Mobile Suit Gundam Franchise: A Case Study of Transmedia Storytelling Practices and the Role of Digital Games in Japan," *DiGRA '19—Proceedings of the 2019 DiGRA International Conference: Game, Play and the Emerging Ludo-Mix*, 2019, http://www.digra.org/wp-content/uploads/digital-library/DiGRA_2019_paper_235.pdf.

13. Stevie Suan, *Anime's Identity: Performativity and Form beyond Japan* (Minneapolis: University of Minnesota Press, 2021).

14. James Welker, ed., *Queer Transfigurations Boys Love Media in Asia* (Honolulu: University of Hawaii Press, 2022); Thomas Baudinette, "Lovesick, The Series: Adapting Japanese 'Boys Love' to Thailand and the Creation of a New Genre of

Queer Media," *South East Asia Research* 27, no. 2 (April 2019): 115–32, https://doi.org/10.1080/0967828X.2019.1627762; Jinying Li, "The Platformization of Chinese Cinema: The Rise of IP Films in the Age of Internet+," *Asian Cinema* 31, no. 2 (2020): 203–18, https://doi.org/10.1386/ac_00022_1.

15. Aurélie Petit, "'Do Female Anime Fans Exist?' The Impact of Women-Exclusionary Discourses on Rec.Arts.Anime," *Internet Histories* 6, no. 4 (October 2, 2022): 352–68, https://doi.org/10.1080/24701475.2022.2109265; Steinberg, *The Platform Economy*.

16. Tressie McMillan Cottom, "Where Platform Capitalism and Racial Capitalism Meet: The Sociology of Race and Racism in the Digital Society," *Sociology of Race and Ethnicity* 6, no. 4 (2020): 441–49, https://doi.org/10.1177/2332649220949473.

17. Wendy Hui Kyong Chun, *Discriminating Data: Correlation, Neighborhoods, and the New Politics of Recognition* (Cambridge, MA: MIT Press, 2021); Leo Ching, "Yellow Skin, White Masks: Race, Class, and Identification in Japanese Colonial Discourse," in *Trajectories: Inter-Asia Cultural Studies*, ed. Kuan-Hsing Chen (London: Routledge, 1998), 65–86.

18. Bryan Hikari Hartzheim, "Pretty Cure and the Magical Girl Media Mix," *The Journal of Popular Culture* 49, no. 5 (2016): 1059–85, https://doi.org/10.1111/jpcu.12465; Shinji Oyama, "Japanese Creative Industries in Globalization," in *Routledge Handbook of New Media in Asia*, ed. Larissa Hjorth and Olivia Khoo (Abington: Routledge, 2016), 322–32; Yoko Nishioka, "Over-the-Top (OTT) Video Service," in *Perspectives on the Japanese Media and Content Policies*, ed. Minoru Sugaya (Singapore: Springer, 2021), 245–61, https://doi.org/10.1007/978-981-15-4704-1.

19. Matthew Hockenberry, Nicole Starosielski, and Susan Marjorie Zieger, eds., *Assembly Codes: The Logistics of Media* (Durham: Duke University Press, 2021); Yuriko Furuhata, *Climatic Media: Transpacific Experiments in Atmospheric Control* (Durham: Duke University Press, 2022); Rahul Mukherjee, *Radiant Infrastructures: Media, Environment, and Cultures of Uncertainty* (Durham: Duke University Press, 2020); Alexander Zahlten, "Before Media Mix: The Electric Ecology," in *A Companion to Japanese Cinema*, ed. David Desser (Hoboken, NJ: Wiley, 2022), 469–92.

20. Sugawa-Shimada and Annett, "Introduction."

21. Thomas Poell, David B. Nieborg, and Brooke Erin Duffy, *Platforms and Cultural Production* (Cambridge: Polity, 2022).

22. Ernest dit Alban, "Pedestrian Media Mix."

Media Mix Perspectives

Makers in the Mix

A Production Studies Approach to Studying the Media Mix

BRYAN HIKARI HARTZHEIM

While less recognized outside academic and industrial circles term, the phrase "media mix" has become synonymous with Japan-produced media such as anime, manga, games, and its associated ancillary industries. Rather than belabor this historical connection, in this short provocation I'd like to look at what the study of media mix has offered and continues to offer in studies of media production, both in its novel contributions and where I hope it can continue to be a beacon for certain types of media studies beyond Japan.

On a fundamental level, the study of media mix is a novel contribution to the study of serial production, particularly of drawn and animated media. Marc Steinberg's pioneering book on anime's media mix came out during a time of exciting scholarship that asked questions about the history, economics, and technologies of convergent, serial, and franchised media.[1] Henry Jenkins's *Convergence Culture,* and in particular his chapter on "transmedia storytelling," has inspired some of the most interesting and innovative analyses of Hollywood serial production, from examinations of the industries or histories behind licensed media franchises to studies of franchise special effects and narrative complexity.[2] Similarly, Steinberg's and Ōtsuka Eiji's work on media mix helped shift the study of isolated anime or manga texts from more ideological or speculative readings to scholarship that focuses on the contexts that enable and sustain their serial possibilities, from "gameic" media mixes involving the commodity role of video games within larger media ecologies to the role of urban networks and pedestrian actors in remixing and recycling media images.[3] Where these texts diverge in national or generic focus, they share some common methodological traits: digging through history via archival research, application of critical theory to explain complex social phenomena, and an attention to media-related things—specifically, the creation and management of serial texts and ancillary paratexts, licensed products and merchandise, and coordinated promotional and marketing strategies.

But the study of media mix is also the study of people. This might not seem apparent, with foci of analysis tending toward the permeability of narratives and characters rather than studio labor and production committees. Even in the existing examples of media mix as "things," there is a great deal of attention paid to the systems that maintain them such as publishing networks and talent agencies, not to mention more specific analyses of the time-saving decisions of artists and animators, the protean and affective attributes of idols and business managers, and even the slippery divide between creators and fans. While advocates of fan studies have done admirable excavations into the affective and immaterial labor of audiences and derivative work—as well as the blurry lines that have long existed between "prosumers," who identify as both consumers and producers—my own research questions and tendencies gravitate toward ground zero in the media mix: to the people both above and below the labor line who are responsible for making the "things" we consume and comprising the dense industrial "systems" that enable their production.

Part of this interest is due to my background working as a reporter for media and newspaper outlets based in Japan. Speaking with editors of manga magazines, managers of budding idol groups, and animators for pachinko slot machine displays revealed to me the layers of diffuse labor and creativity that were present in these interrelated industries, with the people heavily responsible for making what we see and hear far away from production sets, press conferences, and academic articles (which, at the time, lacked writing on anime production). This interest in the less glamorous aspects of creation that grease the wheels of transmedia and media mix franchises naturally led me away from auteur-driven entertainment directed by the likes of Takahata Isao or Oshii Mamoru and toward media franchises mass-produced for television, marketed toward children, financed by toy sponsors, and structured around genre demographics and formulas like *shōnen* battle or magical girl. Interning at Toei Animation allowed me to see this system in practice, where producers, writers, series directors, and advertising reps worked with (though not necessarily alongside) episode directors, animators, colorists, editors, sound mixers, and production coordinators to produce episodes of animated series, again and again, over the course of a year.

Such an interest in this mix of above and below the line labor and economics is the provenance of a subset of media industry studies known as production studies. This focus on the industrial margins and less prestigious media forms gravitated toward the global television economy (and female media professionals in particular). Examples range from Vicki Mayer's redefinition of "producers" to include casters, cameramen, and TV set assemblers to Erin Hill's history of Hollywood's mostly female production assistants and secretaries.[4] These studies all share a desire to make visible hidden labor and highlight production on the margins. The poster child for this approach is John Thornton Caldwell's *Production Culture*, though I'd like to draw attention to his earlier book, *Televisuality*.[5] Not only did *Televisuality* bring academic attention to industrial practice, worker-generated theory, and medium reflexivity a decade prior, but it also continues to provide a useful template for how to combine the analysis of production culture and television aesthetics. What we see on the screen is determined as much or more by network programming decisions and distinction-mining, new technological equipment implemented by cameramen, and digital interfaces applied in postproduction studios as any creative decision levied by directors or showrunners. It also provides a useful way to apply the kinds of speculative theory that film studies and critical theorists are so good at toward atypical texts and contexts. Based on such an approach inspired by production studies but also in line with studies of style and aesthetics, I suggest a few additional areas for media mix production research below.

1. *Media mix as production culture.* If scholars have productively applied concepts from reception studies to examining the practices and communal identities formed through fan cultures of anime and manga, the same cannot yet be said about anime's varied workers, who negotiate their own labor conditions and environments when producing content for the media mix. A large impediment to this kind of research is obviously access: fan communities are more open and accommodating to aca-fans, whereas the media industries have long been secretive and suspicious of any academic incursions, a fact of life that has been exacerbated through the coronavirus pandemic. An exception and model to studying anime's workers is Ian Condry's thoughtful ethnographic exploration of anime's backrooms, which inspired me to knock on many digital doors as a graduate student and pitch my project to the sympathetic ears of Toei.[6] But any access granted was much more to do with the brilliant and generous spirit of unconventional producers like Seki Hiromi, Kinoshita Hiroyuki, Umezawa Atsushi, and Wakabayashi Goh than any kind of grit and determination. Access is also a Faustian bargain, as it necessitates emphasizing certain areas of production while downplaying other systemic issues. If entering planning meetings or script-writing

rooms was difficult for the participant observer before COVID, such access arteries are further clogged in the shift to remote work, Zoom, and the continued precautionary absence of all informal gatherings. Researchers still have options beyond taking on work as production assistants for the sake of networking. As a major studio within the industry, Toei represents many of its strengths and problems, but many other studios, institutions, and organizations also present their own complex cultural phenomena: smaller outsourcing firms, animator support organizations, art and design universities, niche publishers, mobile game developers, playing-card tournament organizers, and industry-sponsored networking and promotional events all are ripe for further investigation and reveal unique issues within their own cultures of production. Researchers also need not focus on the present for understanding today's work worlds and practices. Diane Wei Lewis's examination of *shiage,* or the inkers and colorists of anime who "finish" animation cels, as well as Kimura Tomoya's exhaustive study of Toei Dōga show how contemporary labor conditions can be productively explained through archival means.[7]

2. *Media mix as production programming.* Media mix studies have carefully incorporated theories and methods from political economy, shifting the focus of deriving meaning from anime and manga as authored texts to their status as materials and commodities. This has allowed a welcome shift to studying anime and manga less as discrete works and more as they exist in reality: as half-submerged trees sticking out of a massive multimedia swamp. As others have pointed out, a large chunk of this media mix is televisual, made up of everything from children's programming to TV ads to late-night otaku bait, but rarely do scholars besides Thomas Lamarre, Rayna Denison, and Jonathan Clements nod to the debates and contributions of television studies.[8] Anime has historically been produced not for discount DVD box sets, KissAnime, and Adult Swim, but for pricey single-issue OVAs, TV broadcasts, and (increasingly) Crunchyroll. Watching bootleg VHS tapes of Japanese programs recorded in two-hour chunks replete with commercials with my mom as a kid made ignoring the programming block and distribution conditions impossible, a fact that many who consume anime in the present era ignore at their peril. This industrial noise is smoothed away with most audiences now getting their anime and manga fix via OTT platforms or digital manga apps. As Mimi White

has demonstrated in her analysis of daytime soaps and the commercials that finance them, understanding how anime is produced on the macro level—the roles of television broadcasters, corporate sponsors, distribution companies, and the placement of a show within a particular channel niche or network-programming schedule—is crucial to understanding how a show is organized the way it is.[9] This was one of the things I tried to show in my article on *Pretty Cure*: the fact that animation writers, sponsors, television producers, and advertising agencies all spoke the same language, to the point that commercials independently produced from the animation series—not to mention the other films, events, and performances in the *Precure* media mix— seamlessly incorporated the style of the series itself.[10] This sort of research might not require researchers to be "on the ground" when it comes to seeing how these interstices are produced, though it does require a sensitivity to how these various interests are represented in the program as it is broadcast—or, today, released via SVOD platforms—in real time.

3. *Media mix as production style.* Speaking of television, while I suggested that Takahata and Oshii were auteurs who were above "slumming" in television, it is now common knowledge that both of these celebrated filmmakers toiled in television for years before becoming the established art-house names they are known as today. But rather than look at television as obstacles on their inevitable paths to notoriety, it is more instructive to see how working in the medium for so many years informed how they thought about animation and what effect reduced budgets, condensed schedules, ratings or sales pressures, contractual sponsor and publisher demands, and the long and unwieldy serial format had on the kinds of stories they told and on the techniques they honed. Fresh trends and concepts almost always come from television anime, as dozens of new series premiere every three months eager to stylistically stun audiences immediately. But even long-running shows like *Heidi, Girl of the Alps* or *Urusei Yatsura* reveal as much distinct formal and narrative experimentation as anything from *The Tale of Princess Kaguya* or *Ghost in the Shell*. More to the point, television (or any collaborative media) is not just about the name at the top; these directors and countless others started in various roles from key animator to episode director, learning the ins and outs of the craft, before being charged with projects of their own. In short, it is no

coincidence that so many well-known names in anime began in minor roles on shows like *Crayon Shin-chan* and *Ojamajo Doremi*. While commercials, television, and franchises (or, gasp, commercial television-based franchises) might be culturally denigrated when compared to Cinema, particularly by those trained in literary or film studies, their longer production timeframes, established labor networks, and constant need for output can mean that novice creators are able to refine or redefine their craft while also collecting a paycheck. If the rigid production schedules, risk aversion, and generic predictability of TV franchises act as creative straitjackets, they are ones that can allow for breathing room to innovate, as Stevie Suan has claimed, with new kinds of animation expression in the margins.[11]

4. *Media mix as production stress.* At least, the above is what is hoped for *in theory*. In reality, as the cultural industries have long feasted on underpaid, overworked, frequently contracted workers, growing attention has focused on the anime industry, which harbors some of the *most* underpaid, overworked, and near universally contracted within Japan's cultural industries. This exploitation has been covered by wide shows, industry blogs, and other fan/media outlets, but academics of production studies can also play a role in shining a spotlight on this exploitation. As Miranda Banks argues, a production studies methodology at its core shares affinities with feminist film studies, often resisting or complicating "traditional power hierarchies," containing origins in a "non-binary interdisciplinarity" and possessing a "capacity to highlight cultural inequities."[12] On one level, this involves the sort of intense and dedicated fieldwork that researchers like Nagata Daisuke and Matsunaga Shintaro are engaging with on the micro level, interviewing animators and illustrators about their working conditions, lives, frustrations, and pleasures.[13] Even here, however, is an incomplete picture, as workers can only be so discrete about their conditions when they're looking over their shoulder at their bosses or the potential fallout of a misattributed comment. If studying production no longer means being "on set" (if it ever truly did), then this means sites of observation and discourse are everywhere. Producers, directors, animators, mangaka, editors, voice actors, and production coordinators are all on informal digital channels on social media and leave traces of work in blogs, live chats, and other self-publishing forums. These industrial disclosures reveal much about how these

workers view their own labor, both from the carefully massaged and managed spin from producers to the anonymous cries for help from distressed staff. Researchers can try reaching out, but they can also digitally observe this worker chatter and take notes on what was once the domain of smoking rooms and after-work parties. Applying the theories of Stuart Hall and John Fiske to this worker-generated discourse also means that fan studies and production studies need not be methodologically opposed (a distinction that holds even less weight within the anime and manga industries considering the often collaborative or crossover activities between fans and producers).

All of this is to say: production isn't just the context of the media mix; it is the condition of possibility for the media mix and what enables its indefatigable churn. Understanding it at this level means spending time with the people who make it, live it, and make sense and meaning out of it. I've focused on anime for this provocation, but the same methods and angles should be applied to other cultural industries that play an increasingly important role in the media mix, from light novel publishers and SVOD platforms to mobile game developers and theme park designers. Of course, there are considerable barriers such as the ones listed above, many of which are why we see scant production studies of media mix today. Caldwell's command of the terminology and function of these industrial practices developed from a career in postproduction prior to becoming an academic. Having some exposure as a practitioner helps, though it is not always realistic for academics, so being open to spending time reading about and understanding the perspectives of industry workers is essential to conducting accurate and informed fieldwork. And as the media mix is composed of various industries that primarily employ freelance labor both in and outside Japan, one doesn't need to even commit to observing production in a physical location in order to explain or understand alternative modes to production or ask questions of their conditions.

Questions may include: what informs the people who make the "things" of media? Who are the diverse workers that comprise these networks of production, manufacturing, and distribution? How can knowing about these belief and labor systems give us a better understanding of not just how the media mix is created, but of what we consume both on and off screen? The answers to these questions lie in understanding top-down organizational structuring devices like animation technologies, broadcasting and platform exclusives, and the composition of production committees, but also bottom-up lived realities such as studio workflow, production stress, worker theory, and the very beliefs, values, assumptions, and biases of a diverse workforce in multiple interconnected industries.

....

Bryan Hikari Hartzheim is Associate Professor of New Media at Waseda University's School of International Liberal Studies and Graduate School of International Culture and Communication Studies. He is the author of *Hideo Kojima: Progressive Design from Metal Gear to Death Stranding* (2023) and the coeditor of *The Franchise Era: Managing Media in the Digital Economy* (2019). His other work on Japan's anime, manga, and game industries has appeared in *The Journal of Popular Culture, Television and New Media,* and in various edited collections. He is the guest editor of the forthcoming *Mechademia* 16.2 on media industries and platforms (2024).

....

Notes

1. Marc Steinberg, *Anime's Media Mix: Franchising Toys and Characters in Japan* (Minneapolis: University of Minnesota Press, 2012).
2. Henry Jenkins, *Convergence Culture: Where Old and New Media Collide* (New York: New York University Press, 2008).
3. Ōtsuka Eiji, *Media mikkusu ka suru nihon* (Media mixing Japan) (Tokyo: Shinsho, 2014) and *Taisei yokusankai no media mikkusu* (The Imperial Rule Assistance Association media mix) (Tokyo: Heibonsha, 2018).
4. Vicki Mayer, *Below the Line: Producers and Production Studies in the New Television Economy* (Durham: Duke University Press, 2011); Erin Hill, *Never Done: A History of Women's Work in Media Production* (New Brunswick: Rutgers University Press, 2016).
5. John Thornton Caldwell, *Televisuality: Style, Crisis, and Authority in American Television* (New Brunswick: Rutgers University Press, 1995) and *Production Culture: Industrial Reflexivity and Critical Practice in Film and Television* (Durham: Duke University Press, 2008).
6. Ian Condry, *The Soul of Anime: Collaborative Creativity and Japan's Media Success Story* (Durham: Duke University Press, 2013).
7. Diane Wei Lewis, "Shiage: Women's Flexible Labor in the Japanese Animation Industry," *Feminist Media Histories* 4, no. 1 (2018): 115–41; Kimura Tomoya, *Toei Dōga shiron: keiei to souzō no teiryu* (The historical study of Toei Animation) (Tokyo: Nihonhyoronsha, 2020).
8. Thomas Lamarre, *The Anime Ecology: A Geneology of Television, Animation, and Game Media* (Minneapolis: University of Minnesota Press, 2018); Rayna

Denison, *Studio Ghibli: An Industrial History* (London: Palgrave Macmillan, 2023); Jonathan Clements, *Anime: A History* (London: Bloomsbury, 2013).

9. Mimi White, *Tele-Advising: Therapeutic Discourse in American Television* (Chapel Hill: University of North Carolina Press, 1992).

10. Bryan Hikari Hartzheim, "*Pretty Cure* and the Magical Girl Media Mix," *Journal of Popular Culture* 49, no. 5 (2016): 1059–85.

11. Stevie Suan, *Anime's Identity: Performativity and Form Beyond Japan* (Minneapolis: University of Minnesota Press, 2021).

12. Miranda Banks, "Production Studies," *Feminist Media Histories* 4, no. 2 (2018): 157.

13. Nagata Daisuke and Matsunaga Shintaro, *Sangyō hendō no rōdō shakaigaku: Animeetaa no keikenshi* (Labor sociology of industrial fluctuation: A study on animator experiences) (Tokyo: Koyoshobo, 2022).

Media Mix Is Nonsense—
What Can We Do About It?

ALEXANDER ZAHLTEN

Let me clarify the title: media mix is non-sense, or put differently, not
sensible. We have no sense for perceiving a system or a set of relations; we can
only approximate it/them through some of their more sensible expressions.
We do not see, feel (in a tactile or sensory motor capacity), hear, or smell
the *Betty Boop, Kizuna,* or *Astro Boy* media mix. What we sense are a range of
different manifestations of Betty Boop, Enjōji, or Astro Boy, which we claim
are respectively connected by a dynamic system, one called media mix. But
if Jacques Rancière's proposition that politics is a matter of the "distribution
of the sensible" is correct, then we may have a problem if media mix as a
dynamic system that co-shapes our worlds is fundamentally itself out of the
reach of the sensible.[1]

One of the challenges in researching and writing about the media mix
is that research based in the humanities provides no real training to "read"
systems. Students are primarily trained and encouraged to read media *texts.*
Even then the mode of reading is largely one modeled on literature, i.e., rely-
ing on narrative regardless of the media form (be it film, radio, sound, manga,
video games, etc.), and at most students are encouraged to incorporate some
degree of visual analysis. Attempts by scholars such as Franco Moretti to
establish "distant reading" methodologies are still closely tied to quantifying
the content of texts—but skirt the question of systems. We can "read" (and
historicize) Madoka or Naruto as characters defined by certain visual attributes and as embedded in a specific narrative. We can explore and interpret
the fan-related activities around Madoka or Naruto. But for the most part we
have not learned to read, map, or dynamically trace the systemic form of the
Madoka Magica media mix itself.

How then can we gain a better understanding of media mix's systemic
features, its dynamics, the relational structure? Is there a way to understand
the emergent qualities of (a) media mix, its actancy or even agency? How can
we push media mix as system into the realm of the sensible, that is, a politics
that can be researched and engaged with? What are the trappings of thinking

media mix through systems and/or related concepts such as structure, ecology, or emergence? This article aims to sketch some of the possible issues at hand along with the potential payoffs and pitfalls.

Systems, Ecologies, and the Emergence of Emergence

The above problem would seem to call for drawing on theories that have centrally concerned themselves with systems. At least since Heinz von Foerster's work in second-order cybernetics, many of these theories have also dealt with the issue of an inherent "blind spot" that is centrally co-constitutive of any system. The problem, as von Foerster states—drawing a parallel to the blind spot of the human retina—is not in not seeing *something*, but in not seeing that/what we do not see, which in itself is a precondition for seeing.[2] In a way, then, systems theory has made the above outlined question of the sensible itself central to systems theory. Theories of media mix so far—some of which will be discussed below—have often attempted to trace the system, but rarely dealt with its constitutive non-sensibility.

What, then, to draw on? Undoubtedly the interest in systems is rising, and the mainstreaming of media studies over the last two and a half decades itself attests to that. That rise brought with it increasing attention to media technology. Shifting away from "content," narrative, and representation in a broader sense, it instead introduced systemic paradigms. Friedrich Kittler's understanding of "writing systems," or *Aufschreibesysteme*, as paradigmatic discourse generators is one such example influential in media studies that is positioned halfway between Foucauldian theory of discourse and cybernetics' systems theory. Bernard Siegert has discussed the connected shift by what is often called "German media theory" toward the "nonhermeneutic non-sense" as performed via the material media-technological anchors of the system(s), and moving away from the "hegemony of understanding."[3] On the whole, while an attempt to understand the system of media mix may be understood as a way to grasp a given media mix's totality (i.e., all of the live action films, anime, toys, merchandising, consumers, practices or companies etc. co-constituting it), systems theory has generally been applied in the opposite way: as a theory of differentiation. Consequently, it has tended toward the constructionist, the anti-ontological, and the anti-metaphysical; as such, Albrecht Koschorke has deemed its interest in borders and liminality as compatible with cultural studies' and critical theory's shift toward a focus on decentering and their emphasis on peripheries.[4] As an example, this would seem in line with cultural studies' concerns with marginalized fan cultures, subversive readings, etc. Yet overall, systems theory has developed a tense relationship to the humanities even as systems-theory inflected concepts have taken them by storm.

To name an example, the manner in which the term ecology, often used with distinct and purposeful fuzziness, has taken hold of academic vocabulary is one of the huge terminological success stories of recent years. In *General Ecology: The New Ecological Paradigm*, Erich Hörl has provided one of the best accounts of the recent wildfire that is the rhetoric of ecology, along with a very useful outline of its epistemological consequences and what it might mean in its more rigorous usage.[5] Much of the work that now makes use of a term like media ecology is however still largely tied to conventional close reading of representations/narratives (i.e., to "content") and employs an only extremely general usage of the term that gestures toward vague interconnectedness, what we might call "a system of sorts." It is often used, without much theoretical rigor, interchangeably with a term such as media environment, thereby limiting its useful specificity and ignoring the distinct lineages of the terms. Thomas Lamarre's recent work stands out for a much more rigorous use of the term ecology (and in fact positions it *against* a term like system); it is, however, not primarily interested in the relations or dynamics between multiple media channels in the sense of media mix and instead focuses on the ecological quality of more focused relations such as brain and screen (via phenomena such as the Pokémon shock).[6] But in general, the now-common appeal to ecology already shows a trajectory in the works that is moving away from a focus on content. It is instead replaced by a focus on relationality, though not between bounded units but, to draw on Lamarre's phrasing (itself referencing Karen Barad and others), a system of "infra-individual intra-actions."

Emergence, on the other hand, is a concept that has played little role so far in the discussion of media phenomena, but it is deeply entwined with the larger career of the concepts of system and ecology since the late nineteenth century. Marc Steinberg's pioneering *Anime's Media Mix* is one example of the idea of emergence beginning to emerge in the analysis of media. *Anime's Media Mix* still bases much of the analysis of the media mix on formal analysis, most prominently of *Astro Boy's* dynamic immobility.[7] However, he also hints heavily at the new systemic dynamics in speaking, for example, of a "tipping point"—a classically emergentist concept—and mentioning "[t]he autonomous circulation of the character."[8] What that implies is—in line with the idea of emergence—that a system takes shape in which a whole constitutes more than its parts and develops a set of more or less autonomous dynamics that are in some ways unexpected, that couldn't have been predicted from simply summarizing the parts. The book's inclusion of "thing-thing communication" as one of the basic aspects of media mix points to several exciting and disturbing questions about this new dynamic. Prefiguring some of the current discussions around AI, it poses the question: if media mix is at least partially made of non-human communicational systems, then what happens when humans rely on systems that, at least in parts, are not fundamentally concerned with humans?

Conversely, the lineage of discussing transmedia dynamics that runs through Henry Jenkins's concept of transmedia storytelling and convergence culture is considerably more rooted in discussions of narrative. It has in consequence been much less prone to considering media dynamics through the lens of systems. The discussion of media mix in English-language scholarship has, however, been tied to ideas of system, ecology, and emergence from the beginning. It has nonetheless only begun to actually develop methodologies for thinking, mapping, and analyzing systems, ecology, and emergence themselves. Discussions of media mix in Japanese look somewhat different, though several of Steinberg's and Lamarre's contributions have been translated into Japanese and are part of Japanese-language discussions as well.

Where Is "System"?

How, then, do we locate system, or begin to think about the role it plays vis-à-vis media mix? What is the relation of the system to its constitutive parts? For example, how does a frame from the *Revolutionary Girl Utena* (*Shōjo Kakumei Utena*) anime, a sound effect, the anime episode it belongs to, or an *Utena* sticker, a fan practice common at the *Utena* stage play, or a gesture used to steer the character in an *Utena* video game relate to the *Utena* media mix? What is the relation of the always already media-technological human (as one constitutive, barely distinguishable part) to this system, how do these entities and forces overlap into each other?

There are several ways to explore these questions that involve drawing on a variety of theoretical lineages. In sociology, Niklas Luhmann, one of the most prominent system theorists, sought to replace the relation of part to whole with the relation of system to environment, with humans as the environment of social systems. While Luhmann only represents one approach to systems (itself somewhat controversial among many systems theorists), the questions raised here are intriguing and connect to the above-mentioned concerns: Are we simply an environment for the Astro Boy media mix? Does thing-thing communication exclude us, making us simply background for an emergent system? Luhmann's take in fact moves in the opposite direction of *Anime's Media Mix's* proposal that "the network formed among character things or media-commodity forms constitutes the very surface on which other forms of communication could take place."[9] If we have to reverse that perspective, are we simply hosts to a parasitic system, albeit infra-individual ones? Or are we, ecologically speaking, still an intrinsic if decidedly not central part of the media mix system, dissolving into a range of infra-individually intra-acting components of that system? Either perspective assumes (against Luhmann) that the human is part of the system, rather than separate from it. And to return to the opening question of the blind spot: Does that level of co-constitution compromise our ability to analyze and understand media mix? Does it make analysis or understanding a futile exercise, at least when premised on a still-discernible human, even if "in" the system?

Putting those questions aside for a moment, however, it also makes sense to take a look at some "first questions" and challenges we might address in the possibility of thinking media mix as system. This concerns both methodological trappings and inherent limits of a systems approach.

Site Specificity and System Universality

To begin, we might ask what it means that media mix has been discussed almost exclusively through Japan, and how that complicates a systems perspective. On a conceptual level, how has "Japan" skewed the discussion about how the media-technological situation is understood, and how nation, culture, and other identifiers used to secure Japan as a unit or context work with media mix? Patrick Galbraith and Jason Karlin have warned of a facile but already in-place alignment of different models of media dynamics with national contexts. Conventionally, and too often, media mix is associated with Japan. By contrast, the model of media convergence and transmedia storytelling espoused by Henry Jenkins and those who build on his work is more commonly associated with American media.[10] Galbraith and Karlin point to this schematic perspective and its erasure of the presence of both of these models across many different contexts and media industries.[11] However, since systems are not really their concern, they do not mention the fundamental tension between terms like system and culture.

The term "culture" has long been problematized from within area studies, but it also has several declared enemies from within systems theory thinking. Niklas Luhmann famously declared that culture was "one of the worst terms ever invented," a statement that only expresses a usually more latent stance within a fair amount of systems-theoretical thought.[12] More problematically, systems theory tends to be wary of site-specificity (beyond the trappings of "culture") in general. Systems theory, in its early manifestations such as cybernetics, was always more interested in a universal theory of systems, and in fact often averse to thinking systems or systemic principles as site-specific. Despite the obvious problems of (many definitions of) culture, site-specificity is however something few if any area studies scholars would be willing to sacrifice. For area studies, it is precisely site-specificity that offers the ground for politics and analysis.

In fact, this is where some of the basic limitations and trappings of systems approaches come into view. Systems concepts such as (using a broad definition of systems theory) ecology are intended to decenter the human, often in line with attempts to grapple with the destructive effects of human-centric worldviews for life on the planet. However, throwing out the human or flattening it to the figure of "the human" also does away with many of the achievements of cultural studies and critical theory. Careful attention to issues of class, gender, sexuality, and race is deemphasized and exchanged for a universal human cypher. This is a similar trade-off as the one the rise of media studies entailed. At exactly the moment that film studies had begun to more centrally address issues of race, sexuality, or of provincializing the United States and Europe (following work done earlier in feminist film theory), media studies allowed for a return to abstract and philosophical discussions of media technologies' general effects or of media as a metaphysical framework. It is only recently that media studies has seen efforts to concretize and de-universalize again, but that effort is only beginning—the work of Kara Keeling or Tao Leigh Goffe being especially fruitful examples.[13] Some of the interventions in this area can however also be America-centric while not acknowledging themselves as such, adding a wrinkle to the process of de-universalization.

While cybernetics has produced outliers such as Gotthard Günther's theory of polycontexturality that work hard to provide a framework for combining context and (meta) system, on the whole the assumption is one of incompatibility between universalist systems theory that has abandoned "content" and a hermeneutically focused close-reading practice that in the best case mandates historicization. However, these are not necessary pairings, simply entrenched ones. Media mix, by contrast, has in almost all of the significant moments of its theorization stood at the threshold between the problematic pairs of universal system/without content and site-specificity/close reading. It still has the promise of questioning this pattern. Yet arguably media mix theory still has not made sense of the system or, in other words, has not made the system sensible, which may be where part of the problem lies.

Possibilities: Ecosemiotics

To consider media mix's potential for sensing the system we likely need to survey how other disciplines have dealt with similar tensions between the specific and the universal. For example, one possible "third way" may stem from geography. Ecosemiotics attempts to retain the advantages of semiotic approaches with an attention to ecosystems, essentially reunifying the content-system split that is so commonly assumed. The idea is that, as Kalevi Kull and Timo Maran have phrased it, "Ecosemiotics is a view on ecosystems as communicative systems."[14] The ecosystem is understood as fundamentally co-constituted by communicative processes that include nonhuman systems, living organisms of various kinds, their "semiosic activities" and spatial environments. While this might seem to echo Luhmann's more abstract emphasis on communication as constituting systems (and the famous phrase "only communication communicates"), there are decisive differences in emphasis.

Ecosemiotics is then most often concerned with the way that interpretative or communicative processes between a whole span of actors (human, nonhuman, systemic) have shaped physical environments. If we extend the approach beyond the idea of a physical environment, the applicability to media mix becomes plausible and provides the promise of retaining the level of signification or representation (as "content") that a more single-mindedly systemic view might let fall by the wayside. Put simply, we can continue to take the aesthetic expressions of media mix into account—the character design, the sound design, narrative aspects, etc.—while connecting them to the system that co-organizes them (along with the audiences) as much as it constitutes a kind of environment for them.

Is It Too Late For Us?

Ecosemiotics is simply one example of an approach that may allow for integrating into media mix theory what seems to be at odds between systems approaches and cultural studies or critical theory-indebted approaches. We also already see a number of emerging approaches that do not make use of media mix for that purpose, as in recent work by Stevie Suan and Jinying Li.[15] Media mix is not a necessary tool. We might also draw on rich histories of theorizing systems outside of systems theory approaches (analyses of capitalism being one prime candidate). Returning to the issue of the inherent blind spot, we might also reflect on what it means to inch (further) toward systems-theoretical approaches to media mix at this specific point in time. The rapid spread of systems-theoretical concerns in scholarship, along with the immense popularization of the term ecology across the humanities, communication studies, business studies as well as STEM fields may point in fact to this development itself as a symptom rather than an intervention.

Put differently, it may not be all that surprising that scholars who have themselves lived the majority of their lives as (infra-individually) part of media mixes and technosocial networks will be nudged toward conceptual models that are systemic and prone to endorsing ecological models. In fact, interpreting the popularity of ecology, system, and emergence in academic work over the last decades as a symptom of immersion in systems is the more ecological view than understanding the current trends in scholarship as the result of deliberately devised interventions. Thinking of the surge in popularity of the conceptual tools of ecology and systems as an intervention in fact presents a perspective that relies on models of agency and human autonomy that ecological thought itself challenges.

It may also be no coincidence that Harold Innis, one of the forerunners of today's version of media studies, dedicated much discussion to Minerva's owl and the fact that it only takes flight at dusk—that knowledge needs distance and is generally belated vis-à-vis what it attempts to understand. The more disturbing, postmodern, and aggressive version of such a late-realization model is the central obsession of the characters in Thomas Pynchon's *Gravity's Rainbow*: a rocket so fast that it explodes its target first, with the sound of its impending arrival coming later. One metaphor points to a longing for a distanced yet immediate access to understanding our situation, the other to an urgent fight for survival in an atmosphere of impending doom. Which of these we lean toward may influence our sense of urgency around the questions at hand. Both return us to the problem I opened with here: how to render the media mix *sensible*. In any event, though, it seems paramount to broaden the toolbox of media mix studies and understand the system(s) that constantly are in danger of remaining non-sense, and to grapple with their consequences for us—or rather the mesh of us-in-them and them-in-us.

....

Alexander Zahlten is Professor of East Asian Languages and Civilizations at Harvard University. His work touches on topics such as the dramatic changes in the Japanese film industry after 1960 in his book *The End of Japanese Cinema* (2017), "amateur" film production, and media ecology and the entangled history of electricity and media in Japan. Publications also include his co-edited volume *Media Theory in Japan* (Duke University Press, 2017, with Marc Steinberg) and the article "Between Two Funerals: Zombie Temporality and Media Ecology in Japan" (*positions: asia critique* 29.2, 2021). He has curated film programs for the German Film Museum in Frankfurt, Germany, the Athénée Français Cultural Center in Tokyo and the Parasophia Festival of Contemporary Culture in Kyoto, and was Program Director for the Nippon Connection Film Festival, the largest festival for film from Japan, from 2002 to 2010.

....

Notes

1. Jacques Rancière, *The Politics of Aesthetics: The Distribution of the Sensible* (New York: Continuum, 2004).
2. Heinz von Foerster, *Understanding Understanding: Essays on Cybernetics and Cognition* (New York: Springer, 2003).
3. Bernard Siegert, *Cultural Techniques* (New York: Fordham University Press, 2014), 2.
4. Albrecht Koschorke, "Die Grenzen des Systems und die Rhetorik der Systemtheorie," in *Widerstände der Systemtheorie: Kulturtheoretische Analysen zum Werk von Niklas Luhmann*, ed. Albrecht Koshorke and Cornelia Vismann (Berlin: Akademie, 1999), 49–62.
5. Erich Hörl, *General Ecology: The New Ecological Paradigm* (London: Bloomsbury Academic, 2017).
6. Thomas Lamarre, *The Anime Ecology: A Genealogy of Television, Animation, and Game Media* (Minneapolis: Minnesota University Press, 2018).
7. Marc Steinberg, *Anime's Media Mix: Franchising Toys and Characters in Japan* (Minneapolis: Minnesota University Press, 2012).
8. Steinberg, *Anime's Media Mix*, ix, 132.
9. Steinberg, *Anime's Media Mix*, 125.

10. Henry Jenkins, *Convergence Culture: Where Old and New Media Collide* (New York: New York University Press, 2006).

11. Patrick Galbraith and Jason Karlin, "Introduction: At the Crossroads of Media Convergence in Japan," in *Media Convergence in Japan*, ed. Patrick Galbraith and Jason Karlin (New Haven: Kinema Club, 2016), 1–29.

12. Niklas Luhmann, *Die Kunst der Gesellschaft* (Frankfurt am Main: Suhrkamp, 1995), 398 (my translation).

13. Kara Keeling, "Queer OS," *Cinema Journal* 53, no. 2 (Winter 2014): 152–57; Kara Keeling, *Queer Times, Black Futures* (New York: New York University Press, 2019); Tao Leigh Goffe, "'Guano in Their Destiny': Race, Geology, and a Philosophy of Indenture," *Amerasia Journal* 45, no. 1 (June 2019): 27–49.

14. Kalevi Kull and Timo Maran, "Ecosemiotics: Main Principles and Current Developments," *Geografiska Annaler: Series B, Human Geography* 96 no. 1 (2014): 41.

15. Stevie Suan, *Anime's Identity: Performativity and Form Beyond Japan* (Minneapolis: University of Minnesota Press, 2022); Jinying Li, "The Interface Affect of a Contact Zone: Danmaku on Video-Streaming Platforms," *Asiascape: Digital Asia* 4, no. 3 (2017): 233–56.

The Force Field of the Bullet Curtain

An (Unusual) Archaeology of Danmu

JINYING LI

Marshall McLuhan once famously said: "the 'content' of any medium is always another medium."[1] Like many "McLuhanisms," the argument was meant to be polemical, meant to challenge the long-standing content-centric approach in studying media forms, arguing for a conceptual and methodological shift toward studying the organizations and patterns of media technologies. But the side effect of this radical argument is to render these two entities--content and medium--virtually indistinguishable. For McLuhan, the "content" is nothing but a media condition. This conflation between content and medium, however, masks a key problem, which is the confrontation between the two notions. In fact, some of the most productive, and sometime troublesome, puzzles in media studies often center on the complex relations between the two rather than their supposed equivalency, especially when we are dealing with the expansive and ever-changing transmedia systems known as the "media mix," which operate precisely on the shifting boundaries and intersections between media and contents.

An illuminating case in question for thinking through these problems in the context of the media mix is *danmaku,* or *danmu* (弹幕) as it is called in China. Danmaku is a digital interface originally designed by the Japanese video-sharing platform Niconico to render user comments flying over videos on screen. Danmu was later widely adopted in China in various media contexts such as video-streaming platforms, social media, television, and theatrical cinema (Figure 1). As I have argued elsewhere, it quickly became a prominent device that intermediates among different media forms, contents, and users in regional media mix systems that have largely been platformed in East Asia.[2] As a crucial nexus for organizing the transnational, transmedial systems on digital platforms, danmu also began to draw growing academic interest from diverse fields ranging from culture and media studies to communication studies to area studies.

Situated between video contents and platform connectivity, danmu has been taken as a default interface intermediating the troublesome relationship between content and medium in both the operations and the studies of media mix, along with the troublesome term *platform* that is sometimes used as a substitute for media.[3] There thus emerges a key question: what exactly is danmu? Is it the content of the medium, that is, the user comments generated on the video-streaming platforms? Or, is it the medium of the content, that is, the interface that represents and organizes the user comments? The fact that danmu is also called "comment" (コメン) in Japan further complicates the question. Is it the interface or the content of that interface or something in-between? This ambivalence between content and medium is manifested by the two diverging methodological approaches in the increasing number of studies of danmu. One approach focuses on the textual, paratextual, and intertextual elements of danmu comments as digital contents of a certain sort, which are often analyzed as a form of writing, translation, subtitles, or online chats, as seen in the works of Daniel Johnson, Yizhou Xu, and Yuhong Yang.[4] The other takes danmu's media function as its center of gravity and focuses on its interface effect and affect, such as its intermediation between social communication and video streaming, in organizing and managing media mix systems, as seen in the works of Jinying Li, Marc Steinberg, and Xuenan Cao.[5] This methodological division may be somewhat correlated with the disciplinary and regional cultural differences (e.g., literary studies vs. media studies, China vs. Japan), as the transnational spread of the media mix model, which decenters

Figure 1. The *danmu* interface on the Chinese video streaming platform Bilibili.

its geography from Japan to broader East Asian territories, associates danmu with transcultural, translingual practices such as translation and subtitling in non-Japanese contexts. But the foundation of danmu's ambivalent status is deeply rooted in one of the central problems not only in the logics and operations of media mix but also in media studies broadly. What exactly is the distinction between medium and content? How are they related to each other? The methodological confusion regarding danmu—to study it as a textual content or as a media interface—is merely the latest manifestation of a long-existing problem at the very foundation of media mix, whose assumption that media can "mix" is based on the pretense that medium and content are one and the same, a problematic equation that was prescribed but obscured by McLuhan's above-quoted famous saying.

In what follows, I try to tackle this fundamental problem of the content-medium relationship in media mix by interrogating the meanings and functions of danmu, a key mechanism in media mix systems to manage this problematic relationship on platforms. I do so here in order to signal ongoing theoretical issues—methodological and otherwise—raised by the media mix. By briefly tracing the archaeology of danmu, I call for a theoretical rethinking of *media mix* through an archaeological inquiry, whereby the material and conceptual developments of what we know as "media" cannot be easily "mixed" with the so-called content. However, unlike the conventional approaches in media archaeology that often centers on technological developments, my approach rather focuses on the conceptual development of the metaphorical notion, danmu. I examine the logographic configuration and transformation of the Chinese characters (*kanji* in Japanese) in the word, 弾 (*dan*) and 幕 (*mu*), as a pictorial-symbolic representation of the material history of media development. In other words, I take the etymology of the concept as the basis for an archaeology of the medium. What results is a methodological experiment that may shed new lights to the hidden overlaps between the discursive and the material in media history, because these crucial overlaps are also the dynamic intersections where contents meet media.

Etymology as Archaeology: Between the Curtain (幕) and the Bullets (弾)

To understand what danmu really is, let us begin with where the term comes from and what it means. It is originally a Japanese term, written in kanji

(Chinese characters) and translated as "bullet curtain," to describe the type of shoot-'em-up games in which the bombarding bullets cover the entire screen (Figure 2). The kanji phrase "bullet curtain," or "弾幕," was then borrowed to describe the interface effect of the over-the-video comments that resemble a barrage of bullets flying across the screen on platforms such as Niconico in Japan and Bilibili in China. It is a metaphorical concept that characterizes a combinatory *dispositif*, as in Jean-Louis Baudry's reinterpretation of Foucault's concept of dispositif in which a media system can be characterized as both a discursive formation and a material assemblage.[6] The danmu dispositif has two basic elements, corresponding with the two Chinese characters in the word: 幕 (*mu*), the curtain, as the primary media condition, and 弾 (*dan*), the bullets, as the content of the medium. The configuration and function of danmu thus can be examined and understood through the relationship between the curtain (幕) and the bullets (弾) in the formation of this dispositif.

Let's begin with 幕 (*mu*), the curtain. The Chinese character 幕, in its ancient form in the pre-Qin period (220 BC and earlier), has a strong pictographic tendency: it represents the structure of a tent made of curtains (Figure 3). The character then developed into a logogram with two components: the lower

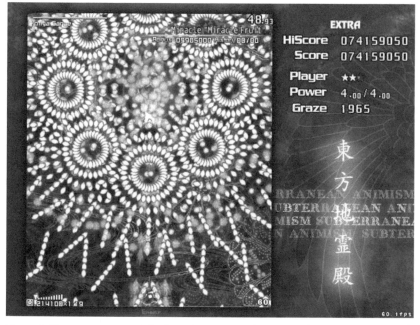

Figure 2. The screen capture of a *danmaku* game, *Touhou Project* (Team Shanghai Alice).

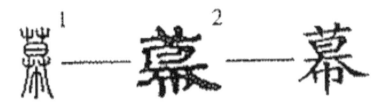

Figure 3. The logographic formation and transformation of the Chinese character 幕 (*mu*). Image source: Xueqin Li, ed., *Zi Yuan* (*The Origin of Chinese Characters*) (Tianjin Ancient Works Publishing, 2013), 690.

part, 巾 (*jin*), is an pictogram referring to fabrics; the upper part, 莫 (*mo*), is both phonetic and ideographic, indicating the meaning of the word as something that covers.[7] The combinatory character 幕 simply means "the covering fabric on top (帷在上曰幕)," as it is defined by the ancient dictionary, *Shuowen Jiezi*, in the Han dynasty (100 AD).[8] Often referring to a curtain, a tent, or a veil, 幕 is a spatial device: it is a layer of structure that covers and blocks a space. Its function of covering and blockage makes 幕 a metaphorical sign for concealment and obscurity, such as its usage in the words 幕府 (*mufu*) or 幕僚 (*muliao*), which refer to military and political powers hidden from public views. It is also its function to cover and block that makes 幕 a prominent device in modern media systems when it was introduced to theaters as a curtain over the stage. As a media device, 幕 is the curtain that covers the screen (referred to as 屏 [*ping*] in Chinese). The association between 屏 (the screen) and 幕 (the covering curtain) in such settings led to the formation of the concept 屏幕 (*pingmu*) that emerged in the twentieth century to describe optical screens in modern media.[9] By and large, 幕 (*mu*), as either a media device or a metaphorical concept, is always tied to its logographic form and meaning that are defined as a spatial structure that covers. Even as an integrated element in modern screens (as in 屏幕), 幕 (*mu*), in its primary media function, is not so much to display or represent as it is to block and obscure.

If 幕 (*mu*) is a medium of blockage rather than representation, what does that make 弹幕 (*danmu*)? Can we describe danmu as a form or a representation of content when its primary function, as a metaphorical curtain, is precisely to block and obscure the very content as such? But if not content, what are those words and sentences written on danmu? What are the functions of the textual elements on a blocking curtain? In fact, a curtain almost always has woven patterns or images on it. But their function is less representational than structural: they serve as a technical means to distinguish between front and back, between inside and outside. This structural function of making distinctions recalls the famous theory by German architect Gottfried Semper about the shared origin between *wand* (wall) and *gewand* (garment) in German. The textile patterns of the garment, according to Semper, are the structural precursors of the wall, as they serve to distinguish "the *inner life* separated from the *outer life*."[10] Therefore, the curtain, which is simultaneously a textile garment and a blocking wall, is the medium *par excellence* of making structural and ontological division and distinction. As Bernhard Siegert argued, "the curtain is the medium of an operational ontology, which brings to light the reason for its existence."[11]

If danmu is to be understood as a metaphorical curtain, what is its "operational ontology" (to borrow Siegert), "the reason for its existence"? Like the textile patterns on a curtain, the textual comments on danmu serve as a technical means to divert our gaze away from what is behind the curtain, that is, the video content on screen. The reason for danmu's existence is thus to divide, an ontological shield between the diegetic and the nondiegetic, between the cinematic gaze and the cybernetic operation, between the content and the platform. Therefore, the danmu comments cannot be merely understood as textual or paratextual content, because this misunderstanding conflates the curtain with the screen. The curtain (*danmu*) is the cover that blocks the screen (the video) but is not the screen itself. For the same reason, I argue against interpreting danmu comments as onscreen translations or subtitles, because to equate danmu with subtitles is to ignore the perverse logics of both: the desire for transparency and seamlessness on the part of subtitles and the gesture of distancing and distraction on the part of danmu. The ultimate goal of subtitles is to be a transparent, integral part of the video on screen, but the logic of danmu is precisely the opposite, because it is, after all, a curtain, whose primary function is to cover, block, and obscure.

The function of danmu as a system of blockage is further underlined by the element of 弹 (*dan*), the bullets. The ancient origin of the Chinese character 弹, as it was recorded in the oracle bone script, is the pictographic representation of an opening bow with a pulled string that is about to shoot a bullet (Figure 4). The emphasis is less the bow or the bullet than the action and the force of shooting. The character later developed into a logogram with two components: the left part, 弓 (*gong*), is an pictogram referring to a bow; the right part, 単 (*dan*), is primarily phonetic but with pictographic and ideographic elements, which characterizes shooting a slingshot with a pronunciation (*dan*) that echoes the sound of a strike (Figure 5). The combinatory character 弹 thus describes, in graphic and sonic means, a forceful process, an act of shooting. As defined by *Guangyun*, a Chinese dictionary in the Song Dynasty (1008 AD), "*dan* means to shoot (弹, 射也)."[12] It characterizes a weaponry system whose focus is not so much the object of the weapon (the bullets) as it is the action of an instant strike (shooting the bullets). As such, 弹 (*dan*) is what Cornelia Vismann called the "medium verb form," because it describes "what media do, what they produce, and what kinds of actions they prompt" and is thus "standing in for verbs."[13]

Figure 4. The logographic formation and transformation of the Chinese character 弹 (*dan*). Image source: Xueqin Li, ed., *Zi Yuan* (*The Origin of Chinese Characters*) (Tianjin Ancient Works Publishing, 2013), 1126.

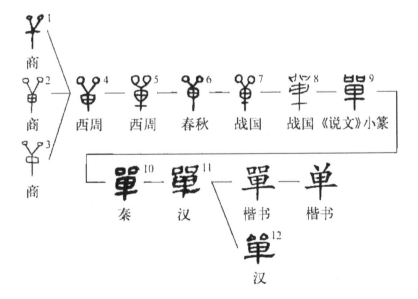

Figure 5. The logographic formation and transformation of the Chinese character 单 (*dan*). Image source: Xueqin Li, ed., *Zi Yuan* (*The Origin of Chinese Characters*) (Tianjin Ancient Works Publishing, 2013), 101.

In the danmu *dispostif*, dan refers to the on-screen comment feeds what appear like flying bullets. But if dan is the "medium verb form" that describes more an action than an object, what does it tell us about the danmu comments? It first raises the question of whether or not those over-the-video comments, the metaphorical "bullets," are actually meant to be read. They simply fly too fast! Bullet time, indeed. The interface organizes the comments in such a way—fast flying, overlapping, and covering the entire screen—that they don't seem to be presented for close reading. After all, bullets are not to be gazed upon, but to be feared. Since the meaning of dan characterizes the action of an instant strike, the function of the danmu comments is to generate the physical and psychological impacts of that strike. They are more affective than discursive. Those "bullet comments" are blasted by the danmu interface to make the viewers *feel* their power, speed, and overwhelming presence. Thus, as I have argued elsewhere, digital platforms shift the center of gravity in media mix systems from discursive contents to affective modules.[14] They constitute a technical structure of feeling rather than a textual content for reading, because they are the metaphorical bullets whose meaning is about an action, a force. Even though some viewers do read the danmu comments, such activities require additional efforts: one often has to pause the video in order to read the comments because they fly too fast to be read at full speed. The reading is thus to be conducted *against* the interface affordance of danmu rather than with it, because the logic of this interface design is fundamentally against reading. The force of the bullets is to be *felt*, not to be *read*.

Danmu as a Force Field

The above etymological analysis argues against taking danmu comments merely as textual contents for reading and instead asks us to examine the production, organization, and reception of danmu comments as powerful forces. It also calls for a methodological reconsideration of media mix, shifting from how it franchises content to how it generates and organizes forces. Consequently, it is more productive to study the affective economy of the media mix (e.g., para-sociality, movements, and conflicts) than to analyze its textual meanings. Furthermore, the meaning of mu as a curtain that covers suggests we should interrogate danmu as a media interface of blockage rather than representation. It calls for examinations of how danmu blocks, disrupts, and interferes with the video content rather than how it represents it. Since danmu is the curtain that blocks the view, it should be understood as an inter-fering signal instead of a paratextual element (e.g., translation or subtitles). The curtain metaphor also underlines danmu's peculiar relationship with the screen, which is often metaphorically described as a "window."[15] As a cur-tain that covers the window, the danmu interface points to the fundamental contradiction and incoherence between medium and content in the media mix. As a medium of blockage, the content of the "bullet-curtain" is *absence*, because it denies the very existence and access of content as such.

How to understand such incoherence between medium and content? If the only content of danmu is absence, then the overt obsession with content in the media mix industry—cue the famous motto "content is king"—seems to be nothing but a fetishistic trap to disavow the lack or insignificance of content in the systems. We are so distracted by the fetishistic logic of danmu in the form of its baffling ambivalence (e.g., is it the content or the interface of content?) that we forget that platforms have already moved away from meaningful content and toward informatic contact for sustaining data flow. The bombarding bullet curtain is delivered to us not as a content but as a façade, a fetishistic perversion that serves to conceal and to attach us to the very absence of content in the platform systems of media mix.

How to avoid falling for this fetishistic trap? I propose to examine danmu as neither a content nor a medium but rather, in rethinking this bullet-curtain *dispostif*, a structure of blockage (*mu*) with instant strikes (*dan*), as a powerful force field. In physics, a force field is a vector field acting upon the particles with noncontact forces so that its position and direction can be felt. This sci-entific concept is adopted in structural biology as a mathematical method for modeling protein structures by estimating the forces between atoms and molecules to calculate the potential energy of the system.[16] If we consider danmu as a force field, then it is neither a textual content to be represented nor a mediating vessel to deliver content. Instead, it is a complex structure with potential energy that acts upon platform users with powerful forces from various positions and directions, that is, a blocking curtain that affect you with the strike of bullets. Like the force field in biology that organizes protein structures with forces and energy, danmu as a force field organizes the media mix system through: (1) the bonding forces with and among the users; (2) the nonbonding forces with and against the video content; and (3) the potential energy of users' affective feelings.

In fact, force and energy are the two key words that are frequently high-lighted by the user community to characterize the experience of danmu. For

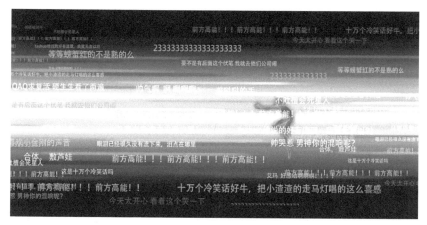

Figure 6. The appearance of *danmu* as a diegetic element in the animation feature film *One Hundred Thousand Bad Jokes* (2014). Note: this fictional danmu contains and highlights the popular phrase "high energy ahead!" (前方高能!).

instance, the video segments that are covered with a high density of danmu comment feeds are often described as "high energy" (高能 *gaoneng*), and one of the most popular danmu comments on Chinese video platforms is "high energy ahead (前方高能)," which is to warn viewers that the next video segment will contain an overwhelming amount of "bullet comments." This "high energy" of danmu is imagined as the source of a powerful force. In the Chinese animation film, *One Hundred Thousand Bad Jokes* (2014), danmu is no longer an interface but becomes a diegetic element in the fictional universe: at the film's climax, the hero unleashes a barrage of danmu (like actual bullets) as a deadly force to strike down the enemy (Figure 6).[17] Associating danmu with force and energy, users often describe the extreme instances when the videos are covered by too many danmu comments as "brutal" (凶残 *xiongcan*), which recalls the origin of the concept as a type of violent shooter game. After all, the force field of the bullet curtain is a violent one.

In conclusion, I want to argue for a methodological shift in our approach to the media mix from the content-medium debate toward the force-energy mechanism, a shift that also calls for a theoretical model to *rethink media formations as force fields*. As Thomas Lamarre reminds us, the ecology of media mix is structured through the bifurcation between the distributive and the totalizing forces, and the tension between them generates and potentializes a field that is experienced affectively.[18] To study the media mix as a force field, therefore, is to examine how the system, like a complex protein structure, is folded and unfolded with actions, forces, and energy that insinuate tendencies and limits, as well as how such forces and energy are felt by different users in various geocultural settings. The numerous unique features of danmu, for example, can be examined as constitutive elements of the force field. These elements include both attractive forces that enable participation, such as the anonymity of commenters, the rewarding effects of virtual liveness and pseudo-simultaneity that are generated by seeing comments by oneself and others appear instantly on a video, and the sense of immersive community created by danmaku, as well as repulsive forces that block participation, such as the visual density of the text and the rapid, fleeting speed at which comments fly past, the temporal disjunctions created by the layering of older comments and newer responses, and the incoherence between platform and content discussed above. Table 1 summarizes these elements and illustrates how they create what I have termed in a previous work the "interface affect."[19]

Table 1. *Danmu* as a force field

ATTRACTIVE FORCES	REPULSIVE FORCES
anonymousness	visual blockage
virtual liveness	fleeting speed
pseudo-simultaneity	temporal disjunctions
immersive community	incoherence between the content and the platform

POTENTIAL ENERGY: THE INTERFACE AFFECT

The anonymity of the comment feeds, on one hand, creates an identifiable and immersive environment for a user community, and so does the pseudo-simultaneity in the temporal structure of danmu's virtual liveness. Both generate attractive forces that bond the viewers with the platform as well as among the viewers themselves. On the other hand, the blocking effects of danmu (the "curtain") versus a transparent vision of the video (the "window") generate repulsive forces that polarize the interface as a contact zone of incoherence between the platform and the content. The bonding, attractive forces and the polarizing, repulsive forces clash and interact with each other, forming a powerful force field whose potential energy is felt as the affective experience. Such is how a media mix is constituted: not by the supposed content-medium equation in a "mixing" media convergence, but by the dynamic force-energy reaction in an affective force field.

....

Jinying Li is Assistant Professor of Modern Culture and Media at Brown University, where she teaches media theory, animation, and digital cultures in East Asia. She is the coeditor of *The Oxford Handbook of Chinese Digital Media* (Oxford University Press, forthcoming), and she has coedited two special issues on Chinese animation for *The Journal of Chinese Cinemas*, as well as a special issue on regional platforms for *Asiascape: Digital Asia*. Her essays have appeared in *Camera Obscura, differences, Asian Cinema, Film International, Mechademia, International Journal of Communication, Journal of Chinese Cinemas*, and *Asiascape*. Her first book, *Anime's Knowledge Cultures*, is forthcoming with the University of Minnesota Press. She is currently working on her second book, *Walled Media and Mediating Walls*.

....

Notes

1. Marshall McLuhan, *Understanding Media: The Extensions of Man*, Reprint edition (Cambridge, MA: MIT Press, 1994), 8.
2. Jinying Li, "The Interface Affect of a Contact Zone: Danmaku on Video-Streaming Platforms," *Asiascape: Digital Asia* 4, no. 3 (2017): 233–56.
3. Marc Steinberg and Jinying Li, "Introduction: Regional Platforms," *Asiascape: Digital Asia* 4 no. 3 (2017): 173–83.
4. Daniel Johnson, "Polyphonic/Pseudo-Synchronic: Animated Writing in the Comment Feed of Nicovideo," *Japanese Studies* 33, no. 3 (2013): 297–313; Yizhou Xu, "The Postmodern Aesthetic of Chinese Online Comment Cultures," *Communication and the Public* 1, no. 4 (2016): 436–51; Yuhong Yang, "Danmaku Subtitling: An Exploratory Study of a New Grassroots Translation Practice on Chinese Video-Sharing Websites," *Translation Studies* 14, no. 1 (2021): 1–17.
5. Li, "The Interface Affect"; Marc Steinberg, "Converging Contents and Platforms: Niconico Video and Japan's Media Mix Ecology," in *Asian Video Cultures: In the Penumbra of the Global*, ed. Joshua Neves and Bhaskar Sarkar (Durham: Duke University Press, 2017), 91–113; Xuenan Cao, "Bullet Screens (Danmu): Texting, Online Streaming, and the Spectacle of Social Inequality on Chinese Social Networks," *Theory, Culture & Society* 38, no. 3 (2021): 29–49.
6. Jean-Louis Baudry, "The Apparatus," *Camera Obscura* 1, no 1 (May 1976): 104–26.
7. Xueqin Li, ed., *Zi Yuan (The Origin of Chinese Characters)* (Tianjin Ancient Works Publishing, 2013), 690.

8. Yucai Duan and Shen Xu, *Shuowen Jiezi Zhu* (*Commentary on Shuowen Jiezi*) (Shanghai: Shanghai Bookstore Publishing, 1992), 628.

9. Jinying Li, "Toward a Genealogy of the Wall-Screen," *Differences* 33, no. 1 (2022): 28–59.

10. Gottfried Semper, *The Four Elements of Architecture and Other Writings*, trans. Harry Francis Mallgrave and Wolfgang Herrmann (Cambridge: Cambridge University Press, 1989), 127.

11. Bernhard Siegert, "After the Wall: Interference among Grids and Veils," *GAM* 09, *Walls: Spatial Sequences* (2013): 32.

12. Xueqin Li, *Zi Yuan*, 1126.

13. Cornelia Vismann, "Cultural Techniques and Sovereignty," *Theory, Culture & Society* 30, no. 6 (2013): 83.

14. Jinying Li, "The Platformization of Chinese Cinema: The Rise of IP Films in the Age of Internet+," *Asian Cinema* 31, no. 2 (2020): 203–18.

15. Anne Friedberg, *The Virtual Window: From Alberti to Microsoft* (Cambridge, MA: MIT Press, 2006).

16. Daniel M. Zuckerman, *Statistical Physics of Biomolecules: An Introduction* (Baton Rouge: Taylor & Francis Group, 2010).

17. Jinying Li, "From Media Mix to Platformization: The Transmedia Strategy of 'IP' in One Hundred Thousand Bad Jokes," in *Transmedia Storytelling in East Asia*, ed. Dal Yong Jin (London: Routledge, 2020), 225–42.

18. Thomas Lamarre, *The Anime Ecology: A Genealogy of Television, Animation, and Game Media* (Minneapolis: University of Minnesota Press, 2018).

19. Li, "The Interface Affect," 233.

A 2.5D Approach to the Media Mix

The Potentialities of Fans' Produsage

AKIKO SUGAWA-SHIMADA

This article and provocation aims to demonstrate how the 2.5-dimensional (hereafter 2.5D) cultural approach could advance the theoretical framework and methodology of media mix studies. 2.5D here means "a space between the two-dimensional (fictional space where our imagination and fantasy work) and the three-dimensional (reality where we physically exist)."[1] In the context of Japanese popular culture, 2.5D culture primarily refers to cultural products based on anime but enacted in live-action contexts, such as stage plays (theatrical adaptations from manga, anime, and games), used as a new category in Japanese entertainment business. But it also includes users' and fans' cultural practices such as appreciating 2.5D stage plays and live concerts by voice actors/characters, cosplaying, performing as VTubers, and so on, where 2D fictionality and 3D physicality intersect via the help of human body. It is an emerging cultural phenomenon in Japan and beyond, impacted by the development of social media, the dissemination of the media mix, and character-oriented consumption since the early 2000s. In my view focusing on 2.5D can call much-needed attention to fans' deep involvement in the media mix—as players who "activate" or "dynamize" the media mix. The ways in which fans activate and engage the media mix will be my focus in what follows, through a consideration of the concept and practices around 2.5D.

Let me start with overall discussions of the media mix. As is well known, "media mix" (or *media mikkusu*) is a Japanese loanword borrowed from the English term. As such, its definition and meanings are vague in nature, and vary depending on the context in which it is used even in Japan. In the context of the Japanese popular culture industry, however, the media mix is generally understood as a media franchise marketing strategy in which cultural contents in multiple works are produced or distributed across multiple media platforms. In this perspective, analyses of the media mix have tended to focus on how the media mix functions in the Japanese entertainment industry, or how it differs from or is similar to its counterparts in other countries, such as media franchising in the United States and South Korea.

Such approaches based on regional or local specificities (including Japanese cultural specificity), however, have served as catalysts for productive arguments about the economics of popular culture production and consumption in Japan and abroad.[2]

Yet, if we take media mix as a phenomenon, as Marc Steinberg suggests,[3] the media mix can serve as a system in which consumption, use, and production vibrantly and energetically interact with one another. In this view, what matters is how fan audiences, as active participants, can activate the media mix. Put another way: the media mix does not exist without its fans, and the specificity of fan interactions—including the specificity of media used in these interactions—make the media mix what it is. This is to say that fan interactions make the media mix *matter* differently. In the digital age in particular, fan audiences or users of popular culture products have become more powerful driving forces of media mixes, especially through using social media platforms such as Twitter, Tumblr, Instagram, and so on. Fan audiences are no longer merely consumers but *producers and users*, that is "produsers."[4] There are of course counter-arguments about how historically new active audiences actually are.

As Henry Jenkins argues, fan audience/users' intense commitments to popular cultural contents are vital in convergence or participatory culture to nurture a well-functioning grassroots democracy.[5] However, their commitments are also criticized in that fan audience/users are easily manipulated and exploited by authorities.[6] Ōtsuka Eiji, for instance, in his *Media Mix Mobilization* (*Dōin no media mikkusu*), reconsiders the role of audience participation in Japan's wartime media mix. He explores how they could be linked to fascism by examining their creative commitment to manga comics during the Asia Pacific War.[7] He elucidates how both professional and amateur manga artists were deftly made complicit in Japanese wartime propaganda when the Imperial Rule Assistant Association created the *Yokusan Family* propaganda manga, which modeled the ideal behaviors for patriotic families. This work was drawn by multiple artists, and amateur artists were also encouraged to send in their own illustrations and comic strips featuring Yokusan Family characters for a chance at publication in national newspapers.

While not during wartime, a similar case can be observed in a recent fans' produsage regarding the official character of Osaka Expo 2025, Myaku-Myaku (which literally means "ceaselessly"). According to the official website, Myaku-Myaku is "a mysterious creature born from the unification of cells and water. Its identity is unknown"[8] (Figure 1).

Figure 1. Poster of Expo 2025, Osaka, Kansai, Japan. Image used with permission of Japan Association for the 2025 World Exposition.

The goal of this Expo is to contribute to the achievement of the United Nations' Sustainable Development Goals (SDGs) and to promote Japan's national strategy of Society 5.0, described as a system "that combines both cyber and physical spaces in a sophisticated manner."[9] For this purpose, the Japan Association for the 2025 World Exposition attempted to involve the general audience by permitting and even encouraging secondary use of Myaku-Myaku so long as it is not for commercial purposes. The character was named Myaku-Myaku on July 18, 2022, and soon after this announcement, anonymous Twitter users began to create and post stories using the character. A computational social scientist, Toriumi Fujio, noted that numerous Twitter users started to call it Myaku-Myaku-sama, adding the suffix "sama" within some hours after the name Myaku-Myaku was announced, as if they worshiped it as a god. (In this context, adding the suffix "-sama" shows respect and awe toward someone with charismatic power.) Within two days, over 70 percent of all the posts referred to the character as Myaku-Myaku-sama and the respectful title became established as the norm.[10] Many derivative works, such as illustrations of Myaku-Myaku-sama, were posted on Twitter and Pixiv (a Japanese social media site specializing in illustrations and manga), providing fictional backstories that depicted it as a godlike creature or a yokai demon. Between 3D reality (the existence of the official mascot character for Osaka EXPO, Myaku-Myaku) and 2D fiction (multiplied stories using Myaku-Myaku-sama as if the character was real), Twitter users played at embodying Myaku-Myaku-sama, which I shall call "pleasurable 2.5D play." This typifies fans' creative produsage, but simultaneously, they were (unknowingly, perhaps) contributing to the promotion of Japan's national strategy of Society 5.0. Here, a sense of 2.5D, or users' expanding imaginative power, is vital to construct the media mix that Expo 2025 intended to produce. Japanese popular culture critic Sayawaka has argued that the Vocaloid Hatsune Miku is "a blank slate that is receptive to any narrative," enabling fans to create a wide variety of works around her.[11] Similarly, in the case of Myaku-Myaku, its mystery and lack of a backstory left large gaps for active fan audiences to fill in. That this action ultimately contributes to the realization of the national mission of producing Society 5.0, demonstrating how fans can be mobilized into national and nationalist projects—both during wartime and in the present.

Fans' creative power, however, can also sometimes threaten corporate or nationalist media mix strategies. Allow to me to provide one intriguing example: King Records' *Hypnosis Mic, Division Rap Battle* (hereafter *Hypnosis Mic*), a unique character rap project launched in 2017, featuring eighteen male characters (all dubbed by voice actors). The initial plot of *Hypnosis Mic* is as follows: "In H-age after World War III, the world was dominated by women. Conflict was replaced not by force of arms but by a special microphone that interfered with the human psyche. This is 'Hypnosismic' [*sic*]."[12] In the setting of the *Hypnosis Mic*, men are not allowed to dwell in the Chuo (Central) Ward where women rule. The areas where men are confined are divided into six units called "Divisions," such as Ikebukuro, Shinjuku, Shibuya, Yokohama, Osaka, and Nagoya Divisions. Each Division has a representative rap-music group, and each group is organized by three handsome male anime-style characters. For instance, the members of "Mad Trigger Crew" in Yokohama Division are Aohitsugi Samatoki (a yakuza gang leader), Iruma Juto (a policeman), and Rio Mason Busujima (an ex-Navy private). As soon as *Hypnosis Mic* was released, it immediately attracted female audiences. Clues about this eccentric combination and the characters themselves were limited to brief character profiles and minimal background information, prompting fan audiences to want to know more about them. This media mix kicked off with music "battle" CDs that contain short dramas (2017–ongoing) and live concerts by the voice actors (2017–ongoing),[13] followed by manga (2019–ongoing), 2.5D stage plays (2019–ongoing), and finally TV anime (2020) and live concerts by 3D CG characters (2021-ongoing).[14] This project was designed to inspire the fan audience's participation through what Patrick Galbraith calls "the labor of love,"[15] or their fanatic devotion to their favorite character(s). In *Hypnosis Mic*, the winner of each rap battle in the ongoing story is selected by voting from fan audiences. A voting code is inserted in the CDs that each Division puts out, so devoted fans purchase as many CDs as possible to help their favorite group win. By purchasing CDs and voting, they can connect the world of *Hypnosis Mic* (2D) to reality (3D), thereby generating the 2.5D space of fandom. Manga scholar Iwashita Hosei suggests that "*Hypnosis Mic*'s project offers fans a sense of contribution to the story, and to the lives of the characters," noting that it "also enhances fans' influence on the project."[16]

The influence of fan participation in the *Hypnosis Mic* project is not unusual because the system whereby fans purchase CDs and vote for their favorite idols was already introduced and popularized by AKB48, one of the most popular female idol groups in Japan. Fan participation is built into the commercial system from the start. However, it is noteworthy that there was a moment when fans' power wielded immense influence on the authenticity of *Hypnosis Mic*.

As mentioned above, although 2D characters' visuals and simple profiles were shown, fans have had to guess the stories behind them using the slightest hints. These open gaps triggered hot debates among female fans on Twitter over the questions such as "When did the H-age start?," "How was each rap group formed?," "Why do they have to compete with one another, and what are they trying to win?," and so on. Some answers were provided to fans when the manga version of *Hypnosis Mic, Hypnosismic* [*sic*]—*Before the Battle*—*The Dirty Dawg*,[17] began to be serialized on Kodansha's *Shōnen Magazine Edge* in 2018. It depicts the story of the rap group "The Dirty Dawg" before the present rap groups were organized. Immediately after its publication, a number of Hypnosis Mic's fans posted their comments on the serialized narrative on Twitter, criticizing it with the term "misinterpretation (*kaishaku chigai*)." The use of the term could be taken in two ways: either fans' misinterpretation/ misunderstanding, or misinterpretation on the company's side. It is natural to assume that their Tweets referred to "fans' misinterpretation," given that the manga was the official publication. That is, fans failed to correctly guess the characters' backstories. However, it seems that some fans meant to point out the *company's misinterpretation*, indicating that the story the manga illustrates did not ring true (at least not to them). As Iwashita argues, the two possible ways of using "misinterpretation" are perhaps equally true; meaning that the stories the company officially provides are not treated by fans as absolutely authentic but merely one possible interpretation of the characters.[18] It seems contradictory to say the creators' authenticity is not always legitimate. None-theless, within this type of media mix project—and arguably the media mix in general—fans and their produsage serve as an essential player to support and even adjudicate the truthfulness or accuracy of the media mixes of popular cultural contents.

A similar example is found in the fan audience in the *Tōken Ranbu* media mix. *Tōken Ranbu-Online* (2015–ongoing) is one of the most popular online games, featuring personified Japanese swords as hunks. The story is set in 2205 when "Historical Revisionists" attempt to change Japanese history by sending their demonlike army to the past. The personified swords called Tōken Danshi are sent into the past by the government to prevent the Revi-sionists' plot. In the game, a player can forge new swords with raw materials and organize teams of Tōken Danshi for combat against the History Retro-grade Army sent by the Historical Revisionists. Along with being a sensational hit, this game has been adapted into 2.5D stage plays (musicals and dialogue plays) (2015–ongoing), live concerts by actors who play the role of the charac-ters (2016–ongoing), anime (2016–ongoing), manga (2016–ongoing), and live action movies (2019, 2023), among other media.

The basic plot of the game is as simple as *Hypnosis Mic*, so it enables pro-dusage among fans, including derivative works. Although *Tōken Ranbu* fans attempt to guess the stories behind the characters based on hints, as *Hypnosis*

Mic fans do, they seem to interpret the characters and the stories in different ways. In *Tōken Ranbu, the Stage* (eleven titles as of 2022), for instance, there are several timelines, with different stories unfolding in each timeline. Most characters are played by the same actors (e.g., Suzuki Hiroki as Mikazuki Munechika), but other characters, such as Tsurumaru Kuninaga, have been played by two different actors in the different titles of the plays. Fans understand which is the first Tsurumaru and which is the second Tsurumaru, depending on the actor playing them. The producer and president of Nitroplus, Kosaka Takaki, intended to offer different stories on multiple media platforms, using a media mix strategy, so that fans can find their own favorite stories and interpretations of characters.[19] His remark points to fact that, as argued throughout this short article, the "official" stories and the interpretations of characters that a media company provides are just one of the numerous possibilities. Hence, we can say that the power relationship between a copyright holder and the fans of a given property is not hierarchal but equal, or at least multidirectional.

In sum, the media mix is not merely a marketing strategy by which a given cultural content is distributed to passive fans, as it has sometimes been presented, but also a site where producers, performers, and fans interactively influence and engage one another. Fans as "produsers" take pleasure in using and creating numerous narratives featuring 2D characters, thereby becoming indispensable players within the media mix. By applying a 2.5D approach to media mix studies, we can bring out how media companies have involved fans from the outset, and also how fans continue to activate media mixes, thereby making the media mix possible. Although a sense of 2.5D totally depends on fans' imaginative and pleasurable interplay between the fictional and the real, a cultural approach to 2.5D emphasizing fan activism may help bring out the regional and local specificities of media mix practices, and hence offer new directions for media mix studies.

....

Akiko Sugawa-Shimada, PhD, is a professor in the Graduate School of Urban Innovation at Yokohama National University, Japan. Dr. Sugawa-Shimada is the author of a number of books and articles on anime, manga, and cultural studies, including *Girls and Magic: How Have Girl Heroes Been Accepted?* (2013), which received the 2014 Japan Society of Animation Studies Award, *2.5-dimentional Culture: Stages, Characters, Fandom* (2021, in Japanese), chapters in the books *Japanese Animation: East Asian Perspectives* (2013), *Teaching*

Japanese Popular Culture (2016), *Shojo Across Media* (2019), *Contents Tourism and Pop Culture Fandom* (2020), and *Animating the Spiritual* (2020), *Idology in Transcultural Perspective* (2021), *War as Entertainment and Contents Tourism in Japan* (2022), and as co-author, *Contents Tourism in Japan* (2017). Her recent works are *Cultural Approaches to Studio Ghibli's Animation* (2022 in Japanese) joined as coeditor and *Mechademia: Second Arc* vol. 15.2, "2.5D Culture," joined as guest editor. Her website is: akikosugawa.2-d.jp.

....

Notes

1. Akiko Sugawa-Shimada, "Emerging "2.5-dimensional" Culture: Character-oriented Cultural Practices and 'Community of Preferences' as a New Fandom in Japan and Beyond," *Mechademia Second Arc* 12 no. 2 (2020): 124.

2. Kathryn Hemmann, "Queering the Media Mix: The Female Gaze in Japanese Fan Comics," *Transformative Works and Cultures* 20 (2015), http://dx.doi.org/10.3983/twc.2015.0628.

3. Marc Steinberg, *Anime's Media Mix: Franchising Characters and Toys in Japan* (Minneapolis: University of Minnesota Press, 2012); trans. Nakagawa Yuzuru as *Naze nihon wa "media mikkusu suru kuni" nanoka* (Why is Japan a "media mixing nation"?) (Tokyo: Kadokawa, 2015).

4. Axel Bruns, *Blogs, Wikipedia, Second Life, and Beyond: From Production to Produsage* (New York: Peter Lang Publishing, 2008).

5. Henry Jenkins, *Convergence Culture: Where Old and New Media Collide* (New York: New York University Press, 2006).

6. Steinberg, *Naze nihon wa*, 329.

7. Ōtsuka Eiji, *Dōin no media mikkusu—"sousaku suru taishu" no senjika, sengo* (Media mix mobilization: The wartime and postwar for "the mass of people who create") (Tokyo: Shibunkan, 2017).

8. "About the Official Character," Expo 2025 Osaka, Kansai, Japan, https://www.expo2025.or.jp/en/overview/character/.

9. "Purpose," Expo 2025 Osaka, Kansai, Japan, https://www.expo2025.or.jp/en/overview/purpose/.

10. Toriumi Fujio, "Myaku-Myaku-sama wa itsu Myaku-Myaku-sama ni nattanoka" (When did Myaku-Myaku-sama become Myaku-Myaku-sama?), *Yahoo News Japan*, July 21, 2022, https://news.yahoo.co.jp/byline/toriumifujio/20220721-00306480.

11. Sayawaka, *Kyara no shiko hou: gendai bunka ron no appu guredo* (The characters' way of thinking: upgrades of contemporary culture studies) (Seidosha, 2015), 20. Translation is mine.

12. "What's Hypnosismic?," *Hypnosis Mic, Division Rap Battle*, https://hypnosismic.com/about/.

13. "Hypnosis Microphone 5th Live," trailer, YouTube, August 2020, https://www
.youtube.com/watch?v=A3LhYRt_L6M.

14. "Hypnosis Microphone—Division Rap Battle—3DCG Live "Hyped Up-01,"
trailer, YouTube, January 2021, https://www.youtube.com/watch?v=9_Rd1Vl
_3tY.

15. Patrick W. Galbraith, "The Labor of Love: On the Convergence of Fan and Corporate Interests in Contemporary Idol Culture in Japan," in *Media Convergence in
Japan,* ed. Patrick W. Galbraith and Jason G. Karlin (Kinema Club, 2016), 234.

16. Iwashita Hosei, *Kyara ga riaru ni naru toki: 2jigen, 2.5jigen, sono saki no kyarakuta-
ron* (When a character becomes real: On characters in 2D, 2.5D, and beyond)
(Tokyo: Seidosha, 2020), 185.

17. *Hypnosismic—Before the Battle—The Dirty Dawg,* story by Evil Line Records,
illustration by Karasuzuki Rui, screenplay by Momose Yuichiro, 4 vols. (Tokyo:
Kodansha, 2019, 2020).

18. Iwashita, *Kyara ga riaru,* 192.

19. Kosaka Takeki, "Gēmu kara butai e to hana hiraku *Tōken Ranbu* no sekaikan
(The blooming world of Tōken Ranbu from the game to the stage plays)," *Bijutsu
Techo Special Issue 2.5jigen bunka* (July 2016): 53.

Gender, Politics, and Power

Exploding Girls, Imploding Strategies
Media-Mixed Bodies in Late 1970s to 1980s Japanese Women's Professional Wrestling

KIRSTEN SEUFFERT

In an analysis of sociocultural events in Japan paralleling the emergence of the term "otaku," cultural critic and media theorist Ōtsuka Eiji asks, "What kind of year was 1983?" Mapping out the terrain—e.g., the opening of Tokyo Disneyland and the first MUJI store, the release of Nintendo's Family Computer, and publication of theoretical work by Asada Akira and Yoshimoto Takaaki as well as manga by Ōtomo Katsuhiro—he argues that 1983 was "the year that all of the 1980s phenomena appeared on the surface all at once."[1] Ōtsuka's list is clearly not intended to be exhaustive, yet he makes one significant omission—the formation of the tag team Crush Gals by professional wrestlers Nagayo Chigusa and Lioness Asuka.

In mid-1980s Japan, Crush Gals (*Kurasshu Gyaruzu*) images and performances saturated the mediascape along with those of other wrestlers from the promotion All-Japan Women's Pro Wrestling (*Zen'nihon Joshi Puroresu*, hereafter Zenjo). Established in 1968 by Matsunaga Takashi and several of his siblings, Zenjo was the only major women's promotion active in Japan from the late 1970s until the 1986 launch of Japan Women's Pro-Wrestling (*Japan Joshi Puroresu*) and as such wielded considerable influence in this period in both Japanese professional wrestling (*puroresu*) and the wider mediasphere.[2] Although puroresu and women's wrestling (*joshi puro*) in particular tend to be neglected in scholarly discussions of postwar media, visual culture, and performance in Japan, the industry and the bodies that enable it played a significant role in the late 1970s–1980s media environment and the everyday experience of consuming popular culture. Crush Gals achieved what is often termed an "explosive" (*bakuhatsuteki*) popularity from 1983 until both members' 1989 retirement from Zenjo. Especially popular with junior high- and high school-aged girls, their media presence rivaled that of mid-1980s men's puroresu stars such as Antonio Inoki and Fujinami Tatsumi and formed an integral part of the social and cultural environment Ōtsuka describes.

However, what sets Crush Gals and Zenjo in this period apart from other moments in joshi puro history and 1970s–1980s men's wrestling in Japan is the extent to which they transcended the ring and populated other media spheres. Zenjo wrestlers not only wrestled in live venues and on TV but were also extremely active in other entertainment areas—cutting records, singing and dancing in the ring and in concerts, appearing on TV dramas and variety and music programs, and lending images and performances to television commercials (CMs), video games, and a wide range of material goods. In doing so, they infiltrated media spaces densely populated at the time by idols (*aidoru*), combining puroresu's violent, aggressive performance styles with trendy, approachable "idol-like" performances to create a novel product. It is now commonly accepted that puroresu is a genre that blurs the lines between sports, theater, and entertainment. However, I argue, the promotional strategies that Zenjo, its wrestlers, and affiliated media companies such as Fuji TV employed during this period blurred these lines even further, capitalizing on the popularity of idol culture to create cross-media commodities that played on and increased the porosity between two (already multimedia) entertainment industries. Zenjo marketed its characters, narratives, and performances—including the wildly popular feud between Crush Gals and *Gokuaku Dōmei* (The Atrocious Alliance), led by Dump Matsumoto—via a unique set of "media mix" strategies that (however unconsciously) plugged in to contemporary media practice and discourse. While much credit should be given to the wrestlers whose labor and physical sacrifices sustained it, the resulting 1980s Zenjo "boom" was also a product of Japan's growing idol-friendly media mix infrastructure, which supported cross-pollination between music, TV, and live performance.

Zenjo's wrestling, singing, dancing, acting bodies permeated the idol image economy in late 1970s–1980s Japan, reaching a mid-1980s peak in diversity of marketing strategies, exposure, and fan enthusiasm. Yet, what is significant about Zenjo's media mix experimentation is that rather than the de-corporealized images often linked in criticism to idol marketing and fandom as well as characters (*kyara*) in Japan, the actors behind these strategies foregrounded and capitalized on wrestlers' material, fleshy bodies and performances. As a performance form centered on muscle, sweat, fat, blood, pain, and violent physical confrontation, joshi puro markets bodies that are excessive and resist flattening—even when circulated within a late 1970s–1980s image economy that privileged more "2-D" idols and anime and manga characters. Zenjo's media mix depended as much on its non-normative, extremely physical "wrestler" bodies and performances as it did on its more mainstream "idol" appeal and in fact benefitted by mixing the two. Ambiguous wrestler-idol bodies not only propelled Zenjo to peak profitability in this moment but also represent—as does joshi puro—a rich site from which to rethink the media mix's relation to embodiment and performance, particularly considerations of gender, sexuality, embodied labor, and affect. This article attempts such a rethinking by tracing Zenjo's expansion into new media territories—in particular, idol content and performance—and the strategies and actors facilitating it. It then explores the historical and theoretical implications of marketing material bodies through the media mix and, finally, offers suggestions for further inquiries into the intersection of bodies and media mix histories, practice, and discourse.

Zenjo Bodies on Idol Turf

The atmosphere on Fuji TV variety show *Yūyake nyan nyan* (1985–87) was rarely what one would call understated. A vehicle for female idol group Onyanko Club, it offered a fast-paced combination of youthful exuberance, musical performances, skits, and gags targeted mainly at those under age twenty. Yet, the show was rarely as chaotic as when Dump Matsumoto blustered onto the set, whacking furniture with her signature bamboo sword and sending idols scattering in (mostly) mock fear (Figure 1). Due to her highly promoted feud with "babyface" (hero) Chigusa, Dump and her "heel" (villain) stable, *Gokuaku Dōmei* (hereafter Gokuaku), were also welcomed into the spotlight. Chigusa, Asuka, Dump, and Gokuaku's Bull Nakano became well-known media personalities throughout mid-1980s Japan, appearing not only on match broadcasts but also on TV variety and music shows, dramas, and CMs. As Dump's appearance on *Yūyake nyan nyan* demonstrates, in this moment, Zenjo bodies and idol bodies shared media, material, and affective spaces, with significant porosity between the two. Yet, wrestlers' larger bodies (particularly Dump's) and aggressive behavior contrasted sharply with those of idols found on TV and movie screens and in trendy magazines, complicating ideas about which sorts of bodies could be marketed in these spaces. Patrick W. Galbraith and Jason G. Karlin define "idols" in the Japanese context as "highly produced and promoted singers, models, and media personalities" who appeal widely and spread their performances and images across media and genres.[3] For them, idols function in the media economy as

Figure 1. Dump Matsumoto and Bull Nakano wreak havoc on the set of Fuji TV's
Yūyake nyan nyan.

"interchangeable and disposable commodities" that are "produced and packaged to maximize consumption" and utilized to advertise other commodities.
While this definition would not apply to every mid-1980s Zenjo wrestler,
it resonates with the ways by which Crush Gals and Gokuaku turned their
images and performances into highly marketable products, aided by Zenjo
management and media and business companies looking to capitalize on the
latest trend. However, while they shared sets, screens, and printed pages with
idols whose appearance and behavior hewed more closely to societal norms
for femininity, their wrestler bodies were *different* idol bodies that introduced
excess and ambiguity into the media mix.

Zenjo's popularity and media exposure peaked between 1985 and 1987,
with fans supporting its wrestling—which was violent and often bloody—
and a wide spectrum of performance. After debut album *Square Jungle* (1984),
Crush Gals released many singles and several more albums on the Victor label,
including *Healthy* and *Crush A Go Go!!: Best of Crush Gals* (1985), *Twin Beat*
(1986), and *Forever Crush Gals* (1987) (Figure 2). Chigusa's and Asuka's idol-like
babyface appeal helped them sell records, book performances on programs
such as *Yoru no hitto sutajio* (Evening hit studio) and *Yan yan utau sutajio* (Yan
yan singing studio), and lure audiences to concerts—a media-crossing perfor-

mance trajectory shared with idols. Other wrestlers such as Devil Masami and Jumping Bomb Angels also cut singles, and Zenjo released several compilation albums of wrestler singles and ring entrance songs. Dump's villainous appeal increased Crush Gals' popularity and also earned her fans and opportunities of her own. She released mini-album *Dump the Heel: Gokuaku* on Victor in 1985 (including music by Sakamoto Ryūichi) and achieved national name recognition as an "image girl" in CMs for Nissin's Takoyaki Ramen. Heel characters are central to puroresu narratives, yet Dump's ubiquitous media presence in mid-1980s Japan demonstrates that in this context, not only idols and baby-faces were mobilized to sell products and bring new energy to content. Zenjo's media mix marketed diverse performance styles and a variety of body types, drawing in new fans and competing for consumer attention.

Aside from its Fuji TV match broadcasts, Zenjo's highest level of mid-1980s media exposure arguably came from appearances on TBS (Tokyo Broadcasting System) drama series. Joshi puro-themed *Kagayakitai no* (1984, I want to shine) features an original script by Yamada Taichi and performances by

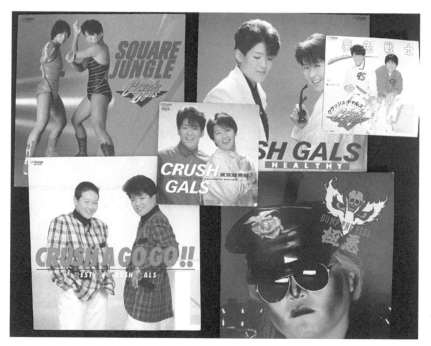

Figure 2. A selection of 1980s Zenjo albums and singles released on Victor. Author's personal collection.

wrestlers Ogura Yumi, Devil Masami, and Jaguar Yokota as well as Sugawara Bunta and Wada Akiko. TBS then featured Dump and Bull on the first season of *Natsu, taiken monogatari* (1985, Summer: A story of experience) alongside idols Nakayama Miho and music group Shōjotai. However, *Maido osawagase shimasu* (1985–87; Sorry for disturbing you) proved a huge promotional vehicle, with Crush Gals cast in the first two seasons as neighborhood wrestler-trainers and Dump and Bull guesting in season two as villainous antagonists (Figure 3). While their roles are peripheral, wrestlers' appearances exposed viewers to Zenjo and promoted singles such as Crush Gals' "*Tokyo bakuhatsu musume!*" (1985; Exploding Tokyo girls), which serve as theme music for training and fight scenes. In this way, Zenjo's tie-ups with TBS extended its brand to trend-conscious content with a wide reach, increasing marketability. Nonetheless, TBS's tendency to cast joshi puro stars as side characters or comedic talent suggests that certain media entities remained unsure of what to do with these newly popular wrestling bodies—a trend that seems to hold true for puroresu in general.

Zenjo's media mix mobilized other products, including concerts and the Takarazuka Revue-like all-Zenjo musical *Dainamaito kiddo* (Dynamite kid); wrestling and music videos released by Zenjo, Victor, Fuji TV, and Fuji Pony;

Figure 3. Crush Gals offer advice to junior high school students on TBS drama *Maido osawagase shimasu.*

radio appearances; video games for arcade and home console such as SEGA's *Gokuaku Dōmei: Dump Matsumoto* (1986); in-person events such as Crush Gals' December 1984 Hawaii fan tour; puroresu and pop culture magazine coverage; and books by and about wrestlers. Venue merch tables and Zenjo mail order also sold material goods, providing fans with alternative ways to connect with wrestlers physically and affectively. Crush Gals and Gokuaku character goods included NTT phone cards, toys, models, a Bandai board game, clothing, wallets, badges, headbands, stationery products, stickers, sports towels, decorative plates, posters, bromides, and more. Curiously, 1970s–1980s Zenjo's crossover to cinema and manga does not seem to have been as robust, though puroresu had made inroads in both decades earlier, the spectacle of fighting female bodies that it provides seems ideal for popular cinema, and Fuji TV had begun producing films in the early 1980s.[4] Exceptions exist, including Tōei Tokyo's 1977 film *Byūti Pea: Makka na seishun* (Beauty Pair: Prime of youth), directed by Naitō Makoto with production support from Zenjo, and Takahashi Miyuki's Crush Gals-themed manga series *Kurasshu densetsu* (Crush legend, 1986–87). However, what becomes clear when surveying the wide range of performances and media and material objects carrying wrestlers' images that flooded the market in this moment is that Zenjo's media mix aimed to access as many media and produce as much content as possible. Due to its dependence on aging, injury-prone bodies and an always-fickle entertainment industry, puroresu tends to follow a "grab what you can when you can" business philosophy, and Zenjo was no exception. Then-president Matsunaga's characterization of joshi puro as "*kiwamono*"—a faddish or ephemeral product—suggests that for Zenjo, the decision to adopt a media mix strategy for its wrestlers to ensure maximum media mobility might have been easy.[5]

Yet, Matsunaga did not develop these strategies alone. A 1985 *Yomiuri Shinbun* article describing an upcoming episode of Fuji TV's *Omoshiro baraeti* (Amusing variety) titled "How to Enjoy Women's Professional Wrestling a Thousand Times More Intensely!" provides a view of Zenjo's promotional landscape that includes many central participants and strategies.[6] The episode—hosted by Crush Gals—featured Zenjo wrestlers demonstrating wrestling skills and modeling fashions, with Gokuaku hosting an "Open Letter" segment. The article promises that wrestlers would reveal details about their training and everyday lives and that viewers of all ages could learn about joshi puro by tuning in. Key Zenjo media mix strategies are visible here. First, "wrestler" (physical skills, strength) and "idol" (trendiness, approachability) appeal and performance are combined within one product. Second,

Zenjo images and performances are spread across a range of media forms and content with prime product placement (here a "Golden Time" broadcast slot). Third, babyfaces are spotlighted with heels functioning as backup. And finally, Zenjo aims to reach as wide a demographic as possible while keeping in mind crucial support from young girls and women. Significantly, the article also identifies key players who read the media-marketing zeitgeist and crafted and implemented these strategies—Zenjo management and wrestlers and Fuji TV. Since the days of Rikidōzan's early postwar matches, television has been indispensable to puroresu. In this moment, Fuji TV—particularly producer Yoshida Hisashi—played a central role in catapulting Zenjo to new markets and mobility.

Galbraith and Karlin date the beginning of Japan's "idol phenomenon" to the 1970s yet mark the 1980s as its "golden age."[7] Zenjo's idol-inflected strategies—what scholar Kamei Yoshie terms its "idolization course" (*aidoruka rosen*)—follow a similar chronology, beginning with the 1974 joshi puro debut of former wannabe idol singer Mach Fumiake and her 1975 release "*Hana o sakasō*" (Let's make the flowers bloom), the first pop single by a joshi puro wrestler.[8] Mach's transition from idol path to joshi puro and subsequent cross-media participation blazed a trail that other Zenjo wrestlers would soon follow—or be forced to. The public and mass media interest behind her novel debut as idol-turned-wrestler—a debut that, according to Kamei, was unusual for joshi puro in that it was televised—attracted the attention of Fuji's Yoshida, and the network began to broadcast Zenjo wrestling regularly for the first time in 1975.[9] Mach's popularity demonstrated to media industry players such as Zenjo management and Yoshida the explosive potential of combining wrestling's raw physical appeal with "idol-like" performances and televising them as a new product.

Zenjo's popularity nosedived after Mach's early 1976 retirement, and a new star—with both wrestling skills and televisual appeal—was required.[10] The development of eye-catching characters and impactful narratives by management and wrestlers is central to puroresu, yet Matsunaga and former Fuji TV ring announcer Shiono Haruo credit Yoshida as the driving force behind Mach's replacement: Beauty Pair. According to both, Yoshida—betting a tag team would sell—paired Jackie Satō with Ueda Maki and chose the team's name, which signaled a socially acceptable femininity that counteracted the violence of their wrestling.[11] Shiono recalls that because Fuji's slogan at the time was "*Haha to ko no Fuji Terebi*" (Fuji TV for mothers and children) with matching target demographics, Zenjo broadcasts had to offer something besides wrestling to remain on brand.[12] Accordingly, he explains, Yoshida pressed first Mach then Beauty Pair into service, establishing singing as a broadcast requirement. Kamei argues that whereas joshi puro had targeted mostly male fans up to and including Mach, Fuji's target audience necessitated an image change, and the singing, dancing, and glamorous costumes the network implemented facilitated a transformation to a more respectable joshi puro with a "gorgeous, bright, and healthy" image.[13] In this way, Fuji TV was instrumental in transitioning Zenjo's brand away from perceived erotic spectacle and solidifying the practice of in-ring song performance—strategies that later helped launch Crush Gals.

Initially, Beauty Pair's singing did not go over well with (mostly older male) live fans, and Matsunaga and Shiono recall jeering and walkouts.[14] Yet, Fuji TV mandated singing, and Zenjo knew that refusal could result in broadcast demotion or cancellation. According to Shiono, a rift over television's necessity developed between the Matsunaga brothers. Toshikuni, he argues, was most in tune with what Yoshida and Fuji were attempting, while Takashi and Kunimatsu were "anti-TV" and preferred Zenjo's traditional methods, with Takashi feeling that Fuji had "seized the initiative" during this era.[15] However, after months of struggle (particularly on Satō's and Ueda's part), groups of young girls began appearing at matches, throwing colored streamers (*kamitēpu*) into the ring and cheering wildly when the duo sang and danced to their 1976 hit "*Kakemeguru seishun*" (Wild-spirited youth), as if attending an idol concert.[16] To Shiono, Yoshida was first to realize that the girls who came to cheer on Beauty Pair were fans of the single—that it had "lit a fire" and appealed more to many of them than the wrestling.[17] He also credits RCA—the company behind the single—and recalls that Zenjo began selling character goods in venues around this time. This transformation apparently won over the more TV-resistant Matsunagas, and a precedent was set: to maximize consumer appeal, Zenjo embarked on a media mix course that would last well beyond Beauty Pair's 1979 dissolution. The strategies and labor of the various actors involved established the infrastructure and fan base needed to support the unprecedented mid-1980s boom to come, when Crush Gals' incendiary fighting style combined with idol-like performances to form a "Zenjo golden age."

Zenjo's annual new wrestler auditions even became televisual. Perhaps sensing the spectacular, melodramatic potential of applicants' physical and emotional struggles, Fuji broadcast the auditions, even holding them in their studio from 1977 to as late as 1986.[18] Mapping out the network's influential role in Japan's "Bubble culture," Hara Hiroyuki cites a 1980s Fuji TV boom in which its content resonated with and helped shape the decade's cultural mood ("*jidai no kūki*"), an argument that demonstrates the reach Fuji offered.[19] By placing its wrestlers adjacent to and within such popular content as *Yūyake nyan nyan*, Zenjo could simultaneously access its target audience of young girls, media insiders, and anyone else who tuned in. Zenjo's attention-grabbing physicality, theatrical performances, and often comical feuds also aligned with Fuji's early 1980s slogan, "If it's not fun, it's not TV" (*Tanoshiku nakereba, terebi ja nai*).[20] Crush Gals' 1983 arrival therefore seems to have satisfied the desires and needs of Zenjo, Fuji, and consumers all at once. Yet, however successful, Zenjo's late 1970s–1980s media mix strategies are perhaps best viewed not as a deliberately crafted media mix "model" but as an unstable mode of adaptation and experimentation, with contributions from multiple actors whose decision-making power fluctuated. The mid-1980s boom, I argue, resulted from complex negotiations between Zenjo's traditional approaches and instinctive flexibility, Fuji TV's crucial intervention and support, interest from other media companies, wrestler and fan agency and labor, and a media mix environment that rewarded novelty and innovative methods of producing and selling. Motivations differed, yet each player had a stake in propelling Zenjo into new markets and increasing its mobility. This mobility, however, relied on different types of bodies than the media mix typically accommodated.

Blood, Sweat, and Tears in the Media Mix

On August 28, 1985, Dump used illegal tactics to defeat Chigusa in one of the most violent matches in 1980s joshi puro. Because this was a "haircut death match" (*kamikiri desumacchi*), the loser was forced to cut off her hair, compounding the shame of defeat. When the match ended, Fuji TV were on hand to capture what they had no doubt been anticipating—images and sounds of young girls crying and screaming as Gokuaku held a bloody-faced Chigusa down while Dump shaved her head with clippers, smiling fiendishly (Figure 4). It may seem difficult to imagine these images and sounds occupying the same marketing universe as the photo insert for *Crush A Go Go!!*, which depicts Crush Gals wearing pajamas, eating apples, and brushing their teeth. Nevertheless, all were circulated by Zenjo's media mix, which appropriated existing cross-media marketing practices yet remained responsive to its core product—the bodies and performances supplied by its wrestlers. Zenjo's media mix marketed an ambiguous product that blended wrestlerness with

Figure 4. A victorious Dump Matsumoto shaves off Nagayo Chigusa's hair during a Zenjo match broadcast on Fuji TV.

idolness, at times privileging one over the other yet often melding them for maximum appeal. What is significant about these strategies for media mix histories, however, is their undeniable dependence on and foregrounding of material bodies. Wrestlers' fleshy bodies and dynamic performances lie at the root of Zenjo's late 1970s–1980s marketing, demonstrating that both image-centric and performance-based brands could function and thrive in this environment and that corporeality and the media mix were not incompatible in this context.

In an argument for the significance of 1960s anime to histories of what would come to be termed the "media mix" (*mediamikkusu*) from the late 1980s, Marc Steinberg demonstrates that different media mix models exist and urges attention to their specificities.[21] Comparing and contrasting what he terms the "anime media mix" with a preexisting "marketing media mix" and models later developed by publisher Kadokawa Shoten, he notes that despite differences and unique histories, certain elements have come to be associated with media mixing over time. As a general definition, Steinberg characterizes the media mix as "the cross-media serialization and circulation of entertainment franchises" or "the phenomenon of transmedia communication, specifically, the development of a particular media franchise across multiple media types, over a particular period of time."[22] According to Steinberg's definition, it can be argued—as he does for anime—that joshi puro has a "media mix legacy."[23] Fleshing out this legacy therefore provides a fuller picture of the various franchises experimenting with cross-media marketing in this moment and the types of commodities they mobilized.

Steinberg explains that in mid-1980s Japan, the term "media mix" was widely associated with Kadokawa, particularly strategies credited to then-president Kadokawa Haruki.[24] It is arguably this model to which Zenjo's late 1970s–1980s strategies most closely correspond, both in terms of temporal context and approach. Both Zenjo and Kadokawa began implementing cross-media strategies in the mid-1970s, though neither would hit their stride until the 1980s. According to Steinberg, Haruki experimented with media "synergy" in the early 1970s, yet the company would not embark upon a dedicated media mix trajectory until he took over leadership later in the decade.[25] Zenjo, likewise, did not begin seriously experimenting with new directions until Mach's wrestling debut and 1975 single. Both Haruki and Zenjo's decision-makers, then, intuitively read Japan's mediascape and developed promotional strategies to fit their products, adapting and expanding as they went. Kadokawa entered into film production and created synergies between publishing, cinema, and music, and Zenjo experimented with music, TV, film, video games, and other media. Precedents exist, of course, and Zenjo built on puroresu cross-media promotional tactics since at least Rikidōzan's era as well as transnational influences. Yet, the breadth and depth of Zenjo's 1970s–1980s expansion and its innovative attempts to turn material bodies into media mix assets mark this moment as unique in puroresu histories.

In an analysis of Kadokawa film production, Alexander Zahlten notes that in the media mix, "each product advertises another product and the locus of desire begins to shift away from the object and toward a brand or image."[26] This gels with Steinberg's reading of Haruki's approach, which "use[d] the films themselves as ads for the novels; the novels as ads for the films; and the films' theme songs on the radio as ads for the records, films, and books," with extensive multimedia advertising.[27] Such a practice resonates with Zenjo's approach, in which wrestling events featured musical performances and mic appeals for singles, and TV appearances functioned as ads for Zenjo wrestling, albums, concerts, goods, etc. According to fan interviews conducted by Kamei and Aiba Keiko, there was no set path to Zenjo fandom and consumption in this period.[28] Pop songs first attracted people who then bought match tickets, others had the opposite experience, and others were lured to matches after seeing wrestlers sing or act on TV. Whatever the entry point, Zenjo's media mix came to function much as Steinberg describes other models—with each performance or product an "in" that enabled consumers to engage in "a continuous mode of character consumption."[29] Zenjo's brand was circulating widely by the mid-1980s, yet its commodified wrestling bodies and performances—not simply its images—facilitated this new mobility.

While I seek to carve out a place for Zenjo in media mix histories, I hesitate to argue that it functioned as a "key player" as Steinberg describes Kadokawa Shoten or a catalyst for wider media transformation, as both he and Zahlten read Kadokawa's strategies.[30] Zenjo did not evolve into the type of transmedia phenomena seen in kyara-driven franchises such as Hello Kitty and Pokémon—often considered media mix "proper"—although it did experiment with turning wrestlers such as Crush Gals and Dump into kyara for use on games, stationery, etc., demonstrating an awareness of image marketing trends (Figure 5). Zahlten views Haruki's experimentation—e.g., centering idol character images rather than narrative—as approaching such a transmedia model and cautions against labeling it a "stunted version of the media mix" in comparison to an ostensibly more communicative model utilized by his brother Tsuguhiko from the late 1980s.[31] It is tempting to read Zenjo's practice similarly—as a transitional moment in the creation of a "world" open to fan creativity and dominated by freely circulating wrestler-characters. Yet, this reading does not quite work.

One possible reason is that puroresu clings to narrative—a crucial selling point and site of fan investment. Henry Jenkins has argued in the late 1990s context of American promotion WWF (now WWE) that television enables professional wrestling narratives to transcend discrete in-ring matches. For Jenkins, WWF narratives "unfold" across multiple televised events such as matches, interviews, and skits, facilitating "a larger narrative trajectory which is itself fluid and open."[32] Sam Ford takes this argument further—toward what Jenkins calls "convergence"—detailing how WWE expanded into transmedia storytelling by the 2010s, mixing old and new media to create serialized narratives that accommodated fan participation.[33] Late 1970s–1980s Zenjo likewise developed narratives via televised wrestling events and specials as Jenkins suggests, yet it also embedded them in other media and genres such as TV dramas, film, videos, CMs, and video games—before joshi puro embraced the Internet. Admittedly, these strategies often facilitated something closer to narrative

Figure 5. Zenjo wrestlers and even "heel" referee Abe Shirō were transformed into kyara for use on promotional goods such as this Bandai board game.

exposure and reinforcement than robust development. Nonetheless, they enabled Zenjo to detach its characters from puroresu narratives and embed them in "idol" stories and media spaces, increasing their mobility and affective appeal. It may not have achieved the same level of "transmedia flexibility" that Zahlten argues Kadokawa had by the 1980s, yet Zenjo's media mix facilitated movement and expansion in a novel way—by deploying ambiguous wrestler-idol characters simultaneously tied to and unrestricted by narrative.[34]

A second—crucial—reason is that Zenjo's media mix relied heavily on not only images but also undeniably real, fleshy, violent, and vulnerable bodies. These bodies are inseparable from puroresu as an industry, and their market-ability and mobility remain tied to performance ability, health, and physical appeal, the latter policed more harshly in joshi puro than men's wrestling. As Kamei notes, joshi puro bodies function as capital and wrestlers circulate, touring cities, suburbs, and rural regions and putting their bodies on the line to entertain fans and earn a living.[35] Zenjo participated in this corporeal circulation throughout the late 1970s and 1980s, yet it also infiltrated and derived much of its success from the idol image economy. Scholars have argued that in this economy, idol images possess a mobility within and between media partly attributable to a "fleshlessness" of sorts shared with kyara—a circulation linked to the accelerated movement of mediatized images occurring within Japan's mediascape. While it plugged its wrestlers into this circulation alongside idols, Zenjo also necessarily foregrounded and commodified blood, sweat, pain, and the spectacular fleshiness of puroresu bodies. Its core product of a sports-performance mix and promotion of ambiguous wrestler-idols lent Zenjo's media mix an excess corporeality that arguably distinguishes it from more image-centric models operating in this context.

According to Galbraith, in Japan's idol image economy, "images of the idol refer to other images, not to a 'reality' beyond them," with "reality" indicating "identifiable human bodies" and lived lives.[36] While carefully noting that idols possess material bodies and agency, what Galbraith emphasizes is the process of their production and consumption, that "there is an economy to producing and reproducing them as images." This resonates with an argument by Ōtsuka, who identifies within mid-1980s idol culture a gendered demand for flesh-and-blood idols to be "bodiless" (shintai naki) originating not only from consumers and producers but also those creating discourse surrounding the idol phenomenon (aidoru-ron).[37] For Ōtsuka, idols in this androcentric system function as simulacra with "diluted" bodies, moving ever closer to an idealized virtual state as de-corporealized information. Zahlten likewise identifies such bodies in Kadokawa Haruki's media mix strategies. Comparing early 1980s "Kadokawa Film" to 1960s–early 1970s pink film (pinku eiga)—which in his view often ties history and politics to corporeal and sexualized images and metaphors—Zahlten argues that Kadokawa had thrown off such "fleshy constraints" in favor of "decontextualized characters," deploying "a very specific kind of pop idol as a freely circulating, nearly blank signifier with a reduced corpo-reality."[38] Likening the function of Kadokawa idol protagonists such as Yakushimaru Hiroko, Harada Tomoyo, and Watanabe Noriko in this model to that of "flexible," "unfixed," kyara-like icons, he stresses that these characteristics lent their images heightened media mobility: they floated easily between print, film, and music and transferred to promotional campaigns and material goods.[39] For Zahlten, Haruki pursued a goal of "radical mobility for the idol image" in part by decentering narrative and shifting idol corporeality to the background—an approach that never would have worked for Zenjo.[40] Galbraith, Ōtsuka, and Zahlten characterize the late 1970s–1980s idol image economy as privileging a production process that downplayed corporeality to suit consumer tastes and marketing trends. We can therefore read Zenjo's media mix—which melded fleshless idol images and performances with indispensable narrative and excessively corporeal puroresu performance—as an alternative and perhaps equally radical approach.

Zenjo differentiated itself from dominant trends in idol and kyara marketing by promoting wrestler-characters who vacillated between intangibility and fleshiness, with both aspects offering something to consumers. Its strategies exploited an image economy that devalued material embodiment, yet certain resistant "wrestler" product elements—corporeal elements inseparable from joshi puro—frustrated attempts to dematerialize and "unfix" Zenjo bodies. Zenjo injected the muscle, fat, blood, sweat, and gestures that form an irresolvable part of puroresu into the media mix, resulting in an excess mobility differing from that of 1980s idol images as often theorized. Idols, of course, also possess performing, laboring, and exploitable bodies. Nonetheless, Zenjo's ambiguous yet difficult-to-dilute bodies demonstrated an excess mobility by circulating within and across media, traveling throughout Japan and beyond, and displaying a dynamic, widely appealing physicality as they flew across the ring.

Idol proximity benefitted Zenjo, yet Zenjo was by the same token not afraid to question the sanctity of the idol image. In a sense, the haircut match between Chigusa and Dump functioned as an iconoclastic act—a site of conflict not just between Zenjo bodies but also between "wrestlers" and "idols," bodies and images. As cameras zoomed in on Chigusa's bloody face and shaved head, maximizing the images' affective impact, what they captured was the abject, embodied reality of joshi puro. The match garnered publicity for Zenjo and fan support for Chigusa, yet it also compromised the Crush Gals "idol image" Zenjo had been so assiduously selling. Nevertheless, the promotional juggernaut carried on, and Chigusa sang, danced, and wrestled with a freshly shaved head. Some fans may not have found it attractive, but her new image— and Zenjo's already diverse bodies and performance styles—challenged mid-1980s ideals for beauty and femininity. In this way, Zenjo wrestling defined for itself the sorts of images it would feed into the media mix.

Conclusion

Matsunaga has claimed that during the Crush Gals explosion, "Everything we did worked."[41] Even so, Zenjo's success proved unsustainable. Crush Gals and Dump retired in the late 1980s, audience numbers fell, and Zenjo overinvested during the economic bubble, opening a Zenjo-themed resort complete with tennis court and swimming pool.[42] Despite a mid-1990s resurgence, a mediascape increasingly enamored with virtual bodies perhaps contributed to Zenjo's late 1990s financial difficulties, and it folded in 2005. Nevertheless, joshi puro benefitted from the media mix groundwork Zenjo laid, later experimenting with, for example, "sexy" photo books and videos as well as new media. Yet, Zenjo's success came at a cost for wrestlers' bodies and physical autonomy. In this, joshi puro and idol experiences again overlap. Both—then and now—are characterized by a degree of bodily control within a gendered, patriarchal industry, fraught by exhausting labor demands and potential for injury, and a disposability linked to age, gender, and wellness. Centering bodies and performance in a discussion of Zenjo's media mix practices allows us to excavate such crucial aspects of the lived joshi puro experience and extend discussion beyond image circulation and the spectacle of the ring. Studies of media mix histories, practice, and discourse can therefore benefit by exploring their imbrication with embodiment and branching out to include underexplored forms of performance.

As this article's focus on Zenjo demonstrates, focusing on excess and ambiguity can open up new areas of inquiry into media mixed bodies. Granted, claiming that there is something ambiguous about professional wrestling is by no means a new argument. Debates surrounding its sports-theater hybridity, babyface and heel porosity, and theoretical and practical questions regarding the "real" and the "fake" have played out in many contexts, with critical debates over puroresu "reality" and "fiction"—including work by Ōtsuka—particularly rich in the context of 1980s Japan.[43] However, as Kamei observes, the majority of such debates focus on men's wrestling.[44] Therefore, much work remains to be done to rethink joshi puro and the bodies that sustain the industry.

In Zenjo's media mix, in particular, a critical ambiguity exists between possibilities for subversion of and complicity with embodied norms. Aiba views joshi puro as an opportunity for women to both perform physical strength and value bodies that clash with Japanese society's gendered ideals. Yet, she acknowledges that wrestlers' experiences and viewpoints vary and in certain ways support rather than resist normative ideas about gender, bodies, and behavior.[45] Gendered labor practices and entrenched gender roles continue to dominate joshi puro, and men still hold the majority of "power" positions: management, trainers, matchmakers, referees, TV announcers and camera operators, photographers, etc. Further, in their complex expectations for wrestler-idols to be young, cute (*kawaii*), healthy, tough, and strong, Zenjo and a portion of its fans promoted somatic ideals that are simultaneously gendered, ageist, and ableist. During the late 1970s and 1980s, Zenjo's media mix promoted wrestler and idol-like performances almost like a tag team—playing off the strengths of each and switching back and forth as needed. As such, it demonstrated that—to use Judith Butler's terminology—there are many ways to "do" joshi puro.[46] Nonetheless, wrestlers were pressured to exude the embodied qualities that best fit social expectations and media trends. Therefore, while Zenjo's media mix found ways to utilize less "idol-like" bodies, it remained an overwhelmingly gender normative (and heteronormative) space. Ultimately, "joshi" puro is an industry whose name itself implies a hierarchy and situates gender within the body, and as such it offers a conflicted experience. Luckily for Zenjo, and notable for media scholars and historians, the media mix could and did accommodate such conflicted, ambiguous bodies.

Kirsten Seuffert is a PhD candidate in the Department of East Asian Languages and Cultures at the University of Southern California.

Acknowledgments
The author would like to thank the University of Southern California for helping to fund this research. I also thank Professor Ayako Kano at the University of Pennsylvania and Professors Akira Mizuta Lippit and Kerim Yasar at the University of Southern California for reviewing an earlier version of this manuscript, as well as Guest Editor Marc Steinberg, the editors at *Mechademia: Second Arc*, and the two anonymous reviewers for their substantive feedback.

Notes
1. Ōtsuka Eiji, *"Otaku" no seishin-shi: 1980 nendai-ron* (A history of "otaku" psychology: A theory of the 1980s) (Tokyo: Kodansha, 2004), 16–17.
2. Matsunaga Takashi, *Joshi puroresu owaranai yume: Zen'nihon Joshi Puroresu moto kaichō Matsunaga Takashi* (The never-ending dream of women's professional wrestling: Former All-Japan Women's Pro Wrestling chairman Matsunaga Takashi) (Tokyo: Fusōsha, 2008).
3. Patrick W. Galbraith and Jason G. Karlin, "Introduction: The Mirror of Idols and Celebrity," in *Idols and Celebrity in Japanese Media Culture*, ed. Patrick W. Galbraith and Jason G. Karlin (London: Palgrave Macmillan UK, 2012), 2, ProQuest Ebook Central.

4. Alexander Zahlten, *The End of Japanese Cinema: Industrial Genres, National Times, and Media Ecologies* (Durham: Duke University Press, 2017), 141–43.

5. Matsunaga, *Joshi puroresu owaranai yume*, 112.

6. "Joshi puroresu o senbai tanoshimu hōhō: Waza ya fasshon mo shōkai: Fuji Terebi-kei" (How to enjoy women's professional wrestling a thousand times more: Fighting skills and fashion to be introduced: Fuji TV), *Yomiuri Shinbun*, October 19, 1985, evening edition, https://database-yomiuri-co-jp.libproxy2 .usc.edu/rekishikan/viewerMtsStart.action?objectId=0h%2Frt%2FnwS3Jkhs M4KwdW0NOKGK%2FxjchE0RwpGndYigY%3D.

7. Galbraith and Karlin, "Introduction," 2–5.

8. Kamei Yoshie, *Joshi puroresu minzokushi: Monogatari no hajimari* (An ethnography of women's professional wrestling: The beginning of the story) (Tokyo: Yūzankaku, 2000), 25.

9. Kamei, *Joshi puroresu minzokushi*, 23–24; Inoue Shōichi, *Puroresu mamire* (Covered with professional wrestling) (Tokyo: Takarajimasha, 2019), 110–11.

10. Matsunaga, *Joshi puroresu owaranai yume*, 122.

11. Matsunaga, *Joshi puroresu owaranai yume*, 98, 122.

12. Matsunaga, *Joshi puroresu owaranai yume*, 123.

13. Kamei, *Joshi puroresu minzokushi*, 24.

14. Matsunaga, *Joshi puroresu owaranai yume*, 98, 123.

15. Matsunaga, *Joshi puroresu owaranai yume*, 124, 127.

16. Matsunaga, *Joshi puroresu owaranai yume*, 123–26.

17. Matsunaga, *Joshi puroresu owaranai yume*, 126–28.

18. Inoue, *Puroresu mamire*, 112–13; "Nihon joshi puroresu 40 nen-shi," special issue, *Lady's shūkan gongu* (November 8, 1997): 7, 20, 48.

19. Hara Hiroyuki, *Baburu bunka-ron: "Posuto sengo" to shite no 1980 nendai* (A theory of Bubble culture: The 1980s as "post-postwar") (Tokyo: Keiō Gijuku Daigaku Shuppankai, 2006), 196–97.

20. Hara, *Baburu bunka-ron*.

21. Marc Steinberg, *Anime's Media Mix: Franchising Toys and Characters in Japan* (Minneapolis: University of Minnesota Press, 2012).

22. Steinberg, *Anime's Media Mix*, viii, 135.

23. Steinberg, *Anime's Media Mix*, xvii.

24. Steinberg, *Anime's Media Mix*, 152–53.

25. Steinberg, *Anime's Media Mix*, 149–51.

26. Zahlten, *End of Japanese Cinema*, 107.

27. Steinberg, *Anime's Media Mix*, 150–51.

28. Kamei, *Joshi puroresu minzokushi*, 85–86; Aiba Keiko, *Joshi puroresurā no shintai to jendā: Kihanteki "onnarashisa" o koete* (Female professional wrestlers' bodies and gender: Beyond normative "femininity") (Tokyo: Akashi Shoten, 2013), 66–68.

29. Steinberg, *Anime's Media Mix*, 144–45, 148.

30. Steinberg, *Anime's Media Mix*, 135–36; Zahlten, *End of Japanese Cinema*, 97.

31. Zahlten, *End of Japanese Cinema*, 120–21.

32. Henry Jenkins, "'Never Trust a Snake': WWF Wrestling as Masculine Melodrama," in *Steel Chair to the Head: The Pleasure and Pain of Professional Wrestling*, ed. Nicholas Sammond (Durham: Duke University Press, 2005), 34.

33. Sam Ford, "WWE's Storyworld and the Immersive Potentials of Transmedia Storytelling," in *The Rise of Transtexts: Challenges and Opportunities*, ed. Benjamin W.L. Derhy Kurtz and Mélanie Bourdaa (New York: Routledge, 2016), 169–83, https://doi-org.libproxy1.usc.edu/10.4324/9781315671741; Henry Jenkins, *Convergence Culture: Where Old and New Media Collide* (New York: New York University Press, 2006).

34. Zahlten, *End of Japanese Cinema*, 150.

35. Kamei, *Joshi puroresu minzokushi*, 63–64, 71.

36. Patrick W. Galbraith, "Idols: The Image of Desire in Japanese Consumer Capitalism," in Galbraith and Karlin, *Idols and Celebrity in Japanese Media Culture*, 186–87, 199.

37. Ōtsuka, *"Otaku" no seishin-shi*, 120–26.

38. Zahlten, *End of Japanese Cinema*, 97–98, 131.

39. Zahlten, *End of Japanese Cinema*, 123–26.

40. Zahlten, *End of Japanese Cinema*, 125, 150–51.

41. Matsunaga, *Joshi puroresu owaranai yume*, 110.

42. Matsunaga Takashi, "Joshi puroresu no shinise ga tōsan: 'Sutā senshu o mō ichido,'" *Nikkei bijinesu* 923 (January 12, 1998): 77–79.

43. Ōtsuka, *"Otaku" no seishin-shi*, 240–54.

44. Kamei, *Joshi puroresu minzokushi*, 8–9.

45. Aiba, *Joshi puroresurā*, 200–205.

46. Judith Butler, *Gender Trouble: Feminism and the Subversion of Identity* (New York: Routledge, 1999).

Imperial Media Mix

Japan's Failed Attempt at Asia's First Transnational Girl Group

MEI MINGXUE NAN

On September 30, 2017, the Formosa Vintage Museum Café in Taipei opened for its last day. The walls of the café were crammed with old photos, advertisements, and movie posters from owner Lin Yu-Fang's private collection of more than ten thousand items from Taiwanese media history.[1] Among the myriad images and artifacts, an advertising poster (Figure 1) was particularly eye-catching. According to Lin, the poster was printed and circulated in 1940 for a tea exhibition in Taiwan. Four flags flutter in the background. These are the national flags of Japan, Manchukuo, and the Republic of China, as well as a triangular gold flag that reads "Anti-Communism and Peace." A medium close-up image of three pleasantly smiling young women is placed in the foreground. From right to left, they appear to represent singer-actresses Okuyama Saiko (b.1916), Bai Guang (1921–1999), and Ri Kōran (1920–2014), members of a short-lived 1940 transnational girl group called Three Girls Revitalizing Asia (興亜三人娘) (hereafter Three Girls).

Representing Imperial Japan, Okuyama Saiko wears a kimono with a floral print of chrysanthemums and cherry blossoms. She holds a tea set engraved with hydrangeas to advertise Taiwanese tea, a top export for the Japanese colonial government. In the middle, Bai Guang represents the Republic of China and wears a blue China dress with the floral print of Formosa lilies endemic to Taiwan. Finally, the one who takes up the most poster space is Ri Kōran, who represents Manchuria and wears a bright yellow China dress with dark blue dragons. On the top right corner, the big red slogan reads: "A cup of green tea / the force to revitalize Asia," evoking the name of the group.

Although many scholars have written on Ri Kōran, given her legendary stardom, none of these studies have provided a detailed account of this girl group and their eponymous debut song released in 1940, which sits near the beginning of her media career. Nevertheless, phonograph records and promotional materials still circulate in vintage markets across East Asia, gaining a life of their own as the remains of times past. Situated at the intersection of East Asian media studies and cultural history, this article investigates the forgotten effort to package and promote Three Girls, Asia's first transnational girl group, by Columbia Records in collaboration with the Japanese Empire in the 1940s.

In this article, I first examine the context from which Three Girls emerged by comparing two different "modes" of what I call the *imperial media mix*: the Nichigeki mode and the Manchuria mode in the 1930s. I then trace the debut and disbandment of Three Girls, highlighting the tensions between mass mobilization and mass entertainment, and explain how Japan's imperial expansions both enabled and *necessitated* the production of a transnational girl group as part of its campaign to promote pan-Asianism throughout the Empire in the 1940s. Finally, I turn to a third "mode" of media mix, one that is based on Ri Kōran's individual star image. Specifically, I analyze how Ri Kōran—the central member of Three Girls—became her own *Ri Kōran media mix*, exceeding and even conflicting with the imperial media mix that produced her.

My concept of the imperial media mix is inspired by Ōtsuka Eiji's discussion of media mix mobilization in 2017.[2] Originally a Japanese industry term meaning a strategy to disperse and coordinate content across various media forms, media mix was first taken up as a theoretical framework by Marc Steinberg in *Anime's Media Mix*. Steinberg's monograph examines the formation of the character-driven media mix in postwar Japan, dating it to the 1960s, when the food company Meiji Seika distributed stickers from the TV animation series *Astro Boy* with its chocolates.[3] Drawing from Steinberg's theory, Ōtsuka proposes the notion of media mix mobilization to revisit Japan's wartime media ecology from 1931 to 1945. He frames media mix mobilization as an attempt to reconsider the totality of wartime propaganda as a media mix, redirecting scholarly attention from studying the media mix as a marketing strategy to understanding its imperial origins and its use in political mobilization.[4]

While scholars tend to explore the success of media mix propaganda, my project examines the girl group Three Girls as a *failure*. Despite Columbia's effort to package Okuyama, Bai, and Ri together in a collaborative effort to promote pan-Asianism, the three members soon disbanded and went their separate ways beyond the Empire's control. The core member, Ri Kōran, even transformed into a character conveying anti-colonial sentiment in 1943 and an anti-war icon in the postwar era. The assembling and disassembling of Three Girls, as well as the singular rise of Ri Kōran to stardom, shed light on

Figure 1. A 1940 advertising poster featuring Three Girls Revitalizing Asia. Harvard-Yenching Library of Harvard College Library, Harvard University.

the contesting forces of convergence and divergence in the intra-East Asian media ecology in the 1930s and '40s.

Existing scholarship on idols and girl groups in Asia is generally on more recent time periods, such as Patrick Galbraith and Jason Karlin's book tracing the evolution of idols in Japan from Onyanko Club to AKB48 and Yang Mingyue, Kim Yoon Kyoung, and Lee Kyoung Hee's analysis of the music and fashion of K-pop girl groups BLACKPINK, TWICE, and Red Velvet.[5] In this article, I turn to Three Girls in part to expand the historical purview of our analysis, tracing the precursors of contemporary industry terms such as "title track," "B-side," "positions," and "center." Illuminating the triangulation of empire, girl group, and media industry, this article's contribution is two-fold: (1) For media studies, it expands media mix theory and context by approaching Three Girls (and Ri Kōran) as the concretization of a complex web of technological, social, and cultural relations; (2) For East Asian cultural history, it examines Three Girls both as a historically bounded phenomenon and as a prototype of Asia's transnational idol groups that have become global sensations today.

The Nichigeki Mode and the Manchuria Mode in the 1930s

The imperial media mix—defined as a fascist use of media featuring a combination of heterogenous media elements—took different forms in Japan and Japan-occupied Manchuria in the 1930s. I term them the "Nichigeki mode" and the "Manchuria mode," respectively. Both were driven by a collusion between the interests of the Empire and capital to exert social control through media management: the Empire sought to ideologically integrate its subjects, while corporations sought to maximize profits by seizing upon the lucrative potential of cross-media tie-ups in new markets. The question for both the Empire and corporations, then, was how to associate the imperial ideology with a consistent set of representations and affects that could translate across media forms and reach audiences from both the metropole and the peripheries. That, in turn, was where the two modes differed: the Nichigeki mode envisioned a stage-based, centrally managed *sōgō geijutsu* (integrated arts), through the establishment of a national theatre (Nihon Gekijō or Japan Theatre, shortened to Nichigeki), an idea informed by Richard Wagner's 1849 concept of *Gesamtkunstwerk* (total work of art). The Manchuria mode, by contrast, was a collaborative mode centering on the film studio, where radio, print, and recording industries joined in a transmedia star-making strategy informed by China's star system with the rise of sound cinema. The Nichigeki mode exemplified a logic of integration, turning heterogeneous elements into a homogeneous spectacle ungraspable by individual perception. The Manchuria mode, following the propaganda of Manchukuo being a utopia where people of different ethnicities work together, embodied the logic of multiplicity and addition, achieving unity as a constellation of heterogeneous elements to which one can endlessly add on. The friction between the two modes reflects a diverse imperial context, where Japan's governance of Manchuria was different from the top-down ruling model in Korea or Taiwan.

In 1932, Kobayashi Ichizō took his hugely successful Takarazuka Revue to Tokyo. He bought out and built cinemas, theatres, and restaurants in the middle-class Hibiya-Yūrakuchō area, aiming to establish a grand amusement district. He acquired Nichigeki in 1935 and envisioned it to be a national theatre that could house an audience of five thousand, open to all social classes and ages as "wholesome family entertainment, a daily necessity for the mass of people."[6] Kobayashi appointed Hata Toyokichi as the director of Nichigeki for his expertise in the entertainment industry overseas.[7] Hata believed in a "comprehensive form of performance," that "harmoniously integrates theatre, dance, music, and film." He saw "the ideal of a producer in the entertainment business" as someone who "synthesizes and controls these various types of arts, which should then constantly generate new forms of entertainment."[8]

Carrying out Kobayashi's ambition, Hata turned Nichigeki into an important part of the imperial media mix for both political mobilization at home and the promotion of Japan's national image abroad.[9] The Nichigeki mode features not only the convergence of theatre, dance, music, and film on stage, but also the convergence of various art forms and performers from the peripheries. For example, the Tōhō Vocal Band recruited many vocalists from Korea and Taiwan.[10] The Tōhō Dance Team accentuated the ambiguity of the race/ethnicity of its dancers, turning their stateless bodies into vessels of Japan's pan-Asianist ideology.[11] It follows that the Nichigeki mode exhibited a wartime collectivism that largely deemphasized individual stardom.[12] Boundaries among media forms, individual voices, and racially ambiguous bodies all dissolved into a single cohesive spectacle ensemble.

Compared to the stage-based, centrally managed Nichigeki mode, the Manchuria mode started with radio and culminated in a collaborative star-making system revolving around film studios. After invading Manchuria in 1931 and setting up the puppet state of Manchukuo in 1932, the Japanese Empire established the Manchurian Telephone and Telegraph Company

(MTTC) in 1933 and the Manchukuo Film Association (shortened to Man'ei) in 1937. Japan's colonial expansion called for the production of disembodied, easily reproducible sounds and images that could be disseminated across the new frontier, with an eye towards cultural infiltration into China. This line of reasoning is similar to Thomas Lamarre's discussion of the "production of distribution," wherein distribution networks usually precede the circulating content, essentially calling for and shaping certain kinds of content.[13]

MTTC and Man'ei faced two problems. First, they lacked talent, especially bilingual talent that could follow Japanese management while attracting Chinese audiences. Second, for content production, they had to balance entertainment with propaganda under wartime censorship. The first problem was solved by selecting and training local talent, while importing staff from Japan and stars from China. Learning from China's star system that developed under the success of sound cinema, Man'ei established its own system, promoting its predominantly female stars through film, magazine, and radio. The second was solved by transmedia co-production and marketing, exemplified by film-adapted radio dramas from 1938 to 1939.[14] On the one hand, MTTC lacked quality scripts for its radio drama program. On the other hand, Man'ei's costly films could only be shown in theaters for a few days. The companies then developed film-adapted radio dramas, where the cast acted the film out over the radio prior to the film's release in theaters. In this way, film supplemented radio with quality content, and radio served as a promotional channel for film, prolonging each film's popularity. Rather than narrative, it was the name recognition of the stars that attracted the audience to both mediums.[15] The star system was sustained by the interdependence of the on-screen and off-screen images of the Man'ei actresses curated by the film studio.[16] The Nichigeki mode of integrated arts dissolved boundaries among media forms and individuals. In contrast, the Manchuria mode hinged on the Man'ei stars' transmedia mobility across different channels.

The two modes were not entirely separate given the transnational and intra-imperial flow of capital and talent. One can take Ri Kōran's career trajectory in the 1930s as an example. Ri Kōran debuted as a radio singer in Manchuria and an actress in a Nichigeki stage show in Japan. In Manchuria, she became a Man'ei star who was unparalleled for her bilingual proficiency and racial ambiguity.[17] In Nichigeki, she played a minor role with other popular singers, and it made little sense to distinguish their roles as they all represented exotic fantasies.[18] However, at that time, neither theater nor film could spread across the Empire as quickly as music records due to the rapid advances in recording technology and the corresponding decreases in the cost of gramophone ownership.[19] The mechanical echoes of *ryūkōka* (popular songs) across domestic and public spaces epitomize Walter Benjamin's observation in 1935 that "the work of art reproduced [had become] the work of art designed for reproducibility."[20] With an entrepreneurial spirit, Ri Kōran hence decided to upgrade her career through a deeper engagement with the recording industry.

The Assembling and Disassembling of Three Girls, 1940

The Nichigeki mode and the Manchuria mode were two forms of media convergence merging multiple media to meet the Empire's demands for the assimilation and standardization of culture. The recording industry, instead, was a diverging factor in its attempt to maintain the production of the commercially successful yet politically incorrect ryūkōka. Ryūkōka was born in 1914 through a symbiosis of stage show, film, print, and recording.[21] It developed rapidly as a genre with the advancement of recording technology. Hiromu Nagahara describes it as the "invention of the recording companies through and through." [22] Wajima Yūsuke puts it under the larger category of "record song," which he defines as "an entertainment song produced by a company on the premise that it is distributed and consumed on a large scale as a commodity through media reproduction."[23] Since 1937, the Japanese authorities attempted to subsume the recording industry into the imperial media mix by "purifying" the suggestive and lowbrow ryūkōka and promoting the educational and wholesome *kokumin kayō* (national songs).[24] The debate of ryūkōka vs. national songs illuminates the complicated relationship between mass mobilization and mass entertainment in wartime Japan.

Columbia Records produced numerous national songs during this period while managing to maintain its production of ryūkōka hits such as "Shina no yoru" ("China Nights"). Released in 1938, "China Nights" was so popular that there was a film spinoff in 1940, starring none other than Ri Kōran. The success of the film further boosted the song's prominence throughout East and Southeast Asia. However, Ri Kōran was not able to benefit from record sales. Although she could perform the song on the silver screen, she was prohibited from releasing her own version as a record because Columbia held the copyright.[25] Observing female stars' crossover stardom in Republican Shanghai (where the most popular actresses were also the most played recording artists, as detailed by Andrew Jones and Jean Ma), Ri Kōran was keenly aware of the lucrative potential of film-and-record tie-ups.[26] She therefore immediately transferred her contract to Columbia. Columbia was shrewd; their first move was to fulfill Ri Kōran's wish by having her release a different song from the same film series.[27] Then, harnessing her transnationally popular Manchu Girl persona, they packaged her with Okuyama Saiko and Bai Guang, marketing them as Three Girls Revitalizing Asia.

There were multiple calculations behind Columbia's decision. To start, Japan's sheer expansion of territory and media infrastructure both enabled and necessitated the intra-imperial distribution of propaganda. Ri Kōran's Manchu girl star persona was a befitting reminder of the slogan "*Nichi man shi shinzen*" ("Friendship among Japan, Manchuria, and China"). It was both intuitive and logical for Columbia to find a Japanese girl and a Chinese girl then group them together, using Ri Kōran's fame to promote the two lesser-known members. This act of political sensitivity also helped cover what the company was truly after: profit generated from the widely popular yet heavily censored ryūkōka (especially the exotic "China melody" genre).[28]

Like Ri Kōran, Okuyama Saiko and Bai Guang were also active in different parts of the imperial media mix in the 1930s, though not as successfully. Okuyama Saiko was the daughter of the influential Columbia Records composer Okuyama Teikichi. Her father wrote two songs for her solo debut in 1939. She then joined the jazz chorus Columbia Nakano Rhythm Sisters. Bai Guang was a Beijing girl trained in Tokyo under famous opera singer Miura Tamaki, who was also Ri Kōran's teacher. When Ri Kōran had become a Man'ei star in 1938, Bai Guang had only played a supporting role in a propaganda film. From the Empire's perspective, the girls were pulled by capital to sing it praises. From the girls' perspectives, however, it was a precious opportunity for them to advance their careers against the decline of ryūkōka under tightening control and censorship.[29]

As shown in Figure 2, two songs were released on the Three Girls record. The title track on the A-side was "*Kōa sannin musume*" ("Three Girls Revitalizing Asia"), a national song in a major key performed by the three girls together. The B-side track was "*Kokoro ni saku hana*" ("Flowers Blooming in My Heart"), a ryūkōka in a minor key also about the three girls but sung by Ri Kōran only. In the recording industry, it was conventional for the A-side to feature a recording that the company intended to sell while the B-side held a secondary recording that was expected to receive less attention. In fact, "China Nights" was initially released as a B-side track given its potentially

Figure 2. The phonograph record released in November 1940.

sensitive content.[30] As the Japanese authority urged media industries to shift priority from profit-making to "public service," ryūkōka managed to survive and thrive as the B-side of propaganda music.[31] On the Three Girls record, the Western-sounding ryūkōka became the B-side of the ostensibly Japanese title track. Similarly, the alluring and racially ambiguous Ri Kōran became the B-side of Three Girls that symbolized propriety and purity.

The title track, "Three Girls Revitalizing Asia," features the Yonanuki penta-tonic major scale (C, D, E, G, A) that is commonly used in traditional Japanese and Chinese music. Its lyrics imitate traditional forms of Japanese poetry by dividing sounds into clusters of five and seven syllables. There are four verses. Okuyama Saiko, Ri Kōran, and Bai Guang each sing a verse on their respective national flowers—chrysanthemum for Japan, orchid for Manchuria, and plum blossom for Republican China—after which they converge into a chorus. As pan-Asianist propaganda, the song was rather well-crafted: on the one hand, it employs a pentatonic scale shared by East Asian music traditions to evoke a sense of commonality; on the other hand, its lyrics flaunt the ability of the Empire and media technology to compress space and time, by describing flowers of different soils and seasons blooming together. More importantly, the song exemplifies how a hybrid genre comprises national songs to forge a sense of "Japaneseness." In the postwar context, Michael Bourdaghs, Wajima Yūsuke, and Deborah Shamoon all analyzed how *enka* managed to shed its origin in the modern, Western-imported ryūkōka and reinvent its image as being authentically Japanese.[32] Similarly, the genre of national songs was a variation of ryūkōka—an imported commodity of foreign capital and cultural influence, performed by Western-trained musicians, yet used to construct a Japanese ethos.

Three Girls was promoted in Columbia Records' *New Scores Catalog* in December 1940 (Figure 3). The Catalog has an interesting visual design. The front cover features an autographed group photo of Three Girls after a live performance with each girl wearing their respective national costumes while smiling and holding flowers. It forms a striking contrast with the bottom cover, which features a male Imperial Japanese pilot ready for battle. The inner pages juxtapose the promotional material of Three Girls with a cartoon of school-aged children singing songs endorsed by the Ministry of Education. These arrangements reveal a gendered militarism that prescribed a static route for women to progress from virtuous girl to good wife to wise mother. Similar to Sabine Frühstück's argument that militarism appropriates children and concepts of childhood to simulate wartime normality, Three Girls was used to simulate closeness.[33] For the Empire, Three Girls helped frame colonialism as a relationship that is both ideal and intimate. For the industry, the female voice was preferred since the birth of ryūkōka as it gives people a sense of affinity.[34] This helps explain why Asia's first transnational idol group was a girl group: the female voice simulates a feeling of affection and closeness, humanizing both the Empire's colonial expansion and the mechanical reproduction of music, enabling a parasocial relationship with the audience.

Compared to other all-female music groups that were competing for popularity at the time, such as the Takarazuka Revue and the Osaka Shōchiku Girls' Revue (*Osaka Shōchiku Shōjo Kagekidan*, or OSSK), Three Girls was different in both genre and origin. Takarazuka and OSSK were musical theatre troupes invented by domestic capital under Western cultural influence. Three

Figure 3a. Cover for Columbia Records' *New Scores Catalog.*

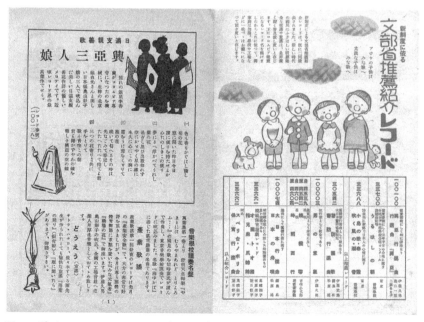

Figure 3b. Inner page promoting Three Girls.

Girls was a ryūkōka group, the result of foreign capital modernizing Japan's music industry with its more advanced recording technology. Three Girls was the first of its kind not only in its transnational production and distribution, but also in the marketing strategy where each member takes up a unique "official position" in the group, getting her own set of semiotic representations consistent across music, print, and visuals. In the promotional material, Ri Kōran as the face of the group is described as "the yearned-after star of the silver screen," Bai Guang the "pure and native Beijing girl," Okuyama Saiko the "beautiful Japanese girl," and the three together form a "flower story of friendship among Japan, Manchuria, and China." In the title track lyrics, Okuyama Saiko is associated with a clear and crisp autumn morning when chrysanthemums gently bloomed; Ri Kōran is represented as an orchid in a dreamy, starry night, where its ephemeral fragrance and the eternal starlight fuse into a contemplative ambience; Bai Guang is compared to plum blossoms enduring frost and snow with resilience and courage.

These motifs correspond to the lyrics of the B-side track "Flowers Blooming in My Heart," which continues the three girls' story:

日本娘の　心の庭に	In the garden of the Japanese girl's heart
ああ飛んで来るのは　どんな鳥	Oh, what kind of bird is it that flies over?
支那の娘の　上衣の裾に	At the hem of the Chinese girl's blouse
ああ吹いてゆくのは　どんな風	Oh, what kind of wind is it that blows?
満洲娘の　小指の爪に	On the fingernail of the Manchu girl's pinkie,
ああちらり光るは　どんな月	Oh, what kind of moon is it that glitters? (Author translation)

Written by poet Satō Hachirō, the B-side track's lyrics are fascinating in how they construct the distinctive images of the three girls. The Japanese girl presents a passive image of waiting for the bird to fly into her heart. The Chinese girl stands against the wind that blows up her hem, alluding to the plum blossoms' resilience in the title track. The portrayal of the Manchu girl is the most intriguing. Alluding to the title track's illusory image of a dreamy night, she is placed in a phantasmagoric scene where moonlight glitters on the nail of her little finger. This is a rather coquettish scene given that, to achieve this glittering effect, the girl would need to slightly raise her pinkie and move it slowly, with herself or her admirer gazing at the shimmer of moonlight on her nail. It is worth noticing that the depictions of the three girls (from heart to hem to nail) become increasingly corporeal, whereas their companion images (from bird to wind to moonlight) become increasingly ethereal. Compared to the Japanese girl waiting for the bird and the Chinese girl standing still, the Manchu girl is allowed the most agency to move, and perhaps to seduce. Released as Ri Kōran's solo single, the song encapsulates her alluring star persona centering the motifs of mobility and transformation, corresponding to Manchuria's ambivalent position between Imperial Japan and Republican China.[35]

Contrasting the cheerful, purportedly Japanese title track that employs the Yonanuki major scale, the B-side track mixes several D minor scales including the harmonic minor scale (D, E, F, G, A, B♭, C♯, D), the natural minor scale (D, E, F, G, A, B♭, C, D), and the Akebono scale (D, E, F, A, B♭) to evoke a melancholic and exotic feeling. The wholesome lyrics of the title track also function to cover up the B-side track's slightly suggestive content. Bundling the two songs, the record demonstrates the contesting forces of convergence and divergence in the imperial media mix, where recording companies attempted to circumvent censorship and gain additional profits. On the surface, Columbia packaged Three Girls to meet the Empire's demands for the transnational distribution of propaganda and the standardization of national culture. In effect, however, it was driven by the market demand for ryūkōka and the business interest in inventing new strategies to sell. The imperial media infrastructure for propaganda became a transnational marketing network for the company and a springboard for the three girls for their career development and intra-imperial mobility.

Nevertheless, Three Girls disbanded quickly. After the light music version of the title track was released in 1941, there were no more mentions of the group or reunions of the members. After the war, Ri Kōran never mentioned Okuyama Saiko in her memoirs and only commented distantly, if not dismissively, on Bai Guang as if they were strangers.[36] In my opinion, there were several reasons why Manchukuo-associated Ri Kōran came out on top while the girl group failed. On the level of group dynamics, the girls were separately trained and hastily put together with no friendship beyond politicized, tokenistic sisterhood. Being the "golden child of the century" (a catchphrase for her 1941 tour in Taiwan), Ri Kōran was simply not motivated to be grouped with lesser-known members and perhaps found it commercially insignificant and politically unwise to mention this experience in the postwar era. On the level of imperial politics, given how Ri Kōran's exemplifies Manchukuo's utopian ideals, her image alone was enough to fulfill the role of Three Girls in the imperial media mix as a self-reinforcing spiral promoting pan-Asianist ideology. After the disbandment, Okuyama Saiko remained virtually unknown outside the Japanese mainland. Bai Guang started to gain fame in Shanghai in 1943 but did not achieve transnational prominence until moving her career to Hong Kong in 1949. Ri Kōran, by contrast, enjoyed continuous stardom throughout East and Southeast Asia. Her celebrity lasted even after her death. She evolved into a new mode of media mix beyond the imperial media mix that produced her—what I term a *Ri Kōran media mix* revolving around a generative star image that transforms and transgresses. The imperial message, in turn, was lost in transmission.

The Ri Kōran Media Mix from 1941 Onward

Despite how Three Girls fell into oblivion, in some sense, Ri Kōran succeeded exactly the way the Empire wanted, gaining a transnational popularity that endured even after the collapse of the Empire. However, she lent herself to different ideologies, defying the initial purpose of her image and her career. When, exactly, did Ri Kōran's star persona spiral out of the Empire's planning and control? Although Ri Kōran had become a huge sensation in the metropole and Taiwan by 1941, her popularity in China was lagging behind given her blatantly pro-Japanese roles. This situation continued until the 1943 film *Wanshi liufang (Eternity)* catapulted her into stardom throughout China.[37] *Eternity* was a commemorative film for the centennial of the 1842 Treaty of Nanjing. It was famous for its interpretive fluidity. By reminding the Chinese audience of the first unequal treaty between China and foreign imperialist powers, the Japanese authority intended to evoke an anti-Western sentiment that would concur with the campaign of the Greater East Asia Co-Prosperity Sphere. The Chinese audience, however, interpreted the film as an act of borrowing from the past to satirize the present and instead deciphered an anti-Japan, anti-colonial message. Ri Kōran performed two songs in *Eternity* and released them as records. Ironically, her songs became immensely popular for their anti-imperialist spirit when she was inserted into the film's otherwise all-Chinese main cast as an indication of Japanese control over the Chinese film industry.[38] After the war, Ri Kōran starred in the 1957 Shaw Brothers film *Shenmi meiren (The Lady of Mystery)* as a patriotic Chinese spy resisting the Japanese invasion. She also became a beloved cultural ambassador between Japan and China after the 1972 Japan-China Joint Communiqué.

How did the poster child of the imperial propaganda machine turn into an anti-imperialist icon? How did Ri Kōran become her own Ri Kōran media mix driven by her star image that outlived the Empire? While it was common for female stars in the 1940s to rely on the diegetic and extradiegetic inter-actions of their songstress image, Ri Kōran was distinctive from her peers in the generative capacity of her star image.[39] For example, both Okuyama Saiko's wartime *otome* (maiden) image and Bai Guang's post-1949 *femme fatale* star persona can be viewed as character archetypes. A character archetype represents specific patterns of human nature that are viewed as universal across history, thus carrying a consistent set of expectations that facilitate storytelling. Ri Kōran's Manchu girl image, in comparison, was derived from popular literature of her time and the myth of her identity.

Ri Kōran played the title role in the stage show adaptation of Koizumi Kikue's widely popular creative nonfiction *Manshūjin no shōjo* (*Manchu Girl*, 1938).[40] In the story, the Manchu girl housemaid becomes an ideal colonial subject—culturally assimilated yet still maintaining colonial differences—through her Japanese mistress' "education."[41] Ri Kōran assumed this ambiv-alent Manchu girl persona with her performance as a purportedly Chinese subject fluent in Japanese on the silver screen and a patriotic Japanese sub-ject fluent in Chinese in real life. Many have commented that Ri Kōran did little to clarify the myths surrounding her nationality. As Griseldis Kirsch puts it, "the illusion of Ri Kōran could therefore hold many identities and none, gaining life according to the desires of the audience."[42] For Okuyama Saiko and Bai Guang, their star images were used to fit into different nar-ratives. For Ri Kōran, it was the narratives that were unfolding around her star image.

It follows that the Ri Kōran media mix historicizes and complicates Azuma Hiroki's postmodernist theory of database consumption centering character design. The Ri Kōran character could be a pro-Japanese Manchu girl in China, an anti-Japanese Chinese spy in Hong Kong, and a Japanese war bride in the United States, without any concerns of compatibility. This was achieved by the mix and match of different appealing fragments of her intricate identities, similar to how, in Azuma's framework, characters are generated by combining various attractive elements and mutate across different productions.[43] For Ri Kōran, the lack of a coherent backstory generated unlimited possibilities, enabling her star image to have a mobility and mutability that gelled espe-cially well with media mix logic. The generative power of Ri Kōran's image enabled her roles to fulfill diverse audience desires and convey conflicting ideologies, drawing people to her films for her character rather than the narratives. The mechanism of the Ri Kōran media mix, i.e., how Ri Kōran morphed from *a character* in the imperial media mix to *the character* driving her own media mix, predates the decline of grand narratives (à la Ōtsuka) or the rise of database animals (à la Azuma). This pushes our interpretation of the contemporary media mix situation for a more historicized understanding.

The Ri Kōran media mix was adaptable to different historical periods and political climates, thus lasting in time. While the Empire and capital thought of Ri Kōran's star image as a convenient vehicle for the distribution of imperial ideology, it turned out that their ideology could be easily replaced. The pan-Asianist propaganda of the Japanese Empire was only one message conveyed by the Ri Kōran character, just like the anti-imperialist message that was conveyed later. As Benjamin noted, new technologies of duplication often threaten existing lines of social control. The Ri Kōran character that was born of the imperial media mix could transform and transgress across space, time, and media channels, gaining the agency to run amok and eventually shedding its imperial origin to signify nostalgia for a cosmopolitan time.

Three Girls emerged at the intersection of the Nichigeki and the Manchuria modes of the imperial media mix. The transnational group image oscillated between the logic of integration and the logic of multiplicity and addition. The examination of the emergence of Asia's first transnational girl group as part of the multimodal imperial media mix, as well as the afterlives of its members, illuminates the complex interconnections among empire's territorial expansion and governance, media industry driven by technology and profit, and individual agency in a broader web of competing imperialist and capitalist interests. It enriches our analytical vocabulary and historical source materials in studies of media ecology. In the end, empires rise and fall. The glamorous image of Ri Kōran remains.

....

Mei Mingxue Nan is a PhD candidate in comparative literature at Harvard University. Her research focuses on modern East Asian literatures, films, and media cultures, with a specific Interest in mediatized memories across the transpacific. Her recent publications in journals and edited volumes include: "Mediated Temporalities: Tsushima Yūko's and Kuo John Sheng's Japanese/ American Passages to Taiwan" (*Transactions of the Asiatic Society of Japan*, 2022) and "Space-Clearing Flânerie: Remapping Hong Kong in Dung Kai-cheung's *Atlas* and My Little Airport's Songs" (*New Directions in Flânerie: Global*

Perspectives for the Twenty-First Century, 2021). She is a recipient of doctoral fellowships from the Social Sciences and Humanities Research Council of Canada and the Japan Foundation.

Acknowledgments
I want to thank Alexander Zahlten, Marc Steinberg, and the two anonymous reviewers for their valuable comments and suggestions. I also benefited from the audience's feedback at the 2022 RMMLA Convention, especially from Linshan Jiang's and Giuseppa Tamburello's comments on gender. I thank the *Mechademia* editors—Sandra Annett and Thalia Sutton—for their editorial support. I am grateful to Kuniko McVey from the Harvard-Yenching Library for her help with finding archival materials. I appreciate my friend Tina Chen for her feedback and editorial support at the final stage of revision. The archival research was funded by a summer travel grant from the Edwin O. Reischauer Institute of Japanese Studies.

Notes

1. Yang Yuan-ting and Jake Chung, "Taipei Cafe that Showcased Taiwanese History Closes," *Taipei Times,* October 1, 2017.
2. Ōtsuka Eiji, ed., *Dōin no media mikkusu: "Sōsaku suru taishū" no senjika sengo* (Media mix mobilization: The masses that create during and after the war) (Kyoto: Shibunkaku Shuppan, 2017).
3. Marc Steinberg, *Anime's Media Mix: Franchising Toys and Characters in Japan* (Minneapolis: University of Minnesota Press, 2012).
4. Ōtsuka, *Dōin no media mikkusu,* 5–6.
5. Patrick W. Galbraith and Jason G. Karlin, *AKB 48* (New York: Bloomsbury Academic, 2019); Yang Mingyue, Kim Yoon Kyoung, and Lee Kyoung Hee, "Eumakbangsonge natanan K-pop geol geurubui paesyeon dijain mit seutail yeongu: BLACKPINK, TWICE, Red Velveteul jungsimeuro" (A study on the fashion style of K-pop girl groups in music broadcasting: Focusing on BLACKPINK, TWICE, and Red Velvet), *Fashion Business* 25, no. 5 (2021): 1–23.
6. Ōhara Yukio, *Kobayashi Ichizō no Shōwa engekishi* (Kobayashi Ichizō's history of Shōwa theatre) (Tokyo: Engeki shuppansha, 1987), 193–95.
7. Washitani Hana, "Ri Kōran, Nichigeki ni arawaru: Utau Daitōakyōeiken" (Ri Kōran appears in Nichigeki: The singing Greater East Asia Co-Prosperity Sphere), in *Ri Kōran to Higashi Ajia* (Ri Kōran and East Asia), ed. Yomota Inuhiko (Tokyo: University of Tokyo Press, 2001), 27–28.
8. Hata Toyokichi, "Taishō goraku ron" (On Mass Entertainment), *Bungei Shunjū* (1936): 196.

9. Qin Gang, "Tōhō supekutakuru eiga songokū ni miru senjishoku" (The color of war shown by the Tōhō spectacle movie Monkey King], in *Dōin no media mikkusu: "Sōsaku suru taishū" no senjika sengo* (Media mix mobilization: The masses that create during and after the war), ed. Ōtsuka Eiji (Kyoto: Shibunkaku Shuppan, 2017), 61.

10. Tarumi Chie, "Ri Kōran o mikaesu shisen: aru Taiwanjin sakka no mitamono" (Looking back at Ri Kōran: What a certain Taiwanese writer saw), in *Ri Kōran to Higashi Ajia* (Ri Kōran and East Asia), ed. Yomota Inuhiko (Tokyo: University of Tokyo Press, 2001), 71.

11. Washitani, "Ri Kōran," 34–35.

12. Washitani, "Ri Kōran," 29.

13. Thomas Lamarre, *The Anime Ecology: A Genealogy of Television, Animation, and Game Media* (Minneapolis: University of Minnesota Press, 2018), 211.

14. Dai Ke, "Sheng yu guang de duanzan jiaohui: Manzhouguo de dianying guangbo ju" (A brief encounter of sound and light: The film-adapted radio dramas of Manchukuo), in *Dongya wenxue chang: Taiwan, Chaoxian, Manzhou de zhimin zhuyi yu wenhua jiaoshe* (East Asian literary field: colonialism and cultural interactions in Taiwan, Korea, and Manchuria), ed. Liu Shuqin (Lianjing, 2018), 205–30.

15. Dai Ke, "Sheng yu guang," 208–9.

16. Ding Shanshan, "Lun Manying de nvmingxing xingxiang ji qi wenhua neihan" (On the image and cultural connotation of Man'ei's female stars), *Jiangsu Social Sciences* 4 (2009): 158–59.

17. Tamura Shizue, *Ri Kōran no koibito: Kinema to sensō* (Ri Kōran's lover: Cinema and war) (Tokyo: Chikuma Shobō, 2007), 62.

18. Qin, "Tōhō supekutakuru," 61.

19. Lin Liang-Zhe, *Liushengji shidai: rizhi shiqi changpian gongye fazhan shi* (Phonograph age: A history of the recording industry during the Japanese occupation period) (Taiwan: Rive Gauche Publishing House, 2022).

20. Walter Benjamin, "The Work of Art in the Age of Mechanical Reproduction," *Illuminations*, ed. Hannah Arendt, trans. Harry Zohn (New York: Schocken Books, 1969), 224.

21. Nagamine Shigetoshi, *Ryūkōka no tanjō: "Kachūsha no uta" to so no jidai* (The birth of popular songs: "Katyusha's Song" and its era) (Tokyo: Yoshikawa kōbunkan, 2010).

22. Hiromu Nagahara, *Tokyo Boogie-Woogie: Japan's Pop Era and Its Discontents* (Cambridge, MA: Harvard University Press, 2017), 3.

23. Wajima Yūsuke, *Tsukurareta "Nihon no kokoro" shinwa: "Enka" o meguru sengo taishū ongakushi* (The constructed myth of "the heart of Japan": History of postwar popular music revolving around "enka") (Tokyo: Kobunsha, 2010), 20.

24. Kaneko Ryōji, *Shōwa sen jiki no goraku to ken'etsu* (Entertainment and censorship during the Shōwa war period) (Tokyo: Yoshikawa kōbunkan, 2021), 75.

25. Yomota Inuhiko, "Ri Kōran nenpu" (A chronicle of Ri Kōran), in *Ri Kōran to Higashi Ajia* (Ri Kōran and East Asia), ed. Yomota Inuhiko (Tokyo: University of Tokyo Press, 2001), 276.

26. Andrew Jones, *Yellow Music: Media Culture and Colonial Modernity in the Chinese Jazz Age* (Durham: Duke University Press), 2001; Jean Ma, *Sounding the Modern Woman: The Songstress in Chinese Cinema* (Durham: Duke University Press), 2015.

27. Yomota, "Ri Kōran nenpu," 276.

28. Nagahara, *Tokyo Boogie-Woogie*, 96.

29. Kaneko, *Shōwasen jiki no goraku to ken'etsu*, 79.

30. Baba Makoto, *Jūgun kayō imondan* (Military song troupe) (Tokyo: Hakusuisha, 2012), 100.

31. Nagahara, *Tokyo Boogie-Woogie*, 88–9.

32. Michael K. Bourdaghs, *Sayonara Amerika, Sayonara Nippon: A Geopolitical Prehistory of J-pop* (New York: Columbia University Press: 2011), 52; Wajima, *Tsukurareta "Nihon no kokoro" shinwa*, 22; Deborah Shamoon, "Recreating Traditional Music in Postwar Japan: A Prehistory of Enka," *Japan Forum* 26, no. 1 (2014): 113–38.

33. Sabine Frühstück, *Playing War: Children and the Paradoxes of Modern Militarism in Japan* (Berkeley: University of California Press, 2017).

34. Nagamine, *Ryūkōka no tanjō*, 36.

35. Washitani, "Ri Kōran," 49.

36. Yamaguchi Yoshiko and Fujihara Sakuya, *Li Xianglan: Wo de qianbansheng* (Li Xianglan: The first half of my life), trans. Gong Changjin and Meng Yu (Beijing: Jiefangjun chubanshe, 1988), 218–21.

37. Shelley Stephenson, "'Her Traces are Found Everywhere': Shanghai, Li Xianglan, and the 'Greater East Asia Film Sphere,'" in *Cinema and Urban Culture in Shanghai, 1922–1943*, ed. Yingjin Zhang (Redwood City, CA: Stanford University Press, 1999), 222–45.

38. Stephenson, "'Her Traces are Found Everywhere,'" 227.

39. Ma, *Sounding the Modern Woman*, 6.

40. Deng Lixia, "Shaonv biaoxiang zhong de zhimin zhuyi: Yi zuopin Manzhouren Shaonv he dianying Zhinazhiye wei zhongxin" (Colonialism in the representation of young girls: Centering on the work Manchu Girl and the film China Nights), *Chuangshang: Dongya zhimin zhuyi yu wenxue* (Traumas: East Asian colonialism and literature), ed. Liu Xiaoli and Ye Zhudi (Shanghai: Sanlian shudian, 2017), 480–503.

41. Kimberly T. Kono, "Imperializing Motherhood: The Education of a 'Manchu Girl' in Colonial Manchuria," in *Reading Colonial Japan: Text, Context, and Critique*, ed. Michele M. Mason and Helen J. S. Lee (Redwood City, CA: Stanford University Press, 2012), 225–42.

42. Griseldis Kirsch, "Gendering the Japanese Empire: Ri Kōran as 'Transnational' Star?" *Arts* 8, no. 4 (2019): 153.

43. Azuma Hiroki, "Database Animals," in *Otaku: Japan's Database Animals*, trans. Jonathan E. Abel and Shion Kono (Minneapolis: University of Minnesota Press, 2009), 42–52.

Anpanman and Patriarchy

Media Mix for Preschool Children in Japan

SANO AKIKO

Within the field of popular culture studies, the media mix has become a topic of increasing interest in recent years. There have been many research studies into Japan's media mix culture, such as works by Marc Steinberg and Ōtsuka Eiji, among others.[1] Many of the previous studies focus on the anime media mix or media mixes that target older children and adults. While adding nuance to our understanding of the connections between anime, popular culture, and commercialization, these studies have overlooked some of the forms media mix has taken in Japan, notably by paying too little attention to media mixes directed at younger children, and thus overlooking the social function of media mixes in child-rearing within Japan's gendered division of care labor. In this article, my focus is on Japanese preschool media mixes, and in particular *Anpanman*, a gentle superhero comedy starring a hero with *anpan* (a popular pastry) for a head, which is popular among children under five.

While there are many examples of the media mix for preschool-aged children, I have chosen to focus on *Anpanman* for several reasons. First, a survey by the toy company Bandai on children's favorite characters also found that, for thirteen consecutive years, Anpanman was the most popular character. In 2015, *Anpanman* merchandise constituted the second best-selling product line in the character goods retail market after Mickey Mouse.[2] After this brief stint in the second spot, Anpanman again rose to the top spot in 2017.[3] Second, the *Anpanman* franchise is a sprawling media mix, moving from print media to television series and annual films, to the many character goods that fill a child's life. In addition to the multiple media forms of the franchise, there are five theme parks in Japan. It is also worthy of note that in *Anpanman*'s case, the commercialization is not limited to one character. In 2009, the TV animation *Soreike! Anpanman* (Go! Anpanman) was recognized by the Guinness Book of World Records for the world's largest number of characters in a single animation series: from the first broadcast in 1988 to March 2009, 1768 characters appeared.[4] Some of these characters appear in various forms across media mixes, from the original picture books of the 1970s to the manga, animated

TV shows, feature films, video games, and products of all kinds that maintain the franchise's continuing popularity (about which more below).

The wild popularity of Anpanman necessitates an examination into the character, its commercialization, and the cultural conditions in which the two occur. Somewhat surprisingly, despite Anpanman's popularity and longevity in Japan (and, more recently, overseas as well), there has been little research into the reasons for the character's popularity from a media mix perspective. Reasons for this relative neglect may be because the target age range is narrow and the character lacks global impact as compared with, say, the Pokémon franchise. However, Anpanman has a large share of the character business in Japan, with a status akin to that of Mickey Mouse. More recently, the series has also been actively expanding its influence overseas, with Bandai Namco Taiwan opening a shop devoted to this character in Taiwan in 2015. It is thus an important moment to analyze Anpanman's longevity and success.

My aim here is to sketch out an analysis of the Anpanman media mix with particular attention to what Marc Steinberg terms the "social and economic ramifications"[5] of the media mix, focusing on the way Anpanman works as a form of child rearing in Japan, given the nation's still patriarchal sexual division of labor—especially as regards child-rearing. Recently, Ōtsuka Eiji, a leader of media mix studies in Japan, analyzed how Japan's media mix during World War II functioned as national policy propaganda, highlighting the effectiveness of the media mix as a propaganda device.[6] This study expands on these and other previous works to focus on the relationship between Japanese-style industrial society (including its media industries) and patriarchy, with a particular focus on social issues such as the inequitable distribution of care, especially childcare, which has received limited attention in previous research. Amidst discussions of the "care crisis" by feminist researchers and in studies of the gig economy, this article takes on the role of popular culture as a kind of care or even care work within contemporary Japanese society.[7]

What I am referring to as Japanese-style industrial society was established during the period of high economic growth in the 1960s. The long working hours established in that period, as well as the expectation of overtime work, remain unchanged. Although the percentage of married women in the workforce has increased in recent years, a "new gender role division" has taken root, one that requires women to bear a double burden, with men doing the work and women doing the work *and* family care.[8] In particular, what has been termed "*wan-ope-ikuji*" or single-operation child rearing, in which one woman is responsible for all aspects of child rearing, is taken for granted. This situation is largely due to Japan's patriarchal system and is proof that the gender inequality issue remains unresolved in Japan, which as of 2022 still ranked 116th out of 146 countries in the World Economic Forum's gender gap ranking.[9] This unequal gender status is closely tied to the legacies of and transformations in Japan's industrial society, within which the media industry is no exception. This article will demonstrate how gender inequality in Japan, especially women's "wan-ope-ikuji," has created a demand for media mixes for preschool children, and how this demand may ironically sustain the Japanese industrial society and patriarchal system, predominantly through the case of *Anpanman*. *Anpanman* is cute and light-hearted on the surface, but just below the surface we can detect the crucial role media mixes play in responding to (and, in a sense, sustaining) Japan's unequal division of care work.

Character Goods and Media as Life Necessities

In considerations of media mix in Japan, scholars have not often taken up the question of how media mixes differ when they are targeting children under six years old. The main factor is that generally preschool children do not buy goods on their own but rather rely on their parents for their wants and needs. A recent survey revealed that most parents start giving pocket money to their children at age six or seven, when children are in elementary school.[10] This means that for preschool children, the sellers are aiming their advertising at both the preschooler and their parents.

A second consideration that must be addressed in a discussion of media mix for preschoolers is the question of why many Japanese parents buy character goods for their children. According to Anne Allison, the appeals of "'healing' and 'soothing' (*iyasu, iyashikei*)" character goods have made not only children but also adults become fascinated with the characters as friends and family members.[11] In addition, Marc Steinberg has expanded this idea, writing:

> In recent years in particular, the idea that character goods allow for inter- or intragenerational human communication has become a privileged explanation for the prominence of characters in Japan. For example, an employee at Sanrio explains that their Hello Kitty character goods can be used as communicational tools for everyday household talk. Mother to child: "Today you're going to brush your teeth with your Kitty-chan toothbrush, aren't you?" This is offered as an example of

the positive form of dinnertime conversation made possible by Hello Kitty. The prominent sociologist Miyadai Shinji and his collaborators have similarly emphasized the importance of character goods for the development of what they term *cute communication* among shōjo girls in the 1970s and 1980s.[12]

Such scholarship indicates that one of the reasons character goods have become an important media mix for preschool children in Japan is the fact that they promote communication between not only the child and their peers, but also the parent and the child.

The above passage also hints at another important reason for the proliferation of character goods: the fact that these goods make caring for children easier. For example, Kaori Manabe, a female entertainer, said:

I keep buying character goods one after the other as my children grow up. My friends who are mothers and I discussed the fact that we could not avoid these characters. For example, my child seriously started using a spoon when we bought some Anpanman dishes, and they memorized a-e-i-o-u [the beginning of the Japanese phonetic alphabet] from Kitty-chan materials. We are so thankful for these products that it seems rude to mention the names without using honorific titles; therefore, I call them Mr. Anpanman and Ms. Kitty, to show my respect![13]

These examples bring us to an important observation about the kinds of goods in children's media mixes as distinct from, say, media mixes aimed at high school students. Character goods for young children in Japan include more than just toys; they encompass many products for daily practical use such as dishes, diapers, potty seats, clothes, sweets, foods, and educational materials, all of which are marketed primarily to mothers with the idea that they can assist the average woman who is responsible for the house and childcare, even though she and her husband may both be professionals.

Recently, this mother-oriented aspect of childcare has attracted attention with the expression "wan-ope-ikuji." This phrase, which was nominated as a U-can neologism and buzzword for 2017, is, as I noted above, a contracted form of the phrase "wan operēshon ikuji," which means "single-operation child rearing."[14] Whether as single parents or part of a married couple, Japanese women are in many cases the sole or primary caregivers for their children, like the lone employees stuck doing all the work by themselves at midnight in most Sukiya beef-and-rice-bowl chain restaurants. The fact that the term has become a cultural buzzword is indicative of the broad cultural trends it reflects. This has profoundly influenced the media mix for preschool children in Japan, as it targets mothers who are often the primary or sole caretakers of their children. In that sense, then, these types of character goods that help mothers take care of young children are more like life necessities than luxury goods. In what follows I refer to these necessities as infrastructural, drawing on the presumption that under particular conditions luxuries or commodities shift to being the required infrastructures of daily life.[15]

Indeed, other scholars have commented on the way character goods can come to fill a gap created by single operation parenting. As Anne Allison has argued:

> Speaking of the recent craze in character/cute goods, an advertising executive describes the relationships formed as both kinlike and (inter) personal. Whether a Kitty-chan key chain, Doraemon cell phone strap, or Pikachu backpack, these commodity spirits are "shadow families": constant and reliable companions that are soothing in these postindustrial times of nomadicism, orphanism, and stress.[16]

What the *Anpanman* media mix makes clear is that character goods begin to create shadow families at a much earlier stage of life than Allison has indicated. In many Japanese families, fathers are frequently absent from the home because of their long working hours. Character goods give the children an enjoyable escape and allow the mother some time to herself and some relief from the daily pressures and stress of childcare while her husband is absent. The next section will introduce how this works through a closer consideration of the *Anpanman* media mix.

The *Anpanman* Media Mix

Anpanman stories tend to be simple. Anpanman is a superhero who has a face made of a bean-jam bun, or "anpan" in Japanese. When he meets people who are hungry, he allows them to eat his face. His primary opponent in the series is Baikin Man, meaning "Virus Man." When Baikin Man does bad things, Anpanman saves everybody. The original author of these simple yet appealing stories, Yanase Takashi, started his career as a graphic designer and became an independent manga artist in 1953. He worked in various fields, such as the stage arts, song writing, radio and TV production, animation, and picture books. *Anpanman* was first published in 1973 in the October issue of *Kinder Ohanashi Ehon* (Children's story picture book), a monthly picture book anthology published by Froebel-Kan. It became popular among children in nursery schools and kindergartens and was first published as both a children's manga and a stand-alone picture book in 1976. In the same year, a musical was staged aimed at adults.[17] Full-scale media mixing began with the animated TV series *Soreike! Anpanman* in 1988, when TMS Entertainment acquired the broadcast rights from Froebel-Kan. Toys were also released in the same year; Bandai, for example, sold dolls and stickers packaged together with Ramune candy.[18] Movies have been released in theaters every year since 1989. Currently, *Anpanman*'s merchandise offerings are diverse. The official portal site categorizes them into "Toys," "Books/CD/DVDs," "Food," "Sundries/Interior," "Fashion," "Digital," and "Services."[19] Many of the daily life necessities for infants and toddlers have been commercialized as *Anpanman* goods, including bedding and clothing, tableware and food, diapers and potties, and even medicine.

Extending beyond the home, there are also many popular sites for family tourism related to *Anpanman*. In 1996, the Kami City Yanase Takashi Memorial Anpanman Museum opened in Kochi Prefecture, Yanase's birthplace. In 2007, the Yokohama Anpanman Children's Museum opened under the operation of the Anpanman Museum & Mall Limited Liability Partnership, which was established on August 22, 2006, with an investment of 1.91 billion yen by twenty-two companies, including Nippon Television Music Corporation, Bandai, Banpresto, SEGA, Fujiya, and other *Soreike! Anpanman* character licensors and licensees. There are currently five Anpanman Children's Museums (actually, theme parks) in Japan (Sendai, Yokohama, Nagoya, Kobe, and Fukuoka). Even modes of transportation have been brought into the mix, as the Anpanman Train has been operating on the JR Shikoku line since 2000, becoming the centerpiece of Shikoku tourism for families.[20]

Along with being pervasive, *Anpanman*'s media mix is comprehensively and rigorously controlled to promote children's exposure to merchandise and animation from infancy. From 1988 to the present, "*Anpanman* meetings" have been held every Tuesday at Nippon Television Music Corporation (the character management and merchandising licensing contact point) in conjunction with the toy manufacturers, and the world view and quality of the original works are rigorously checked. [21] In addition, Yanase previewed and gave his comments on the anime before each broadcast.

Anpanman appeals to children and their parents for several reasons. First, the stories are simple tales where the hero triumphs and in which there are no violent scenes. Second, Anpanman's face is a familiar and comforting food, anpan, which is rendered using round shapes and bright colors that children find appealing. Furthermore, to maintain the franchise's excellent brand image, there is strict quality control of the goods, so parents feel safe offering these goods to their children, which also encourages their consumption.[22] There is an infrastructure that connects the many *Anpanman* media and goods with the parents and children, which means that they frequently encounter *Anpanman* in their daily lives, allowing for easy immersion in the *Anpanman* world. This was a conscious marketing strategy, as is made clear by Watanabe Kazuhiko, one of the instigators who popularized and commercialized *Anpanman* animations. He claimed that *Anpanman*'s popularity was related to the "merchandizing system" where "young children associate Anpanman with the goods."[23] This aspect is quite important and necessitates a detailed examination.

Children can come into contact with *Anpanman* on television, via smartphones, and in supermarkets, where they can buy *Anpanman* sweets, Kleenex, capsule toys (called *gacha-gacha*) and young children's magazines. In *Bebī bukku* (Baby book), which is a young children's magazine targeted at one-to-three-year-olds, and *Mebae* (Sprout), which is targeted at 2-to-4-year-olds, the cover image has been *Anpanman* every month in recent years, and *Anpanman* toys are included as a free supplement when the magazine is purchased.

Steinberg, in his engagement with the models of the media mix that he argues emerge in the 1960s, points out the ways that magazines in particular function as platforms for advertising a given media mix, suggesting that "each media-commodity is also an advertisement for further products in the same franchise."[24] This is all the more true in the case of the children's magazines noted above, this time aiming at an even younger age demographic. For example, in an issue of *Mebae* published in May 2018, at the bottom-left of the page that introduces the "Shopping-Play Corner," there is information about the *Anpanman* television animation series, and on the left side of the page that teaches children how to draw, there is an advertisement for drawing toys (Figure 1). Besides Anpanman, there are several other characters from children's series such as *Thomas & Friends* and *Yo-kai Watch*, for which similar information about TV shows and character goods is provided. In the sixty-three pages of the magazine, there are only nine pages without advertisements. This is an astounding number of advertisements if one recalls that the target age group of the magazine is two-to-four-year-old

Figure 1. Pages from the 2018 issue of children's magazine *Mebae* featuring Anpanman alongside advertisements for the *Anpanman* anime and drawing toys.

children. Furthermore, in the "Present Corner" section of the magazine, there is a chance to win entrance tickets for character theme parks such as the Anpanman Children's Museum. As such, *Mebae* is also an advertisement for the various theme parks. Such advertisements create a cycle of consumption: for example, at the Anpanman Children's Museum in Kobe, half of the facility is a playground, and the other half is a shop, which has a very large area that stimulates children and their parents to buy the goods. While the cover page of *Mebae*, states that it is "educational magazine," it also advertises its wider media mix associations, which include the television animation series *Soreike! Anpanman*, *Anpanman* toys, picture books, and theme parks. This example shows the ways that the child-oriented media mix has built advertising into "education." Moreover, given the ways that these magazines and other goods function as essential aspects of childcare for time-starved mothers, as I have argued above, we also have to remember that these advertisements are not optional but rather necessities or infrastructural.

A further important aspect of this media mix is that the parents and children who view the show are asked to actively contribute to the *Anpanman* television program as well as to social media platforms. The television animation broadcasts character drawings submitted by young fans at the beginning of each show, which encourages parents to help their children draw the characters and send in the pictures. This also ensures that the parents will not miss an episode because of the chance their children's work will be shown, which further boosts *Anpanman*'s popularity and television ratings. Likewise, the formal *Anpanman* homepage also features photos that have been submitted by parents picturing their children enjoying *Anpanman* products and experiences.[25] For example, one might see an image of a baby smiling with the Anpanman toy her parent has bought for her, and another where a toddler is pointing to a display in an Anpanman theme park. These photos also appear on the BS TV program *Ohayō! Anpanman* (Good morning! Anpanman). As with the above-mentioned drawings, this encourages the parents to watch the television program and visit the home page, which of course also promote further consumption activities such as buying toys and going to theme parks to take photos. A photo in which children are making *Anpanman* characters encourages children to create fanfiction. Such activities recall Disney fan activities, for example, when Disney encouraged people to upload YouTube videos of their versions of the "Let It Go" theme song from the movie *Frozen*.

Many people also upload these types of photos on Facebook and Instagram to illustrate their satisfaction with their lives, demonstrating that they are leading a happy life with their children. Many Japanese housewives, some of whom stay at home because they find the areas in which they live to be unfriendly to mothers and children, use this method almost as a fan community to communicate with the outside world. Generally, in Japan, there is a social stigma against bringing young children into certain public places. Many mothers face danger when out with their children, such as being yelled at or their children's strollers being kicked, and the worsening of "hatred against bringing along children" (子連れヘイト *kozure hēto*) has become an issue.[26] The free labor performed by mothers and their children online in an effort to avoid such confrontations ends up further advertising *Anpanman* products to other parents via Facebook and Instagram—to the profit of *Anpanman*'s copyright holders. At this point, the creations of parents and children are benefiting the enterprise, rather than the individuals who are creating them freely. This is important because the children become used to the media mix environment and gradually become longer-term media mix consumers.

Along with fan creations and networks, children's play is also part of the *Anpanman* media mix. The best-selling toy for young children in March and April 2018 was the "*Anpanman kotoba zukan Super DX*" (Anpanman illustrated word reference book Super DX), an intelligence-developing toy from which children can learn two-word sentences in Japanese and English. There are three such intelligence-developing toys among the top five best-sellers.[27] These toys are marketed as educational and ultimately purchased for young children because it is known that the zero-to-three-year-old period is the most critical time for children's mental growth. Mothers in Japan who are committed to early education so that their child can enter a good university and have a happy life are induced to buy Anpanman character-based educational toys—thereby introducing their children to the *Anpanman* universe.

Aspects of the above recall Ōtsuka Eiji's *Teihon monogatari shōhiron* (A theory of narrative consumption). There Ōtsuka argued that the fundamental drive behind children's consumption of Bikkuriman Chocolates was neither the chocolate, nor the sticker, but rather the "grand narrative" behind the product itself.[28] Ōtsuka wrote:

> Be they comics or toys, these commodities are not themselves consumed. Rather, what is consumed first and foremost, and that which first gives these individual commodities their very value, is the grand narrative or order (*chitsujo*) that they hold in partial form and as their background. Moreover, it is by convincing consumers that through

the repetition of this very act of consumption they grow closer to the totality of the grand narrative that the sales of countless quantities of the same kind of commodity become possible (in the case of the Bikkuriman stickers there were 772 in total). *Mobile Suit Gundam* (1979–present, Kidōsenshi Gandamu), *Saint Seiya* (1986–89, Seinto Seiya), *Sylvanian Families* (1987, Shirubania famirii), Onyanko Kurabu—all of these commodities followed this mechanism by setting up their grand narrative or order in the background in advance and by tying the sales of concrete things to consumers' awareness of this grand narrative.[29]

In many cases, Japanese mothers are responsible for organizing their children's education. Borrowing from *A Theory of Narrative Consumption,* we can theorize that mothers buy the *Anpanman* intelligence-developing toy so that the child will get good grades in school, thus using the toy to create her child's happy future, and in a saga-like "grand narrative," all the descendants of the family become happy. To support this grand narrative, the toy makers will then produce a "variation," such as intelligence-developing toys from the "world" of "education" for learning English or mathematics. However, the case of the intelligence-developing toys also differs from the ideas laid out in *A Theory of Narrative Consumption* in terms of how their "grand narratives" or "worlds" are constructed. In the case of general goods, the producer of goods needs to create a "grand narrative," but in the case of intelligence-developing toys, "grand narratives" already exist. The grand narrative is the social expectation and desirability of a happy life for one's child—and the crucial role education plays in this happiness within current Japanese society. The grand narrative is ideological. And yet it is an ideology that is difficult to contest given the pressures on children and by extension on mothers raising children in Japan.

The manufacturer of the intelligence-developing toy hence skillfully mobilizes the existing social and ideological "grand narrative" to generate commercial success. These intelligence-developing toys save time for mothers who are seeking to ensure that their "child's good education = child's happy future" dream will come true. However, if education and success in life are presumed to be the responsibility of the mother to the child, the present state of patriarchy or father-absent families is perpetuated. This, in turn, allows companies to continue to profit from commercially driven educational ventures like *Anpanman* intelligence-developing toys.

It is worth mentioning that some aspects of the media mix do in fact promote effective learning methods. The Ministry of Education and Science recommends the effective use of museums for elementary and junior high school students because young people can learn more by both reading textbooks and by seeing and experiencing authentic objects. Children experience *Anpanman* by watching television, drawing, buying the goods, playing with the toys, and by visiting the theme parks; *Anpanman* infiltrates the lives of both the parents and children. Even after the children have graduated from *Anpanman* at about age five, they continue to consume other hero series or magical girls in the same way as *Anpanman*. *Anpanman* thus sets the stage for further media mix consumption. And yet one must also question the ways that State and commercial enterprises work hand in hand.

Media and the Gender Gap

The importance of products for preschoolers in the Japanese media mix is evident from the fact that preschoolers are included in the target audience for all the top five characters in the 2019 character merchandise retail market. The top five characters (or character-based franchises) are: (1) *Soreike! Anpanman*, (2) *Pokémon*, (3) Mickey Mouse, (4) Snoopy [*Peanuts*], and (5) Hello Kitty.[30] It is predominantly the parents who buy the goods; however, are parents buying goods simply because their children like *Anpanman*? Again, I would argue that it is not only that. In Japan, where "wan-ope-ikuji" by mothers is firmly established, character goods are purchased by mothers because they are means for managing their child-rearing expectations, serving important functions such as improving children's moods and directing children's attention. This is evident in how character goods are promoted to mothers. For instance, the "Chara Walker" character information website offers "Snoopy and other characters to support mothers!" by writing "Let's enjoy our daily lives with the help of cute character goods that can relieve our little worries and burdens!"[31] These phrases are not mere exaggerated advertising claims, but rather point to the excessive burdens that mothers face and the necessary or even infrastructural role of characters in helping mothers manage some of these burdens.

To give a concrete sense of the many burdens on women in Japan, we can turn to a comparison of housework and childcare-related time spent by married couples with children under six years old in 2016 across seven countries. This study showed that wives in Japan spend approximately 5.5 times more time per day on childcare and domestic work than their husbands. Japan leads the list with the highest gender gap, followed by France, where this figure is 2.2 times more than husbands, and Sweden, where the gender gap is lowest, with the figure being 1.6.[32] However, Japan has lagged far behind in recognizing this or even offering support for mothers. Instead, to offer just one example, Prime Minister Kishida Fumio recently stated that he would "encourage women to retrain during maternity leave,"[33] suggesting an obliviousness to the excessive burden of childcare placed on mothers and an assumption that maternity leave is a period of free time.

In 2021 the employment rate of women reached 71.3 percent, celebrated as a "new gender role sharing" trend in Japan.[34] And yet the duties of house-work, childcare, elder care, and nursing, in addition to paid work, still pre-dominantly fall on women. In 2020, women accounted for 54.4 percent of nonregular workers (compared to 22.2 percent for men)[35]; however, these figures indicate that women are working part-time or, even if they are full-time employees, use the "short-time work system" (six-hour workdays in principle) after giving birth, and that women will be undertaking house-work and care work at night when men are working overtime and not home. Although women can avoid losing their full-time positions by taking advan-tage of shorter working hours, they are forced to follow the so-called "Mommy Track," in which women who return to work after childbirth lose their pro-motions and salary increases. Consequently, the ratio of female managers in Japan is "by far the lowest among developed countries" at 14.75 percent, or 167th out of 189 countries.[36] Furthermore, the wage gap between men and women (the ratio of women's wages to men's wages for full-time workers, where the value of men's wages is 100) is 77.5 percent in Japan, compared to an OECD average of 88.4 percent.[37] There is a tacit understanding that women will use the shorter working hour system, and that men do not have time for housework and childcare, a cycle that further entrenches the gendered divi-sion of labor and the gender gap in salary and promotion.[38]

Currently, the Japanese government is debating a ban on long work-ing hours and is also encouraging more women to join the workforce. For example, on the Ministry of Health, Labor and Welfare's website, "efforts towards long-term labor reduction" are listed.[39] However, these goals may be difficult to realize for Japanese companies that have been supported by long male working hours; at present, very few companies have realized these goals. As a result of conditions such as these, Ueno Chizuko has described Japan's industrial society as an "industrial-military type society," suggesting that it is a system in which patriarchy and capitalism mutually support each other.[40] Under this system, men become selfless corporate warriors, while women are assigned the role of bearing and raising soldiers in the family, focusing on household chores, and supporting the home front. This is the most modern division of gender roles and was established on a mass scale in Japan, generating a patriarchal system which differs in quality from the feudal patriarchal system.[41] Japanese industrial society was founded on this system, and discrimination against women in Japan is rooted here.

Characters and the media mix have their own particular place within this system, as I've noted above. Laboring under a system in which women are responsible for unpaid care work such as childcare, women purchase character goods to alleviate this heavy burden, which simultaneously supports an industrial society that marginalizes women further. In addition, children, who are surrounded by character goods from an early age, will become future buyers. Thus, the preschool media mix is an industry that relies on a mutually supportive system of patriarchy and capitalism, and it reinforces gender inequality and the unequal distribution of care.

Conclusion

How the media mix travels to other countries and whether the same unequal, patriarchal conditions of care work are repeated wherever *Anpanman* goes is open to future investigation. Nonetheless, what I have sought to do here is highlight the intersection between care-giving, women's work in child-rearing, and the media mix system within Japan. Media mix theory and analysis must, in my view, focus on the relationship between the market and the "home" that supposedly lies outside the market. To put it another way, the study of the media mix must include the social in its picture. This means that accounts of child-oriented media mixes like *Anpanman* must engage issues of social care, social reproduction, and the unequal division of the labors of care in the home.

Japanese industrial society was established on the premise that the burden of care within the family is borne by a single woman. Currently, industrial society continues to be sustained by the fact that women support it by serving as the bottom of the labor market. The media mix operates fully within this patriarchal division of labor since the media industry also influences and reinforces the unequal distribution of childcare. Child-oriented media mixes are necessities that offer mothers a means of coping with the social burdens society places on them—childcare first and foremost. In exploiting this for commercial ends, we see how the media mix works fully within a system in which patriarchy and capitalism coincide. The narrative of *Anpanman* may be simple, but its role in supporting the gendered division of the labor of care and child-rearing in Japan is, as this article has shown, much more complex.

Sano Akiko is an associate professor at the Faculty of Culture and Information Studies, Doshisha University. Together with Hori Hikari, she coedited *Sensō to Nihon Anime: 'Momotarō Umi no Shinpei' towa nandatta noka* (War and Japanese Animation: What Was 'Momotaro Sacred Sailors'?) (2022). She has served as a joint researcher (2015–) and visiting associate professor (2020–22) at the International Research Center for Japanese Studies (Nichibunken). At Doshisha University, she is conducting joint research on quantitative analysis and archiving of moving images with a faculty member specializing in informatics.

Acknowledgments

The author would like to thank Kathryn M. Tanaka, Marc Steinberg, and Sandra Annett for proofreading and editing this article.

Notes

1. Marc Steinberg, *Anime's Media Mix: Franchising Toys and Characters in Japan* (Minneapolis: University of Minnesota Press, 2012); Ōtsuka Eiji, *Media mikkusu-ka suru Nihon* (The media mixification of Japan) (Tokyo: East Press, 2014).
2. "Uriage 1chō 6,300 okuen no kyarakutā shijō, ninki 2i wa Anpanman, 1i wa? 'CharaBiz DATA 2016(15)' de keisai (Character market with sales of 1.63 trillion yen, the 2nd most popular character market is Anpanman, the 1st most popular is . . . ? Published in 'CharaBiz DATA 2016(15)'), *Print & Promotion*, May 22, 2016, https://p-prom.com/feature/?p=8150 (accessed February 1, 2023).
3. "Bandai kodomo ankēto" (Bandai children's survey), *Bandai* official website, http://www.bandai.co.jp/kodomo/search_cara.html (accessed February 1, 2023).
4. "Anpanman ga Guinness nintei: Kyara saita 1768 tai" (Anpanman recognized by Guinness World Records as having the largest number of characters: 1,768), *Asahi Shimbun DIGITAL*, July 16, 2009, http://www.asahi.com/showbiz/manga/TKY200907160338.html (accessed February 1, 2023).
5. Steinberg, *Anime's Media Mix*, ix.
6. Ōtsuka Eiji, *Taisei yokusankai no media mikkusu: "Yokusan Ikka" to sanka suru fashizumu* (The Imperial Rule Assistance Association's media mix: Participatory

fascism and *The Imperial Assistance Family*) (Tokyo: Heibonsha, 2018); Ōtsuka Eiji, *Dai Tōa Kyōeiken no kūru Japan* (Cool Japan in the Greater East Asia Co-prosperity Sphere) (Tokyo: Shūeisha, 2022).

7. Emma Dowling, *The Care Crisis: What Caused It and How Can We End It?* (London: Verso Books, 2022).

8. Ueno Chizuko, *Kafuchōsei to shihonsei: Marukusu shugi feminizumu no chihei* (Patriarchy and capitalism: The horizon of Marxist feminism) (Tokyo: Iwanami Shoten, 1990), 214.

9. "Japan places 116th in 2022 gender gap report, last among G7," *The Japan Times*, July 13, 2022, https://www.japantimes.co.jp/news/2022/07/13/national/gender -gap-ranking/ (accessed March 15, 2023).

10. "'Kodomo no okozukai' jittai chōsa (Survey on 'children's pocket money'), *O-ucchino*, https://corporate.o-uccino.jp/wordpress2/wp-content/uploads/2015 /10/pr20151016_okozukai.pdf (accessed February 1, 2023).

11. Anne Allison, *Millennial Monsters: Japanese Toys and the Global Imagination* (Berkeley: University of California Press, 2006), 14.

12. Steinberg, *Anime's Media Mix*, 90.

13. Manabe Kaori, "Manabe Kaori no sankaku na kimochi" (Manabe Kaori's triangular feeling), *Nikkei DUAL*, May 31, 2017, https://woman.nikkei.com/atcl/dual /pwr/105/23/ (accessed February 1, 2023).

14. "News Release," *U-Can* official website, November 9, 2017, http://www.u-can.co .jp/company/news/1200236_3482.html (accessed February 1, 2023).

15. Jean-Christophe Plantin, Carl Lagoze, Paul N. Edwards, and Christian Sandvig, "Infrastructure Studies Meet Platform Studies in the Age of Google and Facebook," *New Media & Society* 20, no. 1 (2018): 293–310.

16. Allison, *Millennial Monsters*, 90–91.

17. Yanase Takashi, *Anpanman densetsu* (The legend of Anpanman) (Tokyo: Froebel-Kan, 1997), 14.

18. "Kyarakutā: *Soreike! Anpanman*" (Character: *Soreike! Anpanman*), *Bandai Candy* official website, https://www.bandai.co.jp/candy/products/1988/26098.html (accessed April 1, 2023).

19. "Guzzu Sābisu" (Goods and services), *Soreike! Anpanman Official Website*, https://www.anpanman.jp/goods/policy.html (accessed February 1, 2023).

20. Anpanman Train Official Website, https://www.jr-eki.com/aptrain/rekisi /rekisitop.html (accessed April 1, 2023).

21. Watanabe Kazuhiko and Yanai Kazuhiko, "'Anpanman' anime ka, shōhin ka kara 19 nen: Bijinesu no butaiura" ('Anpanman' 19 years after its animetization and commercialization: The behind-the-scenes business), *Henshū kaigi* 79 (2007): 25.

22. "Ehon kara umareta ninki kyarakutā: Naze, kodomotachi wa Anpanman ni hamaru noka?" (A popular character that was born from picture books: Why do children go crazy for Anpanman?), *Henshū kaigi* 79 (2007): 14–34; Yokota

Masao, "Minna daisuki 'Soreike! Anpanman' no shinrigaku" (The psychology of the beloved 'Go! Anpanman') *Eureka* 631 (2013): 58–65; Nishikawa Hiroko, "Nyūyōji no kyarakutā shikō ni kansuru kenkyu: Naze, kodomo wa 2 sai no toki ni Anpanman ga daisuki ni nari, 5 sai ni naru to 'dasai' to iu noka" (A study of infants' preference toward characters: Why do children fall in love with Anpanman at 2 years old, and start saying 'uncool' at 5 years old?), *Yasuda-joshidaigaku kiyō* 38 (2010): 139–47.

23. Watanabe and Yanai, "'Anpanman' anime ka, shōhin ka," 22–25.

24. Steinberg, *Anime's Media Mix*, 141.

25. "Shashin tōkō: Minna no egao daibosyū!" (Photo Submission: Call for everyone's smile!), *Soreike! Anpanman Official Website*, http://www.anpanman.jp/otanoshimi/form.html (accessed February 1, 2023).

26. "Akka suru 'kozure'" (Worsening 'hatred against bringing along children'), *Life Insider*, September 27, 2019, https://www.businessinsider.jp/post-199568 (accessed April 1, 2023).

27. "Ranking," *Omocha jōhō net* (Toy information network), http://www.toynes.jp/ranking/monthly/ (accessed February 1, 2023).

28. Ōtsuka Eiji, *Teihon monogatari shōhiron* (A theory of narrative consumption, standard edition) (Tokyo: Kadokawa, 2001), 10–11.

29. Ōtsuka Eiji, "World and Variation: The Reproduction and Consumption of Narrative," trans. Marc Steinberg, *Mechademia* 5 (2010): 99–116.

30. "Kyarakutā dētabanku 'CharaBiz DATA 2020(19)' o hakkan: Kyararank 3i wa Mickey, 2i wa Pokémon, 1i wa . . ." (Character Databank 'CharaBiz DATA 2020(19)' published: Mickey ranked 3rd, Pokémon ranked 2nd, and first was . . .), *Print & Promotion*, July 22, 2020, https://p-prom.com/promotion/?p=42419 (accessed February 1, 2023).

31. "Snoopy nado no kyarakutā ga mama wo sapōto!: Kaji ya ikuji ga tanoshiku naru aitemu 5 sen" (Snoopy and other characters support moms! 5 items that make housework and childcare fun), *Chara Walker*, July 20, 2021, https://sp.walkerplus.com/charawalker/topics/topics_1041878/ (accessed February 1, 2023).

32. "Kolamu zu 2.2 6 sai miman no kodomo o motsu hūhu no kaji ikuji kanren jikan (Shū zentai heikin)(1 nichi atari, kokusai hikaku)" (Column 1 Chart 2.2: Housework and childcare-related time (weekly overall average) for married couples with children under 6 years old (per day, international comparison), *The Gender Equality Bureau Cabinet Office Website*, https://www.gender.go.jp/about_danjo/whitepaper/r02/zentai/html/zuhyo/zuhyo01-c01-02-2.html (accessed February 1, 2023).

33. "Kishida shushō 'ikukyūchū no manabi naoshi o shien' hatsugen ni hihan zokushutsu: 'kibō ga zentei'" (Prime Minister Kishida's 'support for relearning while on maternity leave' comment draws criticism: 'Hope is a prerequisite' explanation), *Kyoto Shimbun*, January 31, 2023, https://www.kyoto-np.co.jp/articles/-/964840 (accessed February 1, 2023).

34. "2-2 zu josei shūgyoritsu no suii" (Figure 2-2: Trends in the percentage of women in employment), The Gender Equality Bureau Cabinet Office Website, https://www.gender.go.jp/about_danjo/whitepaper/r04/zentai/html/zuhyo/zuhyo02-02.html (accessed February 1, 2023).

35. "2-2 zu josei shūgyoritsu."

36. "Sekai 'josei kanrishoku hiritsu' rankingu . . . senshinkoku de attōteki saikai, nihon no 'shōgeki no sekai juni'" (World 'ratio of female managers' ranking . . . Japan's 'shocking world ranking' is overwhelmingly the lowest among developed countries), Gentōsha Gold Online, November 18, 2022, https://news.yahoo.co.jp/articles/5d1174c11840333fd385f0d625106d08be307f5c?page=1 (accessed February 1, 2023).

37. "Danjo chingin kakusa (Waga kuni no genjō)" (Wage gap between men and women [Current situation in Japan]), The Gender Equality Bureau Cabinet Office Website, https://www.gender.go.jp/research/weekly_data/07.html#:~:text=%E6%88%91%E3%81%8C%E5%9B%BD%E3%81%AE%E7%94%B7%E5%A5%B3%E9%96%93%E8%B3%83%E9%87%91,%E5%88%86%E3%81%8B%E3%82%8A%E3%81%BE%E3%81%99%E3%80%90%E5%9B%B3%EF%BC%92%E3%80%91%E3%80%82 (accessed February 1, 2023).

38. Hamada Keiko, Dansei chūshin kigyō no syūen (The end of male-centered companies) (Tokyo: Bungei Shunjū, 2022), 56-57.

39. "Chōjikan rōdō sakugen ni muketa torikumi" (Efforts towards long-term labor reduction), The Ministry of Health, Labour and Welfare website, http://www.mhlw.go.jp/kinkyu/151106.html (accessed February 1, 2023).

40. Ueno, Kafuchōsei to shihonsei, 9.

41. Ueno, Kafuchōsei to shihonsei, 196.

Platforms, Characters, and Worlds

The World as Photo Booth

Women's Digital Practices from Print Club to Instagram in Japan

KIMBERLY HASSEL

The practice of taking and uploading photographs using Instagram's filters and effects can be viewed as an extension of *purikura* culture. Purikura, a colloquialism for "print club" (*purinto kurabu*), are photo booths that allow users to take photographs, edit the photographs using a stylus and touch screen, and receive instant prints of these photographs. The term may also refer to the instant prints themselves, which double as stickers and are often small enough to be placed inside of a wallet or pasted onto a phone. Since their introduction in 1995, purikura have been core to girls' culture and sociality, and sometimes but not always coalesce with larger kawaii culture.[1]

Purikura centers bear gendered indexes, as they are often decorated with pink hues and images of young women (Figure 1). This gendered nature is evident in signs within some purikura centers that ban boys and men from using the booths unless they are accompanied by at least one girl or woman (Figure 2). While such signs signal how purikura centers attempt to "protect" this gendered environment of play—one dominated by schoolgirls—it is important to note that this banning practice is exclusionary and poses issues for trans and nonbinary people.

Purikura are material assemblages that also involve a set of practices. First, users pay the fee to use the photo booth using the machine's coin slot and determine the default settings for their session. These settings include default edits related to skin tone and eye size, along with the desired layout of the final print product. Users then enter the photo booth itself via its vinyl curtains. The inside of the booth bears a green screen backdrop and floor, bright lights, a camera, and a miniature monitor that relays visual instructions and suggestions for poses. Users step a certain distance from the photo booth's camera and begin posing for photos. Throughout the process, an automated voice—always feminine—offers instructions and initiates the countdowns.

After the photo-taking process, users head to the *rakugaki* (graffiti) booth to edit their photographs. This process of editing may involve the augmentation or slimming of bodily features, the addition of makeup, the addition of silly stickers such as animal ears, and the writing of text. After this stage, users then select the edited photographs that they wish to have printed. Contemporary purikura allow users to input their email address or mobile phone number to receive digital copies of their edited and original photographs. After selecting their desired photographs, users wait for the photographs to be printed. The prints emerge from a tiny slot located toward the front of the booth. After receiving their prints, users can cut individual photos using nearby scissors and exchange these photos with their friends.

Figure 1. The interior quirks of a purikura center, July 17, 2017. Photo by author.

Smartphones and visual-centric Social Networking Services (SNS) such as Instagram constitute portable purikura. The filters, stickers, and editing features on Instagram are not unlike those found within the process of rakugaki. Most importantly, smartphones and SNS have become enveloped in the media ecology of purikura (Figure 3). Manufacturers of purikura such as Makesoft offer their own smartphone apps that ease the process of saving digital copies of purikura and sharing these copies on SNS. In conversations with young women, I learned that it was not uncommon to "research" potential poses and editing strategies for purikura on Instagram. This saves stress and time during the practice of taking purikura. The prevalence of hashtags such as *#purikura pōzu* (#purikura pose) demonstrate reliance on user-created content as a source of information and inspiration. Purikura *culture* is becoming even more convergent.

Over the course of my fieldwork in Japan, I noticed that the cost of purikura had increased steadily. I asked Hitomi, a high school senior, about the fate of purikura: would these photo booths survive, or would they eventually be displaced by SNS such as Instagram? Hitomi answered that the practice of taking purikura and the practice of taking photographs on Instagram are different experiences. With regards to purikura, individuals are ultimately

Figure 2. A sign banning the presence of unaccompanied men, July 17, 2017. Photo by author.

Figure 3. A spot within a purikura booth, near the machine's main camera, in which users can rest their smartphones and concurrently record videos, November 10, 2019. This highlights the increasingly convergent nature of purikura booths. Photo by the author.

paying for an *experience*, for the practice of "being together." Ultimately, the practice of collectively brainstorming or researching poses, performing these poses, and editing the photographs into a tangible keepsake marked purikura as a distinctive bonding experience.

The visual participatory culture of Instagram is reminiscent of the participatory nature of purikura. During my fieldwork, I observed that several establishments serving food that was deemed *instabae* or "Instagenic" had a designated photo-taking area complete with a backdrop (Figure 4). Such establishments were especially common in Takeshita Street in Harajuku, a hub of youth culture that is also lined with purikura centers. Here, we may consider how the smartphone camera becomes analogous to the camera within photo booths. The smartphone camera's flash, accessories such as ring lights, and the use of lightening filters on SNS such as Instagram become analogous to the lighting assemblage found within photo booths. The *world* becomes a photo booth, and surroundings become a green screen backdrop.

The ubiquity and embeddedness of mobile media and platforms in everyday life—in the case of my research, smartphones and SNS such as Instagram—coincide with media mix's emphasis on the inseparability of

Figure 4. A photo corner in an ice cream store on Takeshita Street, August 15, 2020. Photo by author.

image and lifeworld. In his groundbreaking work on the concept, Marc Steinberg explains that media mix "coincides with the expansion of the media environment into the lifeworlds of human subjects such that it has become increasingly inseparable from all aspects of contemporary life."[2] As an anthropologist, I find this embeddedness or inseparability to be the most generative aspect of media mix, as it yields rich insight into commodification, the intricate social and mediatized lives of subjects, space, and processes of worldmaking.

Scholarship on media mix has understandably centered on anime and fan cultures. Steinberg highlights that the emergence of anime "as a system of interconnected media and commodity forms" in the 1960s—evident in the franchising of Tezuka Osamu's *Tetsuwan Atomu* (*Astro Boy*)—would inspire the development of media mix. In this regard, analyses of media mix cannot be separated from anime.[3] While this scholarship has been illuminating, I propose that there is room for an expansion of media mix to new contexts beyond anime and manga. An expansion of media mix into mobile media studies and platform studies is necessary, given the heightened integration of SNS in transmedia marketing and storytelling. Such an expansion can motivate scholars to concurrently examine the affordances of mobile media and platforms, the embeddedness of these technologies in everyday life, and the social spheres that are mediated by these technologies. These examinations can ultimately pave the way for further expansions of media mix beyond media industries—for example, to industries such as tourism and interior design. To illustrate the possibility of expansions of media mix to other contexts, I want to highlight the growing embeddedness of Instagram in the media mix of girls' culture in Japan. Throughout my fieldwork on digital sociality, instabae culture and Instagram on a broader scale were narrated as primarily dominated by girls and young women. Several "Instagram Lectures" that I attended, which were hosted by marketing specialists in the Tokyo metropolitan area, instructed companies on how to appeal to women consumers via Instagram. One lecture that I attended was even marketed *specifically* for women, offering tips on entrepreneurial usage of SNS.

Gendered social spheres and divisions of labor have long been of interest to anthropologists and ethnographers of Japan. As anthropologist Amy Borovoy has explained, the ideal of *ryōsai kenbo* (good wife and wise mother) was used by statesmen in the Meiji era to promote Japan's projects of "modernization and nation-building."[4] The home became a sphere of authority and empowerment for women, leading to the emergence of the "professional housewives" of the late 1950s and 1960s. Women's labor—emotional and physical—as housewives and mothers served as the backbone of the spheres of schools and companies that were related to the perceived "economic postwar miracle" of Japan.[5] This was and still is evident in mothers' involvement in children's education, especially in the context of the rigorous system of standardized exams in Japan. We also see this intimate care take on other forms in contemporary Japan—for example, the role of "citizen scientist" taken on by mothers in Fukushima as they monitor radiation levels in food sources.[6] With regards to the gendered divisions within the workplace, sociologist Yuko Ogasawara has examined the division of labor in Japanese corporations between salarymen (salaried workers) and "OLs," or office ladies.[7] Sociality among young girls in schools has also been examined, ranging from sociolinguistic examinations of schoolgirl speech to the creation of the subjectivity of the schoolgirl via film and anime.[8] Consumerist play has been noted as a core component of girls' sociality, and is a theme that is especially relevant to my own research inquiries.

In this article, I map the flows of change *and* continuity as they relate to the intersections of gender, sociality, consumerism, and visual participatory culture in contemporary Japan. I propose the inclusion of mobile media and platforms into media mix discourse due to their growing embeddedness in media and social worlds. Using the case study of instabae culture and Instagram use among girls and young women, I highlight how "new" mediatic assemblages involving mobile internet, smartphones, and SNS are extensions of the historical and ongoing forms of gendered socialities and worldmaking practices that characterize the media mix of girls' culture. In doing so, I also gesture toward a theory of media remix that acknowledges the "remixing" of longstanding practices within certain social spheres while also considering the role(s) of the participatory and creative affordances of SNS in contemporary media environments. Examinations of media (re)mix in and of girls' culture, I argue, should address sociality and play alongside questions of dissonance and exploitation. I conclude with a discussion of the promise of media (re)mix in cultivating opportunities for transhistorical and transnational analysis.

Context Matters: Keitai Studies and Instagram

In conducting research on seemingly "ubiquitous" technologies such as SNS and smartphones, we must consider the temporal, spatial, and societal dynamics that impact the localization, use, and imagination of digital technologies in various contexts.[9] In the case of Japan, the smartphone must be discussed in tandem with *keitai* (mobile phones). Anthropologist Mizuko Itō characterizes the keitai as a sociocultural object, a "snug and intimate technosocial tethering, a personal device supporting communications that are a constant, lightweight, and mundane presence in everyday life."[10] What has been noteworthy of the keitai in a historical context is the introduction of the i-mode mobile internet service in 1999 by NTT DoCoMo.[11] This offering of mobile internet in Japan was a stark contrast to internet offerings in locations such as the United States, which centered on personal computers.[12] The perceived particularity of keitai is evident in linguistic terms such as *garakei*. This term combines "Galapagos" and "keitai" to hint that the technological assemblage of the garakei—a flip phone that includes a built-in camera and mobile internet—adapted to the environment of Japan.[13] Marc Steinberg brings attention to the fact that Android and iOS, mobile platforms that currently dominate the global market, were modeled after keitai and the affordances of i-mode.[14]

Keitai culture has been heavily associated with youth culture, particularly schoolgirl culture. Scholars of keitai studies have explained that this association originated with pager culture in the early 1990s—while initially used as a business medium by salarymen, schoolgirls transformed the Pocket Bell pager into a social tool that could also be personalized through decorative stickers. Youths, and schoolgirls in particular, also transformed the keitai in a similar manner through the personalization of the devices as fashion accessories.[15] In dialogue with these scholars, I examine the smartphone and the heightened connectivity afforded by 5G technology as a moment in the genealogy of keitai studies. An updated examination of mobile phones and youth culture in Japan should focus on the amplified affordances of smartphones and the prevalence of SNS, which are often viewed as inextricable from the hardware itself.

Instagram, a visual-centric SNS, brands itself as a platform that fosters closeness with individuals and passions, transcends spatial-temporal borders through the perusal of global content, and builds interest-based communities that encourage self-expression.[16] Instagram originated in the United States. However, Ian Spalter, former head of design of Instagram, comments on Japan as being a point of inspiration in the visual aesthetics embodied by the platform. In a feature episode on the documentary series *Abstract: The Art of Design*, Spalter speaks of his first encounter with Japan. As images of Japanese stationery stores flicker across the screen, viewers listen as he highlights what he perceived to be a high degree of attention to detail in Japan:

> I actually went to Japan the first time with a research trip and I was like, 'Uh, what is this?' When you think about the things we value, the Instagram design team, and things I value personally . . . around attention to detail and craft, there's probably very few cultures that hold that up as high as Japanese culture. It's a place where all the details kind of just tickle you. Everything feels pretty considered. And you're just soaking all that in. So, it's stimulating in a different way.[17]

Spalter eventually moved to Japan and is currently head of Instagram Japan. Within the episode, a team member of Instagram Japan observes that while "selfies" are common among Instagram users in the United States, users of Instagram in Japan do not share selfies as frequently and demonstrate differences in sharing patterns.[18] Spalter raises a question with regard to Instagram's place in Japan's smartphone ecology: "It's a product that people use all the time. So, how does it fit in with the mix of other applications that they may have on their device?"[19]

I am interested in the comments made by Spalter and his team because these comments highlight a necessity to examine the localization of global platforms. Instagram was cited by the young women with whom I spoke as the most popular SNS in Japan at the time of my fieldwork (2019–20). Hana, a *shakaijin* (postgrad) in her mid-20s, described Instagram as a platform where the user may "have fun by looking at images." Conversations with interlocutors revealed that the popularity of Instagram is attributed to its role in allowing users to stay in touch with friends, view their daily updates, and "follow" accounts that embody shared interests and hobbies. Riko, a university student, spoke extensively of her use of Instagram in exploring her interest in home design. This exploration involved following #industrial on Instagram and bookmarking posts that served as inspirations in room decor. Marketing specialist Amano Akira suggests that the act of searching for information via hashtags is displacing the act of searching for information on search engines such as Google—a shift from "googling" (*guguru*) to "tagging" (*taguru*).[20] This shift can be attributed to a sense of trust in user-made content. When users visit a location and document their experiences, other users may view this documentation as more "authentic" than mainstream corporate marketing.

Along with the pursuit of interests, Instagram grants users a degree of self-expression and creativity—or as Grace, a shakaijin, stated, the ability to "broadcast yourself." In this vein, it is not uncommon to have multiple accounts to show different content or "selves" to different audiences. Himawari, a high school senior, mentioned that high school girls can typically have up to ten Instagram accounts. When describing the creation and use of multiple accounts, interlocutors such as Himawari used the categories of "real" or "main" account (*hon aka;* 本垢) and "sub" account (*sabu aka;* サブ垢). In discussions of the dichotomy of hon aka and sabu aka, the former was characterized as curated and public facing while the latter was characterized as "private," or interest based. A third category of *ura aka* (裏垢) was introduced as a "secret" and anonymous account used for darker purposes of cyberbullying.

Vibrant visuality is yet another reason for Instagram's popularity. A discussion of Instagram usage in Japan would be impossible without an examination of instabae (インスタ映え). Possible English equivalents of this term are "Instagenic" or "Instaworthy." However, a more accurate translation may be "Insta-shining," as the term is a combination of "Insta" and "to shine." The term also draws upon *mibae*, or attractiveness. As these nuances suggest, instabae refers to aesthetically pleasing scenes, objects, or sites that are deemed worthy to photograph and upload onto Instagram. Within a Google Image search, instabae is represented by images of pastel-colored objects and places (Figure 5). Suggested search categories that appear on the page's header include "Hawai'i," "photogenic," and "sweets." A search of #instabae on Instagram itself yields images of delectable sweets and young women posing in front of picturesque locations or food (Figure 6). *#Instabae supotto* (Instagenic spots) constitutes one of many popular instabae-related tags (Figure 7). While we see that instabae images bear similar themes of pastel hues and sweetness—in terms of actual sweets and the overall affect of the image—the qualifiers that determine what is or is not instabae are subjective. When I asked young people to define instabae, there was a consensus that there is no "definition" per se, as it is contingent on the gaze of the user. Interlocutors did, however, offer their own interpretations, frequently invoking adjectives such as kawaii.

In discussing instabae and photographic practices in Japan, we must consider the shift to "iphoneography" and the heightened affordances of the smartphone camera.[21] Edgar Gómez Cruz and Eric Meyer have proposed that the smartphone—specifically the Apple iPhone—marks the emergence of a fifth moment of photography characterized by "complete mobility, ubiquity,

Figure 5. Google Image search of instabae. Screenshot, April 19, 2021.

and connection."[22] The integration of the keitai camera in Japan's social fabric in the 1990s suggests that this fifth moment arrived in Japan long before the emergence of the iPhone.[23] Nevertheless, Instagram is a valuable case study of the fifth moment brought about by the smartphone. Instagram—and by extension, the smartphone camera—has become a *lens* for how to view one's own surroundings. Instabae's focus on the picturesque combined with Instagram's filtering affordances ultimately, as Gómez Cruz and Meyer suggest, "changes the politics of seeing the banality of images of everyday life."[24] The experience of *being* becomes strategized as an experience of documenting and being documented based on a particular aesthetic.

Instabae and Instagram are valuable case studies of the contemporary media mix. On one level, the embeddedness of the trend and the platform itself accompanies the embeddedness of smartphones and SNS in everyday life—a mediatization of the everyday. On a second level, the vibrant visuality of instabae and Instagram has become integral to sociality, transmedia marketing, transmedia storytelling, and practices across various industries and (sub)cultures. For example, as instabae becomes a lens for experiencing surroundings, it has subsequently become a central part of *planning* trips and experiences. As I later demonstrate, tourism agencies have jumpstarted campaigns that center on "photogenic travel." In a public address in 2017, former Prime Minister Abe Shinzō even proposed instabae as a potential key to stimulating regional economies, a moment that further highlights the growing commodification and embeddedness of instabae in Japan's media mix and physical landscape.[25]

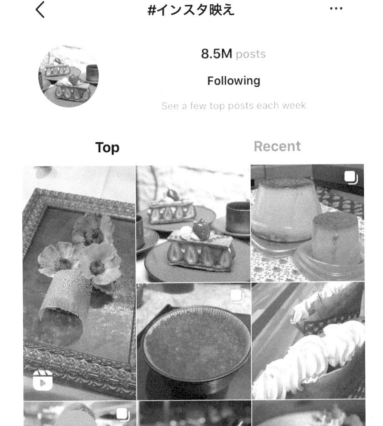

Figure 6. Search of #instabae on Instagram. Screenshot, April 19, 2021.

Hashtag (#)	Romaji and Translation	Quantity of Posts
インスタ映え	*Instabae* (Instagenic)	8.5M
インスタ映えスポット	*Instabae supotto* (Instagenic spots)	277K
インスタ映えスイーツ	*Instabae suītsu* (Instagenic sweets)	109K
インスタ映えカフェ	*Instabae kafe* (Instagenic café)	55.7K
インスタ映え料理	*Instabae ryōri* (Instagenic cooking)	17.9K

Figure 7. Suggested instabae-related tags on Instagram. Quantity of posts as of April 19, 2021.

The visual participatory culture of instabae relies on the transformation of photographic objects and landscapes into vibrant digital representations. This involves the use of the heightened affordances of the smartphone camera, the filtering affordances of Instagram, and the affordances of third-party editing platforms. In this regard, the photographic objects and landscapes become "remixed." Remix is inherent to digital participatory culture, and designates the creative appropriation and reuse of existing media forms to new ends by media consumers, users, and artists.[26] Hart Cohen has explained that since digital participatory culture, modes of engagement, and "authorship" are constantly evolving, concepts such as remediation/remix and convergence must constantly be recalibrated.[27] In this vein, I propose a recalibration of media mix theory that incorporates participatory cultures in/of SNS, which are deeply embedded in the social fabric. A theory of media (re)mix includes an examination of the "remixing" practices that are carried out by user-consumers, along with the ways in which industries and entities—governments, corporations, and the like—aspire for or co-opt this remixing. Furthermore, a theory of media (re)mix involves an acknowledgement of change *and* continuity. After all, "new" media are often an extension or augmentation of so-called old media.[28] Since media, practices, and (sub)cultures are co-constitutive—meaning that they build upon each other across time—any associated theorizations must also account for change and continuity in media industries and cultural practices across time periods and media forms. In the following section, I discuss the integration of Instagram and instabae within the media mix of girls' culture in Japan—a "remixing" of girls' culture.

Digitizing Women's Worlds

Literary and media scholar Tomiko Yoda has pointed out that historically, marketers and tourism campaigns such as Dentsū's "Discover Japan" (DJ) campaign of the 1970s have targeted women consumers. The visuals of this campaign, Yoda notes, did not focus on specific tourist spots—rather, the visuals "foregrounded the ambience heightened by the unexpected chemistry between the women and their surroundings."[29] The dynamics at play within the DJ campaign echo what Yoda characterizes as "girlscape," or the "mediatic milieu, disseminated via a variety of media channels, linking feminine bodies, affects, objects, and environment."[30] Yoda explains that the strategic targeting of young women by tourism campaigns resulted from the perception that young women were not "bound" by societal rules and could thus travel freely and potentially influence other consumer demographics.[31] The appeal of gendered youth marketing furthermore relied on the subjectivity and affect embodying *"girl thinking* and *girl feeling."*[32]

Yoda's discussion of girlscape and the DJ campaign is highly applicable to the transmedia, mobile practices of instabae. While specific locations are featured in magazines or webpages that highlight instabae spots, the *vibrancy* or *potential for vibrancy* is highlighted to a greater extent. There is an emphasis on the "photogenic" nature of these spots, along with the myriad ways in which the embodied vibrancy of these spots can be documented and enjoyed. Visitors are guided on possible forms of engagement with the ambience of the location, which may involve indulgence in local commodities. Another intersecting point between DJ and instabae is an emphasis on self-discovery and "subjective *experience."*[33] Instabae campaigns wield the language of girl journeys (*joshi tabi*) to highlight the solo traveler, the (wannabe) influencer, and the digital auteur. By highlighting journeys, these campaigns also harken to a process of (self-)discovery through intimate time spent alone or time spent with intimate others.

Contemporary marketing campaigns target both women consumers *and* their social use of digital technologies—a remixing of girlscape. One example is the Nippon Travel Agency's (NTA) *#tabijeni* campaign. #Tabijeni is a combination of the terms "journey" (*tabi*) and "photogenic" (*fotojenikku*). The campaign aims to promote local and international sites that center on the photogenic—or more specifically, the "Instagenic."[34] The gendered nature of #tabijeni is made visible through its placement under the "Girls' Trip" (*joshi tabi*) category of the NTA's website. NTA's suggested #tabijeni plans include *instabae meguri* (pilgrimages) within locations such as Kyoto and Melbourne. Yet another part of the #tabijeni campaign is the selection of "tabijeni ambassadors," or Instagrammer travel reporters who post aesthetically pleasing photographs and videos of their travels. These ambassadors are featured on the NTA's #tabijeni page; furthermore, the ambassadors market themselves as part of the #tabijeni campaign on their own Instagram "bios." This relationship can be considered symbiotic, as the NTA benefits from the labor of the ambassadors' posts and the ambassadors benefit from the added "clout" (*eikyōryoku*). This relationship, however, can also potentially be exploitative through lack of compensation for labor—a point that anthropologist Gabriella Lukács makes in her ethnography of women bloggers in Japan.[35]

A second example is Dentsū's continued focus on women's consumption and lifestyles. In late January 2020, Dentsū's GAL LABO, a planning team focusing on girl culture, began an online publication series titled *Reiwa joshi no kizashi* (Signs of a Reiwa girl).[36] The series aims to reduce the misunderstandings between adult women and "Reiwa girls"—those experiencing girlhood in contemporary Japan—by examining current trends in girl culture. In the third publication of the series, Hikino Anna describes the Reiwa girl as a subjectivity embodied by sharing. Drawing upon interviews conducted with six high school girls, Hikino suggests that smartphones and SNS have transformed "alone time" into "sharing time." According to Hikino, "alone time" is decreasing—in other words, even if one is "alone" physically, one is still able to connect with others digitally. Hikino provides the example of *benkyō aka* (study accounts) on Instagram. The visuals associated with these accounts and their associated hashtags include images of neat study desks, cute stationery, and timers. Hikino suggests that such images can serve as a source of motivation for youths who are also in the throes of exams or wish to develop skills in notetaking and the organization of study spaces.[37] I would like to add that youths may feel a sense of solidarity in viewing the efforts of other students, and this is important to consider within the context of Japan's standardized examinations.

Just as transmedia marketing directed at women consumers has been remixed, girls' culture itself has been remixed. When speaking to girls and young women about the role of SNS such as Instagram in their social lives, I observed that the terms *hayari* (trends) and *tsunagari* (connections) were especially prevalent. The participation in trends on Instagram constituted a social practice in and of itself. My conversations with Hitomi and Himawari, both high school seniors, revealed that the consumption and photographing of tapioca drinks—followed by the uploading of these images on Instagram— was a popular practice among young women (Figure 8). The practice of consuming such drinks was so popular that it bore its own verb in youth vernacular: *tapiru*. Connection was facilitated through the creation and use of hashtags, evident in hashtags such as *#oshare na hito to tsunagaritai* (#I want to connect with stylish people). Scholars of digital media have explained that hashtags on platforms such as Instagram can serve as markers of group iden-tity and provide opportunities for connection.[38] My continued conversations with Hitomi and Himawari revealed some of the digital practices that are associated with their identities as *joshi kōsei* (schoolgirls). The status of joshi kōsei (JK) was important to both Hitomi and Himawari—both lamented that their time as schoolgirls was coming to an end. The strength of the "JK brand" as an embodiment of nostalgic youth fosters a sense of pride amongst school-girls that motivates self-branding. Schoolgirls brand themselves by adding the hashtag #jk to their Instagram posts and may denote their year in high school through hashtags such as #ljk (third year; literally "last joshi kōsei").

The visual affordances of Instagram allow users to maintain their social connections through the acts of viewing, sharing, and branding. As Mako, a university student, conveyed to me, sharing photographs of daily activities on Instagram can spark small talk with friends both online and offline. In con-versation with scholars of digital studies, I suggest that such a practice may be considered to be a form of phatic communion or phatic communication.[39] Phatic communion, as originally coined by Malinowski, refers to gestures or remarks that aim to advance social relations rather than convey informa-tion.[40] Scholars of digital studies have suggested that phatic communication is also at play within digital photography and SNS, as the practices of taking and uploading photographs can advance already-existing social relation-ships.[41] I would like to add that visiting instabae locations with friends and documenting the experience online are social practices that can strengthen relationships. The uploaded posts on Instagram, like the material prints of purikura, serve as testaments of these relationships.[42] Purikura booths and participatory culture of visual-centric SNS provide a space for gendered soci-ality and worldmaking.

Figure 8. A strawberry milk tea with tapioca served in a plastic bottle resembling a seashell, September 1, 2019. Photo by author.

Fading Shine: Vibrant Visuality, Worldmaking, and the Question of Dissonance

If media mix worlds, as Steinberg proposes, "define lived experience," there is also much room for ethnographic approaches to the media mix.[43] Doing an ethnography of media (re)mix practices and Instagram grants insight into worldmaking: how interlocutors move through spaces, how they document spaces, how they represent those spaces, and even how they understand the representations of those spaces. Within her ethnography of smartphone usage among young Muslim women in Copenhagen, anthropologist Karen Waltorp illustrates how online spaces are not parallel worlds; rather, these worlds are part of "everyday, emplaced, embodied living and webs of reciprocity." For her interlocutors, "being online" is actually "a fundamentally social practice" of selective visibility.[44] I was intrigued by instabae culture and interlocutors' use of Instagram, so I went to places at their recommendations, and sometimes accompanied by my interlocutors. While sitting at a coffee shop in Odaiba with Mako, she explained to me the sometimes-disappointing dissonance between the "shining" aesthetic of some locations as they are represented on Instagram versus how they actually appear "in reality" (*riaru*). "You said that instabae is better than riaru, why is that?" I asked. "So . . . if it's riaru, it's more *shoboi* (lackluster) than you thought . . . for example, have you been to the Shibuya Scramble Crossing?" Mako remarked, before breaking out into laughter. "Isn't it so shoboi in person compared to how it looks on TV?" Mako asked.

I nodded and laughed in agreement. The Shibuya Scramble Crossing is one of the most crowded crosswalks in Tokyo. Media portrayals of the crossing often feature a bird's eye view of the assemblage of pedestrians—so many in number and shot from such a distance that they appear as ants. The crossing is a popular tourist attraction and is perceived as an embodiment of the hustle-and-bustle of Tokyo life. However, the crossing arguably loses its "shine" in person. In my visits to the crossing, I was pushed around and the experience of joining pedestrians in crossing the iconic intersection was hurried and brief. The fluorescence of the large televisions combined with the booming voices of advertisements overloaded my senses. Yet despite the chaos of the crossing, visitors frequently posed for photoshoots in the center of the swarming pedestrians, scrambling to get their shots in before the walking signal turned red. "It's surprising, isn't it?" Mako began. "You're really like, 'This is it?!' There are so many places like that, but you don't want to show them in that state, right? Since you've made the effort of going."

The experience of encountering this dissonance between online representation and offline experience, or what Mako described as a dichotomy of "shiny" versus "real," was an uncanny one. This ethnographic encounter provokes a consideration of the dissonance between the online representation of experience versus the actual experience. This dissonance is also part of instabae, which is itself a remixing practice. Because instabae and Instagram are so ingrained in the sphere of girl sociality, there is a pressure to participate in trends. There is a socioeconomic element to this, given instabae's emphasis on consumption, travel, and aesthetic. Hitomi commented that she eventually stopped participating in tapiru—the act of purchasing tapioca drinks with friends and documenting the experience—because it was draining her wallet. Young women noted that while Instagram is embedded in their social lives, they are aware that Instagram is not reality. They acknowledged that the pressure to obtain "likes" or represent a picturesque lifestyle was harmful. At the start of my fieldwork, Instagram had selected Japan as a region in which it would test the feature of hiding users' ability to see the number of likes on other users' posts. Himawari and Hitomi commented on this feature with a sense of relief. Himawari confessed that she uses Instagram mostly because it is popular among her peers. She observed that while uploaded photographs on Instagram are "shiny," one cannot truly know if the user is *actually* having fun.

Instabae has also been associated with excess and waste. The term "Insta-flies," pronounced as instabae yet written with the katakana for "house fly" (ハエ), emerged as a jab at instabae. The term implies that participants of instabae are noisy pests that "swarm" around certain sites. A viral Tweet posted in August 2017 by user @ASTROONSEN featured a hand-drawn image of a green fly with square eyes bearing the pink, fluorescent Instagram logo. The image was accompanied by a taxonomic definition of Insta-flies as a parasite that preys on young women and enjoys trendy sweets and treats from Starbucks.[45] In 2019, conservative newspaper *Sankei Shinbun* released an article addressing the connection between food waste and instabae. The article's illustration featured a chef gazing incredulously at two young women, both illustrated with ominous glaring eyes, as they coo: "So pretty!" There is an untouched strawberry parfait on the table behind the young women. The chef mutters in response: "They're barely eating it . . . is this for Insta?"[46] These critiques of instabae hinge on stereotypes regarding age and gender and are not unlike the moral panic discourse surrounding the perceived lack of manners and "acceptable" interpersonal relationships among young keitai users.[47] However, during my fieldwork, concerns regarding waste and the overwhelming influx of visitors to instabae-related sites were indeed vocalized by business owners. In our conversations, Hashimoto, the owner of an upscale British-style pub, recalled stories that had been told to him by fellow restaurant owners in which younger customers ordered dishes for photographic purposes, rather than consumption.

When presenting my research, I am frequently asked if the girls and women who participate in instabae are "dupes." The labor relationship between content creators and corporations—for example, the relationship between tabijeni ambassadors and the NTA—is part of media (re)mix.[48] The creative use of Instagram by young women is a form of "tacit labor" that may benefit the actors who are promoting instabae campaigns.[49] Young women may enjoy this creative use as a form of entertaining engagement without knowing that this engagement actually qualifies as labor that benefits an actor. This dynamic fosters debates regarding deception. In response to similar debates, Yoda has argued that girlscape in the historical context of late 1960s and early 1970s Japan was a political event because it enabled "a new distribution and mobility of feminine bodies in physical spaces and mediascape."[50] I agree that the remixed girlscape of instabae and Instagram also offers empowering opportunities for mobility and the carving of gendered spheres of sociality. However, I would also argue that there is a need for critical inquiries regarding the impact of the infrastructures of extraction and surveillance that are endemic to SNS such as Instagram, which are ultimately managed by multinational corporations aiming to instill neoliberal sensibilities. Instagram users are knowingly *and* unknowingly contributing resources and labor. It is possible to examine media (re)mix and visual participatory culture from the lens of sociality and play while also acknowledging issues and questions of privacy, "agency," the exploitation of user data, and algorithmic influence. Similarly, in the case of instabae culture, we can discuss the carving of gendered spheres of sociality alongside questions of socioeconomic exclusion, waste, disruption, and dissonance. This corresponds with media mix's emphasis on the nuances of marketing and franchising, from production to consumption.

Conclusion: Media (Re)Mix Futures

Despite the "newness" of the circuities of gendered worldmaking in smartphone-enabled social sharing networks in Japan, there are continuities with historical and existing forms of gendered socialities. In this article, I have illustrated change and continuity in social practices and consumerism among Japanese girls and women by introducing the case study of Instagram as a medium of vibrant visuality in the media (re)mix of girls' culture. Media mix theory is generative in that it uses a transmedia and transhistorical approach in describing the nuances of marketing and the embeddedness of media in everyday life. An expansion of media mix analysis into mobile and platform studies can allow scholars to integrate longer histories and existing transmedia practices in their examinations of "new" media forms. Just as purikura should be considered to be a precursor to Instagram, there are intersections between other longstanding playful practices and SNS. For example, anthropologist Sonja Petrovic has already drawn connections between karaoke and lip syncing on TikTok.[51]

Examinations of the intersections between society, social media usage, and smartphone usage have centered on the contexts of Australia, the United Kingdom, and the United States. Such examinations erroneously mark these contexts as a "universal standard." In highlighting Japan, I seek to decenter this overwhelming focus in digital media studies. It is curious that despite its status as a pioneer in mobile communications, Japan is not well-represented in literature on SNS and smartphone usage. The media mix, a concept emerging from Japan and media studies scholarship in/of Japan, only underscores the strength and promise of mobilizing contexts and analytical frameworks beyond those readymade in Silicon Valley.

....

Dr. Kimberly Hassel is an assistant professor in the Department of East Asian Studies at the University of Arizona. She is an anthropologist and digital ethnographer specializing in digital culture, youth culture, and identity in contemporary Japan. Her current book project examines the relationships between Social Networking Services (SNS), smartphones, and shifting notions of sociality and selfhood in Japan, especially among young people. Her examination of the impact of COVID-19 on digital sociality in Japan and ethnographic methods on a broader scale has appeared in *Anthropology News*. Hassel also specializes in diaspora studies, critical mixed race studies, and Afro-Japanese encounters. Her work on digital activism among Black Japanese youths has appeared in *"Who Is The Asianist?" The Politics of Representation in Asian Studies*. Hassel received a PhD in East Asian Studies from Princeton University. Her dissertation fieldwork was funded by a Japan Foundation Japanese Studies Doctoral Fellowship.

....

Acknowledgments

I would like to express my gratitude to the organizers and participants of "Embodiment: Representations of Corporeality in Texts and Images of Japan" at Dartmouth College, where I presented an early version of this article. The comments and feedback provided by Sachi Schmidt-Hori, Junnan Chen, James Dorsey, Samuel Perry, Vyjayanthi Ratnam Selinger, Akiko Takeyama, and Dennis Washburn were helpful in preparing this article for publication. I presented an updated version of this article at the 2022 Annual Meeting of the Association for Japanese Literary Studies, where I received encouraging feedback from attendees. I would like to thank my fellow panelists, Jonathan Abel, Andrew Campana, and Young Yi, for their support and brainstorming sessions. I would also like to thank Amy Borovoy, John Borneman, Ryo Morimoto, Franz Prichard, and James Raymo for their feedback throughout the various stages of this research. I also thank *Mechademia*'s anonymous peer review jury, guest editor Marc Steinberg, editor Brent Allison, and editors-in-chief Sandra Annett and Frenchy Lunning for their comments and guidance throughout the submission process.

Notes

1. Laura Miller, "Graffiti Photos: Expressive Art in Japanese Girls' Culture," *Harvard Asia Quarterly* 7, no. 3 (2003): 31–42.
2. Marc Steinberg, *Anime's Media Mix: Franchising Toys and Characters in Japan* (Minneapolis: University of Minnesota Press, 2012), xi.
3. Steinberg, *Anime's Media Mix*, viii.
4. Amy Borovoy, *The Too-Good Wife: Alcohol, Codependency, and the Politics of Nurturance in Postwar Japan* (Berkeley: University of California Press, 2005), 15.
5. Borovoy, *The Too-Good Wife*, 8–19.
6. Aya Hirata Kimura, *Radiation Brain Moms and Citizen Scientists: The Gender Politics of Food Contamination after Fukushima* (Durham: Duke University Press, 2016).
7. Yuko Ogasawara, *Office Ladies and Salaried Men: Power, Gender, and Work in Japanese Companies* (Berkeley: University of California Press, 1998).
8. Miyako Inoue, *Vicarious Language: Gender and Linguistic Modernity in Japan* (Berkeley: University of California Press, 2006); Sharon Kinsella, *Schoolgirls, Money and Rebellion in Japan* (London: Routledge, 2014).
9. Mizuko Itō, "Introduction," in *Personal, Portable, Pedestrian: Mobile Phones in Japanese Life,* ed. Mizuko Itō, Daisuke Okabe, and Misa Matsuda (Cambridge, MA: MIT Press, 2005), 1–16; Daniel Miller, "Social Networking Sites," in *Digital Anthropology,* ed. Heather A. Horst and Daniel Miller (London: Berg, 2012), 146–61.
10. Itō, "Introduction," 1.
11. Itō, "Introduction," 1; Marc Steinberg, *The Platform Economy: How Japan Transformed the Consumer Internet* (Minneapolis: University of Minnesota Press, 2019), 127–62.

12. Itō, "Introduction," 1–8.

13. Patrick W. Galbraith and Jason G. Karlin, "Introduction: At the Crossroads of Media Convergence in Japan," in *Media Convergence in Japan*, ed. Patrick W. Galbraith and Jason G. Karlin (Kinema Club, 2016), 14–15.

14. Steinberg, *The Platform Economy*, 16–17.

15. Misa Matsuda, "Discourses of Keitai in Japan," in Itō, *Personal, Portable, Pedestrian*, 19–39; Larissa Hjorth, *Mobile Media In the Asia Pacific: Gender and the Art of Being Mobile* (London: Routledge, 2009), 79–118.

16. Instagram, "About" (Webpage), https://about.instagram.com/ (accessed June 28, 2022).

17. "Ian Spalter: Digital Product Design," *Abstract: The Art of Design*, dir. Scott Dadich (2019), 26:43–27:15; available on Netflix (accessed July 5, 2020).

18. "Ian Spalter," 35:33–35:49.

19. "Ian Spalter," 35:50–35:56.

20. Amano Akira, "SNS de jōhō o sagasu jidai he: 'guguru' kara 'taguru' he no shifuto" (Entering the era of searching information on SNS: The shift from "googling" to "tagging"), January 28, 2020, https://dentsu-ho.com/articles/7110 (accessed November 15, 2021).

21. Megan Halpern and Lee Humphreys, "Iphoneography as an Emergent Art World," *New Media & Society* 18, no. 1 (2016): 62–81.

22. Edgar Gómez Cruz and Eric T. Meyer, "Creation and Control in the Photographic Process: iPhones and the Emerging Fifth Moment of Photography," *Photographies* 5, no. 2 (2012): 203–21.

23. Fumitoshi Kato, Daisuke Okabe, Mizuko Itō, and Ryuhei Uemoto, "Uses and Possibilities of the Keitai Camera," in Itō, *Personal, Portable, Pedestrian*, 300–310; Tomoyuki Okada, "Youth Culture and the Shaping of Japanese Mobile Media: Personalization and the Keitai Internet as Multimedia," in Itō, *Personal, Portable, Pedestrian*, 41–60.

24. Gómez Cruz and Meyer, "Creation and Control," 216.

25. "Abe's proposal to boost regions through Instagram seen as shallow," *The Mainichi*, December 29, 2017, https://mainichi.jp/english/articles/20171229/p2a /00m/0na/020000c (accessed June 20, 2022).

26. Lev Manovich, "Remixability and Modularity" (Online article, 2005), *www .manovich.net* (accessed June 15, 2022).

27. Hart Cohen, "Database Documentary: From *Authorship* to *Authoring* in Remediated/Remixed Documentary," *Culture Unbound* 4 (2012): 336.

28. Wendy Hui Kyong Chun, *Updating to Remain the Same: Habitual New Media* (Cambridge, MA: MIT Press, 2016).

29. Tomiko Yoda, "Girlscape: The Marketing of Mediatic Ambience in Japan," in *Media Theory in Japan*, ed. Marc Steinberg and Alexander Zahlten (Durham: Duke University Press, 2017), 185.

30. Yoda, "Girlscape," 176.

31. Yoda, "Girlscape," 180–82.

32. Yoda, "Girlscape," 182.

33. Yoda, "Girlscape," 188.

34. Nippon Travel Agency, "Tabijeni" (Webpage), https://www.nta.co.jp/tabijeni/ (accessed November 1, 2021).

35. Gabriella Lukács, *Invisibility by Design: Women and Labor in Japan's Digital Economy* (Durham: Duke University Press, 2020).

36. Dentsū GAL LABO, "Reiwa joshi no kizashi" (Signs of a Reiwa girl), https://dentsu-ho.com/booklets/391 (accessed November 15, 2021).

37. Hikino Anna, "Benkyō mo ibasho mo shea: Reiwa joshi no hitori jikan wa hitori ja nai" (Sharing study time and whereabouts: The Reiwa girl's alone time is not lonely), February 25, 2020, https://dentsu-ho.com/booklets/391 (accessed November 15, 2021).

38. Lauren Gurrieri and Jenna Drenten, "The Hashtaggable Body: Negotiating Gender Performance in Social Media," in *Handbook of Research on Gender and Marketing*, ed. Susan Dobscha (Cheltenham: Edward Elgar Publishing, 2019), 105.

39. Vincent Miller, "New Media, Networking, and Phatic Culture," *Convergence* 14 no. 4 (2008): 387–400; Crystal Abidin, "'Aren't These Just Young, Rich Women Doing Vain Things Online?': Influencer Selfies as Subversive Frivolity," *Social Media + Society* 2, no. 2 (2016): 1–17.

40. Bronislaw Malinowski, "Supplement I: The Problem of Meaning in Primitive Languages," in *The Meaning of Meaning: A Study of the Influence of Language Upon Thought and of the Science of Symbolism*, ed. C. K. Ogden and I. A. Richards (New York: Harcourt, Brace & World, 1923), 313–16.

41. Jenni Niemelä-Nyrhinen and Janne Seppänen, "Visual Communion: The Photographic Image as Phatic Communication," *New Media & Society* 22, no. 6 (2020): 1053.

42. Richard Chaflen and Mai Murui, "Print Club Photography in Japan: Framing Social Relationships," in *Photographs Objects Histories: On the Materiality of Images*, ed. Elizabeth Edwards and Janice Hart (New York: Routledge, 2004), 190; Mette Sandbye, "Play, Process and Materiality in Japanese Purikura Photography," in *Digital Snaps: The New Face of Photography*, ed. Jonas Larsen and Mette Sandbye (London: I. B. Tauris, 2014), 116–24.

43. Steinberg, *Anime's Media Mix*, xi.

44. Karen Waltorp, *Why Muslim Women and Smartphones: Mirror Images* (New York: Bloomsburg Academic, 2020), 3.

45. @ASTROONSEN, Tweet, August 17, 2017, https://twitter.com/ASTROONSEN /status/898199716264951809 (accessed November 23, 2021).

46. "'Instabae' mokuteki de tairyō tabenokoshi, hōteki sekinin wa toezu?" (Is there legal liability in leaving large quantities of food leftover for the purpose of instabae?), *Sankei Shinbun*, September 20, 2019, https://www.sankei.com/article /20190920-YCPHC7MCNJO2XCGOED7MGHFLPQ/ (accessed November 1, 2020).

47. Matsuda, "Discourses of Keitai," 23–32.

48. Galbraith and Karlin, "Introduction," 21.

49. Abidin, "Aren't These Just Young, Rich Women?," 10.

50. Yoda, "Girlscape," 194.

51. Sonja Petrovic, "From karaoke to lip-syncing: performance communities and TikTok use in Japan," *Media International Australia* (June 2022): 1–18.

The *Genshin Impact* Media Mix

Free-to-Play Monetization from East Asia

JOLEEN BLOM

In the first quarter of 2022, the free-to-play game *Genshin Impact* (2020) surpassed a revenue of $3 billion dollars (US) from their mobile phone players.[1] *Genshin Impact* is currently one of the highest-grossing games on the market since its official launch on September 28, 2020. The above revenue number is from sales through the App Store and Google Play alone, and it does not include the game's PC and PlayStation versions. The game also has a significant global impact; while it makes the most sales in the Chinese market (ranking number one in revenue) and Japan (ranking number two), the United States ranks number three.[2] In 2021, the game's developer, HoYoverse, generated almost $1.5 billion USD in revenue from in-app purchases, a number that was doubled compared to the prior year, with *Genshin Impact* as their top-grossing mobile game.[3]

Genshin Impact can only be described in a multitude of adjectives. It is a cross-platform, free-to-play, open-world, role-playing game with *anime*-inspired characters. Players can roam the virtual world of Teyvat doing just about whatever they want, ranging from completing the main quest, playing through story quests, traversing dungeons, building a home base, fishing, fighting monsters, or just wandering through the world's villages and cities. The game bears a resemblance to Japanese role-playing games (JRPGs); before its official release, the game was considered by entertainment website Polygon to be a clone of Nintendo's *The Legend of Zelda: Breath of the Wild* (2017),[4] and even reported by the game news website Kotaku to be similar to the *Tales* JRPG series.[5] The most lucrative element of this game is its characters. The game operates on a monetization model in which the game itself is free to play but offers in-app purchases. These purchases predominantly take the form of game characters that players can attempt to obtain through a *gacha* mechanic, where players make small purchases to roll for a desired character, which they may or may not obtain.

In light of this special issue of *Mechademia: Second Arc*'s focus on new approaches and analyses of the media mix, this article aims to shed light on the monetization model of free-to-play games within a media mix practice with characters at its center. As Marc Steinberg explains, characters function in media mix practices as the devices that connect audio-visual media (such as *manga*, anime, and video games) and objects while simultaneously forcing the proliferation of these media and objects.[6] *Genshin Impact* both follows and diverges from this aspect, because, although the *Genshin Impact* characters proliferate across different media such as an online manga, an upcoming anime, and even social media like YouTube and Twitter, the free-to-play game is the primary medium to which all these media are directed. As this article shows, the characters are used as a device for the game's monetization strategy to connect its different sources of income into a single game service instead of an entire media mix.

The past decade has seen two major shifts that have had a significant impact on our understanding of the media mix as a practice to spread content across different platforms (more on that in the next section). First, digital games have increasingly become the focal point for many media mixes, where the game has become the main platform from which characters transfer to other media platforms. Second, there has been a global emergence of a platformization of cultural production. The platformization of cultural production is defined by David Nieborg and Thomas Poell as "the penetration of economic, governmental, and infrastructural extensions of digital platforms into the web and app ecosystems, fundamentally affecting the operations of the cultural industries."[7] We may understand this as a broader trend in the platformization of society, where digital platforms—operated in particular by the Big Five tech companies (Alphabet, Amazon, Meta, Apple, and Microsoft)—not only affect the cultural industries but influence how we live and how we organize society in general.[8] Digital platforms are, as defined by van José van Dijck, Poell, and Martijn de Waal, programmable architectures "designed to organize interactions between users," and are "fueled by *data*, automated and organized through *algorithms* and *interfaces*, formalized through *ownership* relations driven by *business models*, and governed through *user agreements.*"[9]

Although the majority of digital platforms, such as popular social media network sites or search engines, are globally created and dominated by the USA, notable exceptions exist in countries such as China, South Korea, Japan, and Russia.[10] Platforms create East Asia as a cultural region (Korea, Japan, and China in particular) through their circulation with content in and around these countries, countering the hegemonic dominance of the USA. To show

how platforms create East Asia as a region, Steinberg describes regionalism as a market construction, where platforms "'coproduce' a sense of the regional (in their reception, distribution, and production), and draw on a preexisting set of cultural tendencies within the region (such as the dominance of a character-centered mass culture)."[11] For example, Steinberg argues that the three chat apps dominant in East Asia (WeChat, LINE, and Kakao) create a commonality of shared experiences and practices among users by borrowing, mimicking, and non-collaboratively coproducing features and content of these apps (particularly shared icons like characters and regional celebrities), thereby effectively producing this idea of cultural regionalization, which refers to the creation of ties between the nations and a sense of regional togetherness.[12] By extension, digital games may also be perceived from a regional lens by how they coproduce the idea of a region through shared content and practices like game monetization approaches.

The global platformization of cultural production has influenced how digital games are monetized, contributing to a shift from premium business models (i.e., one-time sales of physical and digital commodities) to free-to-play business models that now dominate the game industry.[13] This includes games coming from the East Asian region. Media mixes from this region often incorporate licensed free-to-play games, in particular in the mobile game market, to amplify engagement with its host franchise with gacha as the most lucrative monetization mechanic through which players can obtain desired characters and items.[14] *Genshin Impact* is representative of both shifts. Through its success, it occupies a significant spot in the global game industry, demonstrating the impactful global influence of media mixes that center a free-to-play game as their focal point.

The main argument of this article is that the media mix has become a major driver in the global monetization models of free-to-play games, usually associated with lootboxes, which are random boxes that offer players items from a large pool of items.[15] Nevertheless, video games in a media mix and their monetization schemes are often overlooked by scholars from both Japan Studies and Game Studies. The former field tends to pay more attention to manga and anime as media types, whereas the latter field's Western-centered perspective concentrates on games and game cultures created (or translated) for and by native English-speaking audiences. Yet, according to Bjarke Liboriussen and Paul Martin, Game Studies has been undergoing a regional turn with game scholarship increasingly focusing on areas outside of Western Europe and North America.[16] They label this trend "regional game studies" to describe the investigation of games and different regional gaming cultures and the identification of connections between them. This article thus places itself at the intersection of Japan Studies and Game Studies to show that, in fact, the fields can operate in tandem to enrich our understanding of both global and regional phenomena of popular culture.

This article presents a close reading of *Genshin Impact*, a method used in the field of Game Studies that allows scholars to understand how the text (i.e., the game and its related texts) works.[17] The close reading is based on my ten-month gameplay and on me following HoYoverse's advertisement campaigns for new characters, which allowed me to become familiar not only with the gameplay itself but also with its direct and indirect monetization approach for which content is constantly added and updated over a longer period of time.

The close reading is divided into two analyses. The first analysis focuses on the game's direct revenue. It explains the functions of the game's characters and their role in the game's gacha mechanic to demonstrate the workings of the game's direct source of revenue. The second analysis focuses on the advertisement campaign of the character Kamisato Ayato on YouTube and Twitter—the game's indirect source of revenue—to show how characters are promoted as one of *Genshin Impact*'s primary means through which the developer aims to attract and retain players as part of their overall free-to-play monetization strategy. HoYoverse promotes new characters across different social media platforms in different languages, such as across YouTube, Twitch, Facebook, Twitter, Discord, Reddit, Instagram, TikTok, and HoYoverse's own website. To make this analysis concise, I focus on YouTube videos from *Genshin Impact*'s official English-speaking YouTube and Twitter channels that have been outstanding in Ayato's popularization and proliferation across different channels before and during his entry in the game's wish banner. I chose to focus on Ayato because he is a character who was highly anticipated by fans when new content for the in-game Inazuma region was added in the span of ten months.[18] Furthermore, YouTube is HoYoverse's dominant platform to present new video advertisements and is supported by their Twitter channel. I supplement the English-speaking advertisements with *Genshin Impact*'s official Japanese-speaking YouTube and Twitter channels, because the English-speaking audience tends to watch the Japanese-speaking YouTube channel for extra advertisement content not released on the English channels.

In the next sections before the analyses, I provide a background on characters and the increasing growth of digital games as the focal point of media mix practices. The following section then turns to the topic of free-to-play games, also known as freemium games, which refers to a monetization approach toward digital games developed under the global platformization of cultural production over the past decade, encompassing not only the Euro-American game industries but also game industries from South Korea, China, and Japan. After the analyses, I conclude this article by reflecting on what the global platformization of cultural production means for our understanding of the media mix, shedding light on how characters in a media mix strategy do not only attach players to a product but have become premium goods integrated in the game's service model, thereby directly supporting its revenues.

Games and Characters in Media Mixes

The media mix is described by Steinberg as "the cross-media serialization and circulation of entertainment franchises."[19] As Akinori Nakamura and Susana Tosca explain, a media mix ecosystem surrounds fans with a variety of products for them to consume as they please, such as manga, anime, and video games, while simultaneously creating touchpoints for new consumers to a range of products.[20] We may therefore perceive a media mix as a strategic practice to spread content across different media platforms and related products. As I explain elsewhere,[21] media mix strategies belong to the phenomenon of media convergence described by Henry Jenkins as "the flow of content across multiple media platforms."[22] Within this phenomenon, Jenkins' term "transmedia storytelling" is a common concept in Euro-American countries to describe the "process where integral elements of a fiction get dispersed systematically across multiple delivery channels for the purpose of creating a unified and coordinated entertainment experience."[23]

Transmedia storytelling dominantly focuses on storytelling in a unified and coordinated manner across different works to create a franchise. But, in contrast, media mix strategies concentrate mostly on the proliferation of characters across different works to create a franchise. Since the late 1980s, critics and theorists of Japanese media have regarded characters as entities that can exist beyond stories or fictional worlds in cross-media settings to proliferate across different works.[24] They can be recontextualized in a variety of different settings and media types, from more narrative-oriented media like anime or manga to different character goods.[25] Characters often have different functions within a single media mix; they can be seen as fictional actors or mediated performers that adopt any role or function attributed to them.[26] Media mixes hence use characters as means to attract both old and new consumers to a family of products.

Although the media mix has been discussed since the early 2000s in English-speaking academic circles of Japanese Media Studies (albeit not always explicitly under the same denominator) works such as Susan Napier's *Anime from Akira to Princess Mononoke* and Anne Allison's *Millennial Monsters*,[27] usually fly under the radar of scholars in the field of Game Studies. The opposite also occurs; academic works on the media mix from Japan Studies tend to be dominated by a focus on manga and/or anime, with only a handful of exceptions focusing on games, like Steinberg's article on the gameic media mix.[28] As a result, both fields tend to create a tunnel vision of these topics without awareness of their fundamental relevance to the other field. Game Studies risks perpetuating hegemonic, orientalist power relations by positioning Anglophone game cultures at the center and East Asian game cultures at the periphery of research. Meanwhile, Japan Studies risks treating games as media similar to manga and anime while being oblivious to the nuances of how games work as texts. For example, as a form of cybermedia, video games have an underlying mechanical system that makes them switch from one state to another (unlike non-cybermedia such as most manga or anime), which means they require the user's nontrivial effort to traverse the text.[29] The mechanical system of a game is important to take into consideration, especially for textual readings, since it leads to different interpretations and experiences by players stemming from a game's structure. That is, the same game will not show players the same events in the same manner.

Bringing the fields together enriches our understanding of how games from the East Asian region, such as *Genshin Impact*, have been making such a large impact on the global game marketplace. We see this from the fact that although Steinberg's *Anime's Media Mix* has put the term "media mix" on the Anglophone map in the last decade, it was not until the mid-2010s that Game Studies started showing more explicit interest in the Japanese media mix. This is despite the fact that Japanese video games are important products to a media mix ecosystem that, historically, has been providing a dominant contribution to the global success of major popular entertainment franchises.[30] Nevertheless, more works from scholars who locate their work on the junction of Japan Studies and Game Studies have been appearing, including Rachael Hutchinson's *Japanese Culture through Videogames*,[31] and Jérémie Pelletier-Gagnon and Hutchinson's edited volume, *Japanese Role-Playing Games*.[32] It is therefore necessary to gain an understanding of the characteristics of the East Asian regional game industry and culture, as briefly outlined below.

Japan has been a global force in the game industry since its development in the 1980s, but it serves our understanding of *Genshin Impact*'s global impact to frame the game industries of Japan, China, and South Korean as a regional game industry, each with its own idiosyncrasies. According to Martin Picard and Pelletier-Gagnon, the Japanese game industry is part of and works in tandem with other cultural production industries characterized by commercial strategies, specifically the media mix.[33] This industry is shaped simultaneously on a local scale by marketing strategies, on a national scale by industrial transformations, and by creative and technological developments that were established on a global scale.[34] The media mix has had an impact on China and South Korea since the early 1990s, where it has shaped the tastes of youth in their consumption of popular cultural content, including the games they played.

Despite Japan's historical dominance in the global gaming market, the Chinese game industry is actually the largest digital game market in the world at this moment.[35] Nakamura and Hanna Wirman explain that China's game production has seen a steady growth based on knowledge from foreign sources, like Japan and South Korea, which has not only influenced character-dominated mass culture in general but also game monetization approaches.[36] Since the early 2000s, the Chinese game industry has been rapidly expanding into online gaming, where browser-based games, games embedded within social media, and smartphone game apps have been flourishing so much that China has become the largest game playing population in the global market.[37]

South Korea's success in free-to-play mobile games has also played a vital part in the expansion of the freemium model in the East Asian region. The freemium model largely originated from and was popularized by the South Korean game industry.[38] The South Korean government banned the import of Japanese cultural products like physical video games and gaming consoles until 1998.[39] This led to a nationwide uptake of online games with free-to-play monetization elements in the early 2000s, quickly reaching a Chinese market that developed its own free-to-play industry.[40]

Monetization Models of Contemporary Video Games

Simultaneously, with the growing role of digital games in media mixes, the past decade saw a swift change in monetization business models toward video games, which can be attributed to the global platformization of cultural production where cultural commodities have become dependent on digital platforms and are malleable in design.[41] The architectural design of digital platforms enabled a quick shift in game monetization approaches where games were previously treated as stand-alone products, but now they are treated as a service.

In the early to mid-2000s, the logic of cultural production in the digital game industry was dominated by the premium (transaction-based) revenue model, where games were seen as stand-alone products generating value through the sale of boxed or digital units.[42] However, with the rise of smartphones and tablets as gaming devices over the past decade, facilitated by the platformization of cultural production, the monetization model dominating the game industry shifted from premium to freemium, where the game itself is free-to-play but contains in-game purchases.[43] Such a shift occurred in East Asian game markets ahead of Euro-American game markets. As discussed above, this was primarily due to the large national success of South-Korean free-to-play games that became popular globally, reaching Japan, North America, and Europe.[44]

Freemium games rely on direct and indirect revenue streams.[45] Direct revenue streams include in-game purchases through microtransactions for access to additional game content like cosmetic additions; unlocking levels, if players do not wish to wait; or, in extreme cases, paying to gain an unfair advantage in the game, also known as "pay-to-win."[46] Indirect revenue streams include advertising, product placement, and collecting and analyzing user data, which have much in common with social media platforms and search engines.[47] Player-generated data allows developers to inform targeted advertising and, in some cases, customize game content to improve their monetization advertisements and their key performance indicators.[48] As Aphra Kerr explains: "In the platform logic we see business models that valorize sharing, connecting, posting and playing because companies must generate value from these practices to survive."[49]

The freemium model is part of the larger *games as a service* (GaaS) model, where, as Louis-Etienne Dubois and Johanna Wester explain, game studios "indeterminately support and periodically release content incrementally for existing games instead of developing new games or stand-alone sequels. While this generates more stable revenues, it also results in fewer new games since the focus switches to catering to the current player base."[50] For a free-to-play business model to be effective, it relies at its core on player acquisition and retention; previously, developers relied on impact from the release of blockbuster productions common for Triple-A games, but the freemium model favors data-driven design to stimulate players to continue playing, having continuous support with a consistent stream of large content updates, either paid or free.[51] This provides game developers the opportunity to extract revenue from the game for a longer period of time, supporting it with updates and new content for as long as the game is profitable.[52] Since only a small fraction of players are willing to pay for in-game materials or services, all aspects of free-to-play games (production, marketing, usage) must therefore be optimized and measured to effectively generate revenue.[53]

The GaaS model is not without its critics. For the purpose of this article, I limit the critique to two points: data extraction and gambling-like mechanics. Since the model relies on data extraction to acquire and retain players for its financial success, players have effectively become producers of gameplay data for game studios that exploit and substitute user play for company labor.[54] Such data allows game studios to strategically change a game according to what is necessary to optimize their revenue.[55] Another point of critique is that freemium games often contain purchases that employ gambling-like mechanics. For example, lootboxes are often considered to be gambling mechanics at work in the Euro-American game industries.[56] Meanwhile, game industries from the East Asian region use gacha, a long-standing mechanic in Japanese media mixes, often found in the form of playing cards or in console and mobile games. The term gacha derives from the *gachapon*, small capsule machines in Japan that sell balls containing different items. Upon purchasing a ball, consumers may or may not obtain a desired item. Both mechanics have been criticized by scholars and policymakers for their potential fomentation of gambling disorders, and some types of these mechanics are regulated through industry self-regulations or consumer protection laws.[57]

Direct Revenue: Characters in the Gacha Mechanic

As Kati Alha explains, free-to-play games are designed as never-ending experiences in which "playable content never ends as long as the game continues to be profitable. More content is added constantly, and the speed of progression is limited."[58] Following this trend, *Genshin Impact* offers players a continuous stream of new content: new quests, new events, new characters, new stories, and new areas to explore. With these continuous updates, the game has already managed to extract revenue for more than two years.

New characters are an important source for *Genshin Impact*'s monetization model, because they function as collectibles in the game; the affordance to players to use these characters—especially as their avatars—is contingent on their ownership of the character, which depends on if they managed to obtain the character through the game's so-called "wish banners." *Genshin Impact*'s new characters, offered in the wish banners, are one of the game's most lucrative sources of revenue.[59] Every three weeks, HoYoverse offers new characters. Players can then use in-game resources they accumulated over hours of gameplay—or purchased—to obtain the advertised character through a gacha mechanic. Freemium games that use a gacha mechanic are therefore also known as "gacha games," in which players are incentivized "to buy or accumulate in-game currency which can be used to obtain a randomized virtual item that might—to greater or lesser degrees—enhance or progress the game. Currency can be accumulated through repetitive patterns of play ("grinding") and/or by investing real world money."[60]

In *Genshin Impact*, every banner has one featured, rare five-star character whose probability of accession goes up for a limited amount of time (usually three weeks), together with a few four-star characters that players also have increased chances to win. As players pay only for the *chance* to obtain their desired character, the mechanic resembles gambling. The wish banner rewards players with every roll, but most of the time it will be a weapon of low rank with very little use. However, players are always guaranteed a four-star character with every ten rolls and a five-star character with every ninety rolls (more on that below). Players usually cannot obtain highly ranked characters in any other way, which encourages players to make use of the mechanic.

The wish banner is very popular. For example, the fan-made website paimon.moe counts the number of times players globally attempt and succeed to obtain certain characters from the wish banner. One of the highest summoned characters from the wish banner is Raiden Shogun, a rare five-star character whose banner "Reign of Serenity I" was available September 1–21, 2021. Almost five billion wishes in that banner were made by 790,000 users, of which only 1.68 percent of those "wishes" or rolls successfully summoned her—a total of 808,883 times.[61] So, a low number of players actually have the Raiden Shogun as a playable character in their game collection, whereas others can only experience her as a non-playable character in the game's main quests.

Since the odds of successfully summoning the advertised character are so low, there are only a few ways of raising one's chances to pull a desired rare character. The game makes use of what is known among players as a "pity system." The pity system provides players with a guaranteed summon of a rare five-star character, like Raiden Shogun, after ninety attempted rolls in a temporary banner.[62] There is no guarantee, however, that the five-star character will be the one depicted on the banner. Almost needless to say, ninety attempts are a lot of rolls, especially considering that players need to grind for hours for enough resources to be able to try as many rolls as possible. So, players tend to play strategically, often investing more time at the beginning of the game, which leads to fast progression and the saving of time later.[63] This is especially the case if one wishes to play for free, because when a player has invested enough time to have leveled-up a lot, they obtain more resources than earlier in the game.

Indirect Revenue: Character Advertisement Campaigns

Genshin Impact's most lucrative indirect source of revenue to lead old and new players to the game comes from its advertising on social media. As Nieborg explains: "[t]he emergence of the free-to-play business model is fully intertwined with the evolution of online advertising strategies, the global diffusion of mobile devices, and the political economy of ad-supported social media platforms."[64] While Nieborg points mostly to in-game advertisements to lure players to games, I would like to point out that *Genshin Impact* diverges from this approach and dominantly uses social media platforms such as YouTube and Twitter to acquire and retain players through the advertisements of in-game content like old and new characters. Every character is advertised before it becomes available through a wish banner, especially when the characters are new and have not previously appeared in the game as playable. Players know exactly which character will be appearing when and can adjust their strategies to roll for a desired character accordingly. At the time of writing this article, an available character is Kamisato Ayato, currently part of the highest selling wish banner(s) in Japan.[65] For the purposes of this article, I focus explicitly on the advertisement campaign known as "Version 2.6: Zephyr of the Violet Garden" through which this character was introduced.

In the game's story, Kamisato Ayato is the head of the Kamisato Clan on the island of Inazuma, who is known for his cunning and wit. Inazuma became available to players with the game's update to "version 2.0" on July 21, 2021. Ayato's appearance has been somewhat of a mystery until late in the advertisement campaign; his existence as the head of the Kamisato Clan has been mentioned several times in the story's main quest, but it was not until several official teaser videos that it became clear Ayato was likely to become available in a wish banner, released in "version 2.6" on March 30, 2022.

The first hint of Ayato's likely availability in-game came on December 8, 2021, at the end of both the English and Japanese YouTube trailers of Arataki Itto, a character advertised prior to Ayato.[66] However, Ayato's first "appearance" was limited to the sound of his voice speaking a single line. His visual depiction came two months later in the game's story promotional video, in which he is glimpsed only for a single second and is not shown in great detail (Figure 1).[67] Luckily, his official announcement on Twitter came the same day, which included a detailed illustration and a description of the type of game character he would be.[68] Yet, it was not until the official announcement of the advertisement campaign, one-and-a-half months later, that the pace of Ayato's advertisements picked up, as the new character for the wish banner was introduced together with a larger content update of the game.[69]

From mid-March on, HoYoverse released several Ayato-themed advertisements in the span of three weeks. After the teasers, Ayato was first discussed in more detail in the "Version 2.6 Special Program" on the English YouTube channel—a video notably absent from the Japanese YouTube channel. In this special announcement, Ayato's English voice actor, Chris Hackney, explains Ayato's different skills as a playable character (Figure 2).[70] The videos that followed all focus on different aspect of Ayato to create expectations for how players are supposed to use and understand the character, such as the "Character Teaser,"[71] "The Character Demo,"[72] and "Collected Miscellany."[73] Approaching the day of Ayato's entry into the banner, HoYoverse released several Twitter announcements, such as a brief introduction of Ayato's skills and abilities, a notable tweet that announced Ayato's English and Japanese voice actors exclusively on the English channel,[74] a special Ayato-themed web event,[75] and his in-game story quest.[76]

The advertisements did not stop after his entry in the banner. On the day-of and days following his entry, HoYoverse stimulated player participation in and around the game's version 2.6 update by arranging contests in which players could participate by creating content for free for HoYoverse. Contests

Figure 1. Ayato's first appearance (on the right) in the Story Promotional Video, February 4, 2022. Screenshot by author.

Figure 2. Ayato's skills were first discussed in the Version 2.6 Special Program video on March 19th, 2022. Screenshot by author.

included strategy guides created and submitted for the Zephyr of the Violet Garden events in the game's update[77] and a TikTok contest where players were asked to like, create, and share videos with the hashtag #GenshinMoments.[78] Players received several in-game resources as rewards to smoothen and progress their gameplay. Lastly, the final advertisement for Ayato was on April 22, when HoYoverse released a new set of stickers containing Ayato and his sister Ayako to be used in HoYoverse's forums for English-oriented players.[79] However, for Japan, these stickers were released on LINE,[80] a chat app highly integrated within Japan into various media mix strategies through its use of character stickers.[81]

Genshin Impact's Media Mix in the Global Platformization of Cultural Production

The media mix has become part the global platformization of cultural production, transitioning from a practice that focuses on producing stand-alone products in which characters connect the different audiovisual media and objects to a practice that follows the logic of platforms.[82] Digital games play a large role in that logic. They have increasingly been occupying the focal point in the consumption of media mix strategies. However, not every media mix has the same monetization approach. Some contemporary media mixes still follow the premium approach, in which a game is released as a stand-alone product, and the marketing approach is to spread content across a range of different media to create a family of products. For example, for the *Persona 5* media mix released by Altus, the digital game(s)—*Persona 5*[83] and the enhanced version *Persona 5 Royal*[84]—are the figurative mothership, whereas all other types of media, the various official (and unofficial) manga and anime series and even other games serve to either retell or supplement the narrative of the mothership.[85]

However, the global platformization of cultural production in the past decade shows that certain media mixes follow the freemium approach or a variety thereof, in particular the mobile segment. Those that follow the platform logic, like *Genshin Impact*, focus not so much on a family of products consisting of multiple media types but focus on a service in the shape of a freemium game. The game itself has become the main service to which consumers must be attached, supported by a variety of different sources of revenue to make the service a financial success. As a cross-platform game, *Genshin Impact* shows how the freemium approach unfolds in its media mix, where characters are at the heart of its monetization model. In this approach, the functions of characters have expanded in comparison to media mix strategies following the premium monetization approach. In *Genshin Impact*'s media mix, the characters function to acquire and retain players' attention in said service. They have become integrated in the GaaS model. That is, the characters exist to support the various direct and indirect revenues, functioning as the device that connects all these difference sources of income to a single service.

While gacha was initially a peripheral phenomenon in a media mix strategy, its incorporation into the freemium monetization model of the mothership game has brought the gacha mechanic to the center. *Genshin Impact*'s wish banner is almost unavoidable for players to engage with. The game lures players into a repetitive cycle: it rewards players with resources for any type of quest they complete, be it daily, weekly, or monthly new quests. These resources exist to be spent either to level-up characters the players already own or on limited wish banners to obtain new characters. Nothing ensures that players will get the prominent character from the wish banner; just that they have a *chance* at getting it. This cycle reveals the game's true purpose: forcing players through the gacha mechanic of the wish banners. The reward? Repeating the exact same cycle again and again, with the only difference being that with each cycle players will have slightly better characters to accumulate more resources to spend on, once again, the wish banners.

Genshin Impact constantly demands players' time or money to improve their gameplay, which, as a consequence, requires players to act strategically toward the game's monetization model. According to Orlando Woods, players of gacha games are constantly faced with a trade-off between either spending money or spending time to accumulate resources. Consequently, players have become strategically calculative in their engagement with the game, actively avoiding monetary investments in *Genshin Impact* in favor of temporal investments.[86] They must grind to accumulate enough in-game resources to obtain the characters for free, which means that time is of value as the trade-off for monetary investments, which turns the game into a game of capitalist endeavor.[87] This is problematic because such grind can be purchased away; wealthier players can evade the labor of grinding for resources by paying.[88] The game is designed so that avoiding labor has become "a source of revenue for game studios," which means that the boundary between labor and leisure becomes even more insidious.[89]

My analysis of Kamisato Ayato shows that HoYoverse is dependent on social media platforms to reach a large group of consumers, thereby acquiring new players and retaining old ones. The characters dominantly proliferate through social media under the platform logic of advertisement to catch player interest in a variety of ways: for example, as fictional beings with an inner life through their voice actors or through their appealing visual appearance, or as game pieces defined through their in-game skills and abilities.[90] They function as the device that not only connects different platforms but directs consumers to the service of the freemium game. Once the characters have caught players' potential interest, players will enter the direct revenue stream where they can accumulate resources—or pay—to obtain the desired characters through the wish banner.

Even the indirect revenue, however, is not without the exploitation of player labor. Ayato's advertisement campaign shows that once characters enter the wish banner HoYoverse attempts to retain players' interest through the creation of strategy guides and TikTok competitions, demonstrating that they are not only extending their social media strategy to other platforms with potential players (like TikTok) but that they require player-generated content to sustain the freemium model.[91] Player-generated content such as this may be conceptualized as participatory culture[92] but is in reality free labor for the developer.[93] This blurring of the boundary between labor and leisure in *Genshin Impact*'s grinding practices can be identified as "playbor"—a form of exploitation that masks user-generated content as playful, but is, in fact, a commodification of leisure as labor, capitalizing on consumer creative output without compensation.[94] Such labor practices fit within the larger trend of digital games becoming increasingly designed in terms of productivity to manipulate player populations to increase their time and/or spending on the game.[95] In other words, the attractive characters incentivize players to labor away in service of the game studio.

Genshin Impact shows that the freemium approach from the media mix needs to be taken into consideration by scholars of popular culture in a world-wide circulation of free-to-play games and beyond, not only because they have been shown to be successful among audiences in and outside of East Asia but also because they carry with them the negative potential of exploitative immaterial labor that is common for the overall predatory trend of digital capitalism in which users are constantly tracked. As Dal Yong Jin explains, users on platforms have become information commodities as their activities are constantly monitored, and eventually appropriated by large corporations and advertising agencies.[96] We may understand surveillance in digital capitalism in the words of Christian Fuchs as a "control strategy of humans that aims at enhancing productivity and capital accumulation."[97] The emergence of playbor in *Genshin Impact* then is an illustrative example of how digital games nowadays are framed in terms of productivity, since, as Jennifer Whitson and Martin French explain, these games generate and leverage player data to channel player behavior toward consumption, increasing a player's time on the device.[98] Tracking player activities and stimulating players to create free content for the developer under the guise of "play" serves exclusively to optimize player activity and, in turn, the game's revenue. Perhaps players might not think of themselves as being exploited. Nevertheless, they are effectively turning themselves into commodities by grinding for resources to obtain a character while the developer tracks exactly how the players are doing this, precisely to encourage them to continue playing, spending even more time and/or money in the process.

Finally, as the reader may have noticed, I have explicitly taken both a global and a regional approach to the understanding of the role of digital games in the media mix. The media mix is not only a Japanese practice but a regional practice that is global in reach. As Japan has been a dominant force in the development of global game culture, the media mix has been of influence on different game cultures and has been influenced by different game cultures as well. HoYoverse uses the cultural tendency toward character-centered mass culture from the East Asian region in *Genshin Impact* and simultaneously injects and continues that tendency globally by successfully having installed *Genshin Impact* among the global market of freemium monetization models. The impact of the East Asian region on global game culture should therefore not be overlooked; *Genshin Impact*'s global prominence shows that gacha and its connection to characters are another type of highly influential form of monetization in GaaS. *Genshin Impact* is far from the only freemium game from the East Asian region that uses gacha mechanics to monetize its games through both direct and indirect venues. Rather, the East Asian market accounts for the majority of free-to-play revenues, being especially strong in the mobile market, as *Genshin Impact* demonstrates. And given that the mobile gaming market is only expected to grow, especially in the Asia-Pacific, Middle East and African markets, the global impact of the East Asian game industries on game monetization approaches will likely also continue to grow.[99]

As such, the media mix offers an understanding of how East Asian game industries use freemium monetization approaches to have a global impact, and in turn how the media mix is globalized in its travels via freemium games. It reveals that when media mix strategies operate on the platform logic, characters become a powerful means to relegate consumers to a single service of a free-to-play game, in conjunction with exploitative labor practices common to digital capitalism. Therefore, this article shows that it is important to pay attention to the regional particularities of the platformization of cultural production, since studying games from a regional perspective not only allows us to identify connections between different regional game cultures but also serves to critique how the East Asian region's game markets and related cross-media practices contribute to predatory digital trends worldwide.

Dr. Joleen Blom is a postdoctoral researcher at the Centre of Excellence in Game Culture Studies and at the Game Research Lab at Tampere University. She holds a BA degree in Japan Studies, an MA degree in Media and Performance Studies, and a PhD in Game Studies from the Center for Computer Games at the IT University of Copenhagen, where she was a member of the ERC Advanced grant project *Making Sense of Games* (MSG). Her research interests include transmedia storytelling, Japanese games and culture, characters, and parasocial relationships and intimacy through technology and media. She has published on these topics in journals such as *Narrative, ToDiGRA,* and *Replaying Japan,* and edited collections like *Japanese Role-Playing Games Genre, Representation, and Liminality in the JRPG.*

Acknowledgments

This research was supported by the Academy of Finland project Centre of Excellence in Game Culture Studies (CoE-GameCult, [353266]). I would like to thank Kati Alha, Souvik Mukherjee, Olli Sotamaa, Lukas Wilde, Zach Pearl, and the reviewers for their helpful feedback on this article.

Notes

1. Craig Chapple, "Genshin Impact Surpasses $3 Billion on Mobile, Averages $1 Billion Every Six Months," *SensorTower,* https://sensortower.com/blog/genshin -impact-three-billion-revenue (accessed May 11, 2022).
2. Chapple, "Genshin Impact."
3. Statista, "Annual Mobile Revenue Generated by MiHoYo Worldwide from 2015 to 2022," https://www.statista.com/statistics/1265527/mihoyo-annual-app -revenue/ (accessed May 11, 2022).
4. Patricia Hernandez, "That Breath of the Wilde Anime 'Clone' Actually Looks Impressive," *Polygon,* https://www.polygon.com/2019/6/21/18700922/genshin -impact-gameplay-beta-breath-of-the-wild-clone-botw (accessed November 30, 2022.
5. Ari Notis, "Genshin Impact Is More Than A Breath Of The Wild Clone," *Kotaku,* https://kotaku.com/genshin-impact-is-more-than-a-breath-of-the-wild-clone -1845232653 (accessed November 30, 2022).
6. Marc Steinberg, *Anime's Media Mix: Franchising Toys and Characters in Japan* (Minneapolis: University of Minnesota Press, 2012), 83.
7. David B. Nieborg and Thomas Poell, "The Platformization of Cultural Production: Theorizing the Contingent Cultural Commodity," *New Media & Society* 20, no. 11 (April 2018): 2.

8. José van Dijck, Thomas Poell and Martijn de Waal, *The Platform Society: Public Values in a Connective World* (New York: Oxford University Press, 2018).

9. Van Dijck, Poell, and de Waal, *The Platform Society*, 9. Original italics.

10. Dal Yong Jin, *Digital Platforms, Imperialism and Political Culture* (New York and London: Routledge, 2015), 59.

11. Marc Steinberg, *The Platform Economy: How Japan Transformed the Consumer Internet* (Minneapolis: University of Minnesota Press, 2019), 217.

12. Steinberg, *The Platform Economy*, 215–31.

13. Alexander Bernevega and Alex Gekker, "The Industry of Landlords: Exploring the Assetization of the Triple-A Game," *Games and Culture* 17, no. 1 (2021): 47–69.

14. Bryan Hikari Hartzheim, "Transmedia-To-Go: Licensed Mobile Gaming in Japan," in *The Franchise Era: Managing Media in the Digital Economy*, ed. James Fleury, Bryan Hikari Hartzheim, and Stephen Mamber, Traditions in American Cinema (Edinburgh: Edinburgh University Press), 233–55.

15. Ray Holmes, Joe Gonzales, Andy Ashcraft, Paul Stephanouk, Crystin Cox, Giles Schildt, James Ernest, and Linda Law, "Group Report: Ethical Video Game Monetization," The Twelfth Annual Game Design Think Tank, Project Horseshoe, Fat Lab Inc., 2017, https://www.projecthorseshoe.com/reports/featured /ph17r4.htm.

16. Bjarke Liboriussen and Paul Martin, "Regional Game Studies," *Game Studies: The International Journal of Computer Game Research* 16, no. 1 (2016), http://game studies.org/1601/articles/liboriussen.

17. Astrid Ensslin, *Literary Gaming* (Cambridge, MA: The MIT Press, 2014), 40; Espen Aarseth, "Playing Research: Methodological Approaches to Game Analysis," in *Melbourne DAC: The 5th International Digital Arts and Culture Conference* (2003), 1–7.

18. Genshin Impact Official, "Well, I Consider Myself Merely a Serious, Dutiful Public Servant Who Owes His Allegiance to the Almighty Shogun," https://web .archive.org/web/20220326065503/https://www.hoyolab.com/article/3935779 (accessed March 24, 2022).

19. Steinberg, *Anime's Media Mix*, viii.

20. Akinori Nakamura and Susana Tosca, "The Mobile Suit Gundam Franchise: A Case Study of Transmedia Storytelling Practices and Ludo Mix in Japan," *ToDIGRA* 5, no. 2 (2021): 1–33.

21. Joleen Blom, "The Dynamic Game Character: Definition, Construction, and Challenges in a Character Ecology" (PhD diss., IT University of Copenhagen, 2020).

22. Henry Jenkins, *Convergence Culture: Where Old and New Media Collide* (New York: New York University Press, 2006), 2.

23. Henry Jenkins, "Transmedia Storytelling 101" (March 22, 2007), http://henry jenkins.org/2007/03/transmedia_storytelling_101.html (accessed July 5, 2017).

24. Ōtsuka, Eiji, "World and Variation: The Reproduction and Consumption of Narrative," trans. Marc Steinberg, *Mechademia* 5 (2010): 99–118.

25. Lukas R. A. Wilde, "Recontextualizing Characters. Media Convergence and Pre-/Meta-Narrative Character Circulation," *Image*, no. 29 (January 2019): 3–21.

26. Lukas R. A. Wilde, "Kyara Revisited: The Pre-Narrative Character-State of Japanese Character Theory," *FNS* 5, no. 2 (2019): 220–47.

27. Susan J. Napier, *Anime from Akira to Princess Monoke: Experiencing Contemporary Japanese Animation* (New York: Palgrave Macmillan, 2001); Anne Allison, *Millennial Monsters: Japanese Toys and the Global Imagination* (Berkeley: University of California Press, 2006).

28. Marc Steinberg, "8-Bit Manga: Kadokawa's Madara, or, The Gameic Media Mix," *Kinephanos Journal of Media Studies and Popular Culture* 5 (December 2015): 40–52.

29. Espen Aarseth and Gordon Calleja, "The Word Game: The Ontology of an Indefinable Object," in *International Conference of Foundations of Digital Games*, Pacific Grove, CA, 2015. https://www.um.edu.mt/library/oar/handle/123456789/26620.

30. Nakamura and Tosca, "The Mobile Suit Gundam Franchise."

31. Rachael Hutchinson, *Japanese Culture through Videogames* (London: Routledge, 2019).

32. Rachael Hutchinson and Jérémie Pelletier-Gagnon, eds., *Japanese Role-Playing Games: Genre, Representation, and Liminality in the JRPG* (London: Lexington Books, 2022).

33. Martin Picard and Jérémie Pelletier-Gagnon, "Introduction: Geemu, Media Mix, and the State of Japanese Video Game Studies," *Kinephanos Journal of Media Studies and Popular Culture* 5 (December 2015): 3.

34. Picard and Pelletier-Gagnon, "Introduction."

35. Akinori Nakamura and Hanna Wirman, "The Development of Greater China's Games Industry: From Copying to Imitation to Innovation," in *Game Production Studies*, ed. Olli Sotamaa and Jan Švelch (Amsterdam: Amsterdam University Press, 2021), 275–92.

36. Nakamura and Wirman, "The Development of Greater China's Games Industry."

37. Anthony Y. H. Fung and Sara Xueting Liao, "China," in *Video Games Around the World*, ed. Mark J. P. Wolf (Cambridge, MA: MIT Press, 2015), 119–35.

38. Peichi Chung, "South Korea," in *Video Games Around the World*, ed. Mark J. P. Wolf (Cambridge, MA: MIT Press, 2015), 495–520.

39. Kati Alha, "The Rise of Free-to-Play: How the Revenue Model Changed Games and Playing" (PhD diss., Tampere University, 2020).

40. Alha, "The Rise of Free-to-Play," 37.

41. Nieborg and Poell, "The Platformization of Cultural Production."

42. David Nieborg, "From Premium to Freemium: The Political Economy of the App," in *Social, Casual and Mobile Games: The Changing Gaming Landscape*, ed. Tama Leaver and Michele Wilson (New York: Bloomsbury Academic, 2015), 225–40.

43. Aphra Kerr, *Global Games: Production, Circulation and Policy in the Networked Era* (New York: Routledge Taylor and Francis Group, 2017).

44. Alha, "The Rise of Free-to-Play," 37.

45. Kerr, *Global Games*, 74.

46. Nieborg, "From Premium to Freemium."

47. Kerr, *Global Games*, 74.

48. David B. Nieborg, "Free-to-Play Games and App Advertising: The Rise of the Player Commodity," in *Explorations in Critical Studies of Advertising*, ed. James F. Hamilton, Robert Bodle, and Ezequiel Korin (New York: Routledge, 2016), 28–41.

49. Kerr, *Global Games*, 108.

50. Louis-Etienne Dubois and Johanna Weststar, "Games-as-a-service: Conflicted identities on the new front-line of video game development," *New Media and Society* 24, no. 10 (2021): 1–22.

51. Bernevega and Gekker, "The Industry of Landlords," 50.

52. Alha, "The Rise of Free-to-Play."

53. Nieborg, "From Premium to Freemium," 233–34.

54. Miikka Lehtonen, Mikko Vesa, and Tuomas J. Harviainen, "Games-as-a-Disservice: Emergent Value Co-Destruction in Platform Business Models," *Journal of Business Research* 141 (December 2021).

55. Nieborg, "Free-to-Play Games and App Advertising."

56. Joseph Macey and Mila Bujić, "The Talk of the Town: Community Perspectives on Loot Boxes," in *Modes of Esports Engagement in Overwatch*, ed. Maria Ruotsalainen, Maria Törhönen, and Veli-Matti Karhulahti (Cham: Palgrave Macmillan, 2022), 199–23.

57. Leon Y. Xiao, Laura L. Henderson, Rune K. L. Nielsen, and Philip W.S. Newall, "Regulating Gambling-Like Video Game Loot Boxes: A Public Health Framework Comparing Industry Self-Regulation, Existing National Legal Approaches, and Other Potential Approaches," *Current Addiction Reports* 9 (2022): 163–79.

58. Alha, "The Rise of Free-to-Play," 79.

59. Craig Chapple, "Genshin Impact Generates $3.7 Billion on Mobile in First Two Years," https://sensortower.com/blog/genshin-impact-mobile-two-years-analysis (accessed December 12, 2022).

60. Orlando Woods, "The Economy of Time, the Rationalisation of Resources: Discipline, Desire and Deferred Value in the Playing of Gacha Games," *Games and Culture* 17, nos. 7–8 (2022): 2.

61. Paimon.moe, "Wish Tally Reign of Serenity," https://paimon.moe/wish/tally/300018 (accessed November 15, 2021).

62. IGN, "Pity System Guide," https://www.ign.com/wikis/genshin-impact/Pity_System_Guide#What_is_the_Pity_System_and_How_Does_it_Work (accessed April 15, 2022).

63. Woods, "The Economy of Time," 11.

64. Nieborg, "Free-to-Play Games and App Advertising," 30.

65. Kristine Tuting, "Ayato and Venti Genshin Banners Break Records with US$20.3M Estimated Earnings," https://www.oneesports.gg/genshin-impact/ayato-venti-genshin-banners (accessed May 11, 2022).

66. Genshin Impact, "Character Teaser—'Arataki Itto: That's How the Show Should Go!' | Genshin Impact," YouTube, 2021, https://www.youtube.com/watch?v =KGjnRThxe7k (accessed May 11, 2022).

67. Genshin Impact, "Story Promotional Video | Genshin Impact," YouTube, 2022, https://www.youtube.com/watch?v=nU0MnCpsUD4 (accessed May 11, 2022).

68. @GenshinImpact, Twitter Post, February 4, 2022, 11:40 AM, https://twitter .com/GenshinImpact/status/1489534191989575686 (accessed May 11, 2022). @GenshinImpact, Twitter Post, February 4, 2022, 11:40 AM, https://twitter .com/GenshinImpact/status/1489534192006225925 (accessed May 11, 2022).

69. @GenshinImpact, Twitter Post, March 16, 2022, 6:00 AM, https://twitter.com /GenshinImpact/status/1503944145924026368 (accessed May 11, 2022).

70. Genshin Impact, "Version 2.6 Special Program | Genshin Impact," YouTube, 2022, https://www.youtube.com/watch?v=G90nKszpjlU (accessed May 11, 2022).

71. Genshin Impact, "Character Teaser—'Kamisato Ayato: Lanterns in the Night' | Genshin Impact," YouTube, 2022, https://www.youtube.com/watch?v =s3ok84NeMdU (accessed May 11, 2022).

72. Genshin Impact, "Character Demo—'Kamisato Ayato: Fathomless Swirls in the Forest' | Genshin Impact," YouTube, 2022, https://www.youtube.com/watch?v =KxMs7IsSTgs (accessed May 11, 2022).

73. Genshin Impact, "Collected Miscellany—'Kamisato Ayato: Reflection of the Moon and Flowers' | Genshin Impact," YouTube, 2022, https://www.youtube .com/watch?v=E7wDRANQI8I (accessed May 11, 2022).

74. @GenshinImpact, Twitter Post, March 24, 2022, 8:00 AM, https://twitter.com /GenshinImpact/status/1506873445241348096 (accessed May 11, 2022).

75. @GenshinImpact. Twitter Post, March 25, 2022, 6:00 AM, https://twitter.com /GenshinImpact/status/1507205635753996291 (accessed May 11, 2022).

76. @GenshinImpact. Twitter Post, March 28, 2022, 7:00 AM, https://twitter.com /GenshinImpact/status/1508292798113492996 (accessed May 11, 2022).

77. @GenshinImpact. Twitter Post, March 30, 2022, 7:00 AM, https://twitter.com /GenshinImpact/status/1509017572976455683 (accessed May 11, 2022).

78. @GenshinImpact. Twitter Post, March 31, 2022, 4:00 PM, https://twitter.com /GenshinImpact/status/1509515864726405123 (accessed May 11, 2022).

79. @GenshinImpact, Twitter Post, April 22, 2022, 7:00 AM, https://twitter.com /GenshinImpact/status/1517352494791372801 (accessed May 11, 2022).

80. @Genshin_7, Twitter Post, April 23, 2022, 7:23 AM, https://twitter.com/Genshin _7/status/1517720864351211520 (accessed May 11 2022).

81. Steinberg, *The Platform Economy*, 219.

82. Steinberg, *Anime's Media Mix*, 83.

83. P-Studio, *Persona 5*, Atlus, 2016 (Japanese release).

84. P-Studio, *Persona 5 Royal*, Atlus, 2019 (Japanese release).

85. Joleen Blom, "The Manifestations of Game Characters in a Media Mix Strategy," in *Comics and Videogames: From Hybrid Medialities to Transmedia Expansions,*

ed. Andreas Rauscher, Daniel Stein, and Jan-Noël Thon (New York: Routledge, 2020), 201–21.

86. Woods, "The Economy of Time," 13.

87. Woods, "The Economy of Time," 14.

88. Lehtonen, et al., "Games-as-a-Disservice," 6.

89. Lehtonen, et al., "Games-as-a-Disservice," 7.

90. Felix Schröter and Jan-Noël Thon, "Video Game Characters: Theory and Analysis," *Diegesis* 3, no. 1 (2014): 40–77.

91. Kerr, *Global Games*, 108.

92. Henry Jenkins, *Textual Poachers: Television Fans and Participatory Culture* (New York: Routledge Taylor and Francis Group, 1992).

93. Kerr, *Global Games*, 129.

94. Lehtonen et al., "Games-as-a-Disservice," 6.

95. Jennifer Whitson and Martin French, "Productive Play: The Shift from Responsible Consumption to Responsible Production," *Journal of Consumer Culture* 21, no. 1 (2021): 14–33.

96. Jin, *Digital Platforms, Imperialism and Political Culture*, 139.

97. Christian Fuchs, *Social Media: A Critical Introduction* (Los Angeles: Sage, 2014), 117.

98. Whitson and French, "Productive Play," 23.

99. Newzoo, "Global Games Market Report the VR & Metaverse Edition," https://newzoo.com/products/reports/global-games-market-report (accessed June 10, 2022).

Contents Tourism, the Media Mix, and Setting Moé

Toward a Spatial Theory of the Media Mix

PAUL OCONE

In 2017, fifteen thousand people gathered in Yuwaku, situated in the Kanazawa prefecture of Japan, for the annual Bonbori Festival. A procession of attendees snaked through a path illuminated by lanterns, guiding a goddess to the local shrine and then to a nearby pond. By the pond, plaques containing the wishes of participants were ceremonially burned in a bonfire while a priest recited a prayer. This festival continued a tradition—only the "tradition" was invented wholesale by the 2011 anime series *Hanasaku Iroha*, whose setting is a fictionalized version of Yuwaku. Kanazawa Prefecture was devastated in 2009 by floods and landslides, and the anime's producers worked with local officials in order to promote tourism to the area. Soon after the series finished airing, the town recreated the fictional festival in real life, which saw five thousand attendees, a number that kept growing as the festival grew in popularity.[1] In this way, the fictional festival materialized, attracting tourism and local revitalization along the way.

What the Bonbori Festival demonstrates is the increasing importance of contents tourism to fans, to communities, and to the media mix. Indeed, there is a need to more fully consider the role of spaces, and not just characters, in the media mix. Contents tourism, a term for media tourism in Japanese contexts, is the practice of the audience of a piece of media or multimedia franchise visiting locales where the work is set, where the setting is based on, or where there is some other connection to the media.[2] Contents tourism can result from a variety of media, but it often occurs with media such as anime, where it is associated with otaku subcultures. In these contexts, related terms include *seichi junrei* ("sacred place pilgrimage"), *butaitanbō* ("scene hunting"), and "otaku tourism."[3]

Contents tourism has many connections to the media mix, which can be broadly defined as Japanese media franchises, often centered around anime, that proliferate across multiple media forms, or the specific set of industrial practices in creating media franchises used by Japanese companies. A media mix may include many different media forms (including merchandise), where

167

each medium provides equal access to the narrative and creates synergy with the others without one iteration of a franchise dominating as the "definitive" work.[4] Contents tourism is increasingly part of the contemporary media mix, as producers collaborate with locales to explicitly promote tourism and integrate tourist experiences into franchises.[5] However, although there is scholarship addressing the use of physical spaces in the media mix, dominant models of the media mix are inadequate for fully addressing contents tourism.

In Marc Steinberg's foundational scholarship, the media mix is the deployment of characters across multiple media forms, including explicitly narrative media such as manga and anime, as well as media commodities such as toys and candies. Characters are central to Steinberg's model of the media mix: characters bring disparate media forms together and transform these media, creating synergistic relationships and fashioning the media mix into a connected web. Steinberg's focus on characters is related to his elaboration on Ōtsuka Eiji's theory of narrative consumption or world consumption.[6] To recap, Ōtsuka argues that people access narrative worlds through narrative fragments. These fragments can vary in size from brief sketches of a world or character, to an episode of a TV serial, to a whole media work, but they add up to create a narrative "worldview." The worldview is not accessible in its entirety, but parts of the worldview (or "world") can be consumed through these fragments, which also represent different variations or manifestations of that world.[7] In his reading of Ōtsuka, Steinberg draws out the importance of characters in connecting the fragments that create a "world" or media mix franchise. Steinberg sees characters as resolving a central issue of both world consumption and the media mix, namely, maintaining a unity of worldview in light of fragmented variations.[8] For Steinberg, character is the glue that holds together all the variations of the media mix. Steinberg also suggests that in the 2000s, the focus of media mixes shifted from centering *worlds* as the primary object of consumption (in closer alignment with Ōtsuka's original theory) to centering *characters*.[9] In what follows, I explore the implication that the consumption of worlds has declined in importance in the contemporary media mix must be challenged in light of the rise of contents tourism, which suggests a new prominence of place, and, by implication, worlds.

For Steinberg, the character image also plays a major role in the extension of the media world out into real spaces and daily life in the "environmentalization of media," where the presence of character images in space provide constant opportunities to consume characters and worlds.[10] Following this, most literature that considers the role of physical space in the media mix emphasizes character representations in spaces (often spaces of commerce) that provide access to a narrative world. For example, in the work of Edmond Ernest dit Alban (including collaborations with Steinberg), character images connect to spatial practices and relations: characters circulate through the neighborhood and through different media forms in the media mix.[11] Another scholar writing about the relationship of the media mix to physical space is Anya C. Benson, who considers spaces, designed for the marketing of the girls' anime media mix *Precure* (2004–, *Purikyua*) that create the feeling of entering into a narrative world. These spaces all feature merchandise, special events, and activities for children to engage in the world of *Precure*, and the presence of character images in space encourages the narrative consumption of merchandise featuring these characters.[12] This describes a classic media mix regime in which consumption of the narrative is tied to the consumption of characters and narrative fragments.

Character-world models of the media mix provide a useful theoretical paradigm, but the emphasis on character has its limitations: contents tourism does not always involve characters directly and so would not seem to fit inside character-centric models of consumption. Fans can be motivated by an investment more in the setting itself than in characters. Therefore, media mix theory must be expanded and modified to encompass practices of contents tourism that do not involve characters. In exploring the limitations of character-centric models of media mix theory, I open up a space for considering the affective draw of mediatized spaces themselves, or what I call "setting moé." In "character-type setting moé," fans are drawn to the setting as a kind of character, while in "world-type setting moé," fans form attachments to the setting itself. During fan pilgrimage, setting moé is transformed: attachments to the setting and the real place are blurred and heightened. In what follows, I expand on media mix theory to better account for the space-based practices of contents tourism, exploring the concept of setting moé via case studies. I also develop a multipart typology, consisting of setting moé as well as existing theoretical models, of the ways fans engage with places in the media mix.

Contents Tourism and Media Mix Theory

Much of the scholarly literature on contents tourism emphasizes that the narratives inspiring this tourism are found across multiple media forms, positioning contents tourism squarely as a media mix-related practice. In

Contents Tourism in Japan, Philip Seaton et al. argue that "contents tourism" is not only the phenomenon of tourism itself but also an analytic lens used to approach media tourism; what sets contents tourism apart is that it is centered around multiple interrelated media forms (that is, a media mix): "the more that a set of contents . . . reaches fans through multiple media formats, the greater the potential for a contents-tourism approach."[13] Nelson Graburn and Takayoshi Yamamura similarly argue that the concept of contents tourism centers "trans- or cross media experiences of tourists in the mixed media age."[14] The word "contents" (*kontentsu*) itself arose in Japanese discourse as a way to talk about the rise of new media and the many burgeoning media mix franchises in the 1990s[15]; the concept of contents tourism is thus intimately linked to the media mix.

A version of narrative consumption also factors into scholarship and theory on contents tourism, even when Ōtsuka's theory is not invoked directly. For example, Seaton et al. write that "contents tourism begins with the creation of 'narrative worlds.'"[16] As in Ōtsuka's theory of world consumption, a world is created *across and between* different variations of a narrative (or iterations, "fragments," media forms) and accessed via these variations, and this is paramount to understanding how and why people engage with these worlds in real life via contents tourism. Seaton et al. explain this world-centric approach by referring to the example of tourism related to Jane Austen. Because there are many media forms and iterations of Austen's works, it becomes useful to use a contents tourism approach and "focus on the various contents of 'Austen's world,'" including places related to the author, novels, and films.[17] This idea of a world created across the totality of Austen's corpus and related media (the "contents" or "media mix") aligns neatly with Ōtsuka's conception of narrative "worlds," and not individual narratives, being consumed.

The example of Austen's world hints at the physical sites of tourism themselves being part of the broader "world," and the literature on contents tourism also suggests that tourist sites *themselves* become media texts that are part of the media mix. For example, Seaton et al. argue that "the destination is also a form of media" that increases consumption of other media in the mix (i.e., promotes media mix synergy).[18] Graburn and Yamamura refer to this as the "mediatization of tourist sites and mediatization of experiences or creation of tourists/fans" and suggest that the "media mix or transmedia approach of contents tourism . . . embraces various types of media including a 'site' or 'event,'"[19] clearly placing the sites of contents tourism as part of the media mix. Given this, the term "contents tourism" could have two senses: tourism derived from experiences with "contents," and tourism in which locations and experiences are themselves "contents," or part of the media mix.

If physical sites become mediatized through the process of tourism, they are consumed as media by tourists, and Graburn and Yamamura also suggest that tourist practices are related to patterns of comparison in media consumption; these patterns are themselves suggestive of Ōtsuka's theory of world consumption. They write that fans may cross-reference between "narrative worlds depicted in film or anime as media and also narrative worlds expressed in the locations (physical sites) as media."[20] The existence of different narrative variations that nevertheless construct a whole world is key to Ōtsuka's theory, in which people consume across these variations to get at the whole world. When tourist sites become mediatized through contents tourism, they become another (spatial) variation on the world; fans visit the location in order to consume this variation and access more of the total world. This consumption can also involve the comparison between the world as presented in the narrative and the tourist site. Within this framework, we see that contents tourism is also a practice of (or part of) media consumption.

In his article "Avonlea as 'World,'" Brian Bergstrom links Japanese *Anne of Green Gables* tourism to Ōtsuka's theories of world consumption and uses this theoretical link to understand embodied modes of tourist experience. Examining the writing of *Anne* fan Okuda Miki about her time living on Prince Edward Island, Bergstrom contends that her experiences of embodied fandom, "inhabiting a real place as an extension of one's engagement with a fictional world,"[21] can be understood through Ōtsuka's narrative consumption and Steinberg's extension of it. Arguing that Japanese fans of *Anne* are not merely engaging with the original text but also with a myriad of adaptations and related texts, Bergstrom writes that there is a shift "from *Anne* as text to *Anne* as world."[22] For Bergstrom, *Anne of Green Gables* the novel becomes a variation in a series of texts that together create the world of *Anne,* a world that can then be *experienced* by traveling to or living on Prince Edward Island.

Fandom, Bergstrom notes, moves "towards embodied experiences that allow a feeling of inhabiting the world the books describe in longer-lasting, expanded ways."[23] Similar to Graburn and Yamamura's conception of the "mediatization" of tourist sites, Bergstrom argues that Prince Edward Island "has been transformed into an extension of a fictional world" in which there is "a sense that this island can be experienced as a space that points constantly back to the books while always managing to exceed them."[24] However, a difference is that Graburn and Yamamura identify both tourist sites and fan/tourist experiences as texts in the media mix, while Bergstrom sometimes seems to identify the tourist site with the world itself and individual experiences or tourist lifestyles as variations.[25] On this point, I would argue that Graburn and Yamamura are more accurate: a tourist site cannot be the "world" itself, which always eludes capture in Ōtsuka's framework,[26] but it *can* be a text that is a variation on that world. Nevertheless, Bergstrom's contention that fan tourism and embodied experience represent a form of narrative consumption is a valuable contribution that explicitly connects contents tourism to the theories of Ōtsuka and Steinberg.

The Problem of Character

There is an unaddressed theoretical problem with the connection of the media mix and Steinberg's version of world-consumption theory to contents tourism: the issue of *character*. As discussed above, in Steinberg's theory, character is the key element that connects the different media forms in the media mix together: characters unify disparate variations and enable narrative consumption. But the emphasis of contents tourism is the *setting* of the narrative, not the characters of the narrative. The issue of character is not as large within the original text of Ōtsuka's essay: it is in Steinberg's expanded version of the theory that character, in both material and immaterial form, plays such a large role in narrative consumption. But nevertheless, when trying to think about contents tourism as media mix practice, the problem remains: how can we understand the media mix in terms that center fan experiences with worlds? In the remainder of this article, I explore the role of character in contents tourism and the theoretical gaps that remain, as well as outline possible solutions to these problems. I present a typology or framework of tourist experience with the media mix that includes a range of existing theories drawn from the literature, as well as a theory of "setting moé." This typology can more fully account for existing and emergent media mix practices.

One of these types of fan/tourist experience comes via Bergstrom's model of embodied engagement with space, what I term "embodied world consumption." Bergstrom uses a character-centric model of world consumption: like Steinberg, Bergstrom sees the character "circulating as a floating signifier that can attach to various products and experiences and give them value." He finds a continuity between contents tourism (and other embodied fan experiences) and character-centric world consumption, seeing embodied fandom as an experience of *becoming* a character in the storyworld, which connects "Anne as character to emulate and Avonlea as inhabitable world."[27] For Bergstrom, character is still important to contents tourism: emulating or imagining oneself as a character helps provide access to the world.

Another angle to embodied world consumption can be found in Anya C. Benson's work on *Precure* spaces. Benson emphasizes the importance of the idea of "becoming" the characters of the series in these spaces. For example, the entrance to one of these spaces emulates the way the characters of the series enter the magic world, and advertisements for the space emphasize that you can "'become a magician'" by crossing the threshold.[28] Benson's contention is that the marketing of *Precure* and its merchandise encourages girls to emulate the characters in order to play *as* character.[29] This aspect of the *Precure* media mix stands in contrast to Steinberg's analysis of children's media mixes, which largely focuses on the consumption of character images. Steinberg writes about toys in the 1950s that allowed children to emulate characters but argues that with the rise of the modern media mix, these were deemphasized in favor of toys and merchandise only *representing* characters.[30] What the case of *Precure* makes clear, however, is that the character-play style of narrative consumption persists in franchises like *Precure*. This mode of narrative consumption is accessing the narrative world not only through the consumption of character images (as in Steinberg's model of the media mix), but also through the imitation or performance of character: character-as-lifestyle, or the "practice of the text as lifestyle."[31] (This mode can also be expanded beyond contents tourism to describe phenomena such as cosplay.) Both Benson and Bergstrom write about fan engagement with media-inflected spaces as the embodied experience, or lifestyle practice, of character.

Bergstrom also writes that fans can imagine the experience, not of existing characters, but instead of *themselves* as new characters in the storyworld. Analyzing a passage from Okuda Miki's memoirs, Bergstrom writes of a mode that "imagines Okuda as another character in Anne's world . . . a *variation* on the theme of Anne."[32] For Bergstrom, then, character still plays a role in the world consumption of contents tourism, whether it be imagining oneself as a preexisting character or reimagining oneself as a new character. One might classify the phenomena described by Bergstrom and Benson under the name of "embodied world consumption," or a relationship to mediatized space in which one embodies characters as a way of accessing the world(view) of a narrative. This corresponds to what Abby S. Waysdorf, invoking Anglophone fan studies' equivalent theory to narrative consumption, calls the "hyperdiegetic" mode of fan tourist experience.[33]

Embodied world consumption (or hyperdiegetic experience) is certainly a way in which characters can, and do, factor into fans' engagement with space in contents tourism, but it does not adequately cover all of the ways in which fans might engage with space. For example, in the practice of butaitanbō, or "scene hunting," fans search for anime settings and take photographs that precisely match up with the background art of an anime series (Figures 1 and 2).[34] The pleasure for fans here is not in some embodied relation to character, but in finding the setting and getting the perfect shot. While Bergstrom's framework certainly describes some experiences of contents tourism, practices like butaitanbō beg the question: are all fan experiences in mediatized spaces related to an imagined embodiment of character?

Another type of fan experience accompanies the presence of character images in some tourist sites, or the integration of the character media mix into physical space. This follows Steinberg's model of the "environmentalization of media," and much literature (Ernest dit Alban, Benson, etc.) emphasizes that character images or goods mediate audience engagement with physical spaces. Consistent with this paradigm, character images and merchandise can be found at some contents tourism sites, integrating the site into the character media mix. A classic example of this is Takayoshi Yamamura's exploration of tourism induced by the 2007 anime *Lucky Star* (*Raki suta*) in the town of Washimiya, where fans, community members, and rightsholders all collaborated to create events and merchandise. This collaboration ultimately fostered one of the first highly successful and publicized examples of anime contents tourism and was at the forefront of contemporary trends of anime pilgrimage (although anime pilgrimage existed as an underground phenomenon since at least the 1990s, and arguably since the 1970s).[35] Character images appear in this case study in several ways: on *ema* (votive plaques) at the shrine with fanart on them, on a newly-made portable Shinto shrine carried at the local festival by fans, and on official merchandise created in collaboration between the locality and Kadokawa, the rights-holder of *Lucky Star*.[36] Characters ultimately play an important role in this example, and through the collaboration with Kadokawa, they fostered the integration of the tourist site into the official media mix. In the case of Washimiya and *Lucky Star* tourism, characters seem to be an integral part of contents tourism and its relation to the media mix.

Figures 1 and 2. *Hanasaku Iroha butaitanbō*. Photos by Mike Hattsu (https://mikehattsu
.blogspot.com). Used with permission.

Even in the case of *Lucky Star*, however, it becomes apparent that characters are not a requisite part of contents tourism. For example, although it
is true that they soon began drawing characters on ema plaques, when fans
first began to visit Washimiya, there were no character images in the tourist
sites themselves.[37] Additionally, Yamamura cautions against seeing contents
tourism purely in relation to character merchandising, arguing that they are
"not synonymous":

[O]n many occasions contents tourism does indeed overlap with the character business. However, the sale of such character products is only a single element in the context of tourism. More precisely, when considering contents tourism, not only the character business but also many other phenomena must be considered in relation to the copyright holders, localities and fans. . . . The important task . . . is to make the character fans into fans of the locality as well.[38]

As Yamamura argues, engagement with characters can occur but is not the only motivating factor behind the world consumption of contents tourism. And that is not to mention practices like butaitanbō that almost never involve engagement with characters. Characters are not an inherent part of tourist spaces, and fans may engage with spaces (and consume fictional worlds) in ways that do not involve the mediation of characters. The theoretical challenge that arises when considering contents tourism, narrative consumption, and the media mix, then, is to not only consider fan consumption of characters, but also to consider the affective investments fans have in the settings and locations themselves, or what I call "setting moé." It is only after taking these responses into account that the world consumption of contents tourism can be more fully understood.

Setting Moé: Affective Responses to Worlds

If the subcultural slang of "moé" can often be understood as indicating an affective response to characters, particularly within otaku subcultural contexts,[39] then what I call "setting moé" should be defined as an affective response to or investment in (mediatized) space. Setting moé could be considered a variation on narrative place attachment as theorized by Setha M. Low, with a focus on media mix texts and world consumption instead of the mythological or community narratives of place that Low writes about.[40] The use of the term moé, usually used for characters, to refer to spaces is not without precedent: Ikuho Amano explores the phenomenon of "kōjō moé" (factory moé) in Japan, in which people feel attachments to and take nighttime tours of factories and industrial landscapes.[41] Importantly, part of the affective investment of fans in industrial landscapes is due to media such as *Blade Runner* (1982), which suggests that we see kōjō moé in relation to contents tourism.[42] I propose two subtypes of setting moé that can account for different varieties of character-world-fan relationships. In the first, "character-type setting moé," the setting of a text itself takes on a role as a kind of character, and fans' affective responses are to the setting-as-character. The second, "world-type setting moé," is an affective response to mediatized space *itself* without a relation to characters, for example, kōjō moé. In what follows, I elaborate on these concepts through case studies and explain how they resolve the problems left by existing media mix and contents tourism theory.

"Character-type setting moé" is an affective response to a place that takes on aspects of a character—in other words, it is a response to setting *as* character. Following Saitō Tamaki's argument that otaku aim to possess objects of desire through fictionalization,[43] character-type setting moé is the affect that emerges from the fictionalization of space, or the creation of a fictional construct of character out of a setting. World-type setting moé also involves the fictionalization (or mediatization) of space, but with character-type setting moé, the space is fictionalized as character. One might look to Patrick W. Galbraith's work on *fujoshi* desire and play for an analogous example, where inanimate objects—including locations such as roads—become characters in playful yaoi reading practices.[44] Galbraith writes about the ways that real-world spaces can be read as moé through fictionalization, but the situation he describes emerges via improvised play—character-type setting moé could also involve an affective investment in a space that is built up as a kind of "character" in a longer narrative. I would argue that the setting of the anime series *Aria* (2005–21)—Neo-Venezia, or a reconstructed Venice on the planet Aqua (i.e., Mars), and to some extent Aqua itself—might engender character-type setting moé. Neo-Venezia and Aqua are literally and metaphorically characters in the series: in *Aria's* characteristic use of magical realism, Aqua is implied to protect and keep watch over the protagonist Akari. This is made manifest through the character Cait Sith, a deity identified with Aqua itself.[45] Because of this characterization, tourists to the real Venice who are inspired by *Aria* may feel an attachment to an imagined "Neo-Venezia" as a character.

One can perhaps think of these character-settings in terms of the genius loci, or the spirit of a place. This concept has taken on different forms in different contexts: in ancient Rome and Romantic literature the genius loci was a guardian spirit, or literal personification, of a place.[46] In contemporary discourse, meanwhile, genius loci has taken on a more pedestrian meaning: the characteristic appeal or *je ne sais quoi* of a locale.[47] Character-type setting moé approaches the former more than the latter; however, in addition to character-settings (personified genii locorum), where the setting takes on a role as a kind of agentic character in the narrative, there may also be instances where setting is simply seen to have a kind of personality that is character-like, or the contemporary conception of genius loci. In this vein, fans may consider settings as characters in more of a metaphorical sense (a "character" because of a strong sense of place, but not a character with agency), for example a fan in Waysdorf's study who says that the town of Portmeirion is "one of the central characters of [the TV series] *The Prisoner.*"[48] Character-setting as metaphor starts to blur into world-type setting moé, and the boundaries between the two may be porous. Setting moé, then, is a concept that gets at the double meaning, the slippage between character and characteristic of place found in the term genius loci.

In fan accounts of *Aria* pilgrimage to Venice, one can certainly find expressions of attachment to Neo-Venezia/Venice and their characteristics. Tachikichi, who maintains a comprehensive pilgrimage guide to Venice, writes, "Not only the scenery, but also the impressions of *Aria*'s ambience and atmosphere—the whole city itself was the wonderful space of *Aria.*"[49] Another fan, reflecting on an *Aria* pilgrimage to speak to the appeal of seichi junrei more generally, writes that upon experiencing the setting, you invariably "fall in love with the place itself."[50] As these reports testify, certainly fans visiting Venice feel an attachment to the setting of Neo-Venezia and the real Venice (setting moé). In most accounts, however, it is hard to determine how much the "character" of Neo-Venezia plays into these feelings. The difference between world-type and character-type setting moé may be more of a continuum, but these accounts seem to lean toward world-type setting moé. The "character" of Neo-Venezia may still play a role in these fan's experiences, but the fans do not testify to that role. For this reason, I believe that ethnographic research is needed to better understand whether and how character-settings play a role in fan's attachments to mediatized spaces.

However, there is one fan's travelogue that does seem to make connections to the character-setting of Neo-Venezia. The *Aria* pilgrim Mizuya recounts a chance encounter they had with a fellow fan at a restaurant in a nontourist area of Venice. It turns out that they worked at the same company and may have briefly met previously at the wedding of a mutual friend! Mizuya refers to these coincidences as "miracles" ("*mirakuru*") and writes, "I had the strange conviction that these kinds of fortuities piling up would of course happen on an *Aria* pilgrimage!"[51] Here, Mizuya is indirectly referencing the setting of Neo-Venezia and its characteristics. Being a city of miracles is Neo-Venezia's genius loci—in both senses. That is, the city is seen through the eyes of *Aria*'s protagonist Akari (and subsequently the audience; the series' tone departs from her outlook rarely, if at all) as a city of wonder and miracles. This is perhaps the defining characteristic of the setting, and words like "miracle" ("*kiseki*") and "wonderful" ("*suteki*") appear frequently in dialogue and in episode titles. But this genius loci (characteristic) is also tied to the genius loci (character) of Neo-Venezia/Aqua as represented by its guardian deity Cait Sith. Akari's meetings with Cait Sith are miraculous encounters in and of themselves, but Neo-Venezia and the planet Aqua as characters (and Cait Sith as the representation of genius loci) are also implied to help create this city of miracles.[52]

When Mizuya says that "of course" ("*sasuga*") miraculous encounters would happen on an *Aria* pilgrimage, they are connecting the real Venice with the characteristics of Neo-Venezia and imagining the city as Neo-Venezia. But because the series identifies these characteristics with Neo-Venezia-as-character, this moment of connection to the world of *Aria* is also, in a sense, a moment of affective connection to the setting-character of Neo-Venezia—that is, character-type setting moé. Granted, this connection is implicit—nowhere does Mizuya explicitly state an attachment to setting as character. *Aria*'s strong identification of setting with character, however, means that when invoking Venice/Neo-Venezia as a city where miraculous encounters happen, Mizuya is also invoking the character of Neo-Venezia. In any case, Mizuya leaves the chance encounter amazed, "strangely intoxicated from the miracles."[53]

If character-type setting moé is the appeal of place as character, "world-type setting moé" is an affective response to place itself, with little to no relation between characters and place in the response. In some cases, world-type setting moé could be expressed as a sense of returning "home," or the "fan homecoming" that Waysdorf describes.[54] This type of fan response may be the closest theoretically to Ōtsuka's original outline of narrative consumption: in world-type setting moé, mediatized space is a fragment or variation on the narrative world, and visiting this space is one way to access the world. In this respect, it is similar to the embodied world consumption discussed by Benson, but with a key difference: Benson and Bergstrom describe fans becoming characters while visiting mediatized space in order to access the world, but "world-type setting moé" involves no such relation to character. In this type of setting moé, fans form attachments to settings, and they visit those settings in order to access the world, but although their experience is embodied when visiting the setting (or world fragment), they do not necessarily experience character embodiment. Because of the absence of character embodiment, world-type setting moé could also be called "semi-embodied world consumption" when tied to actual tourism.

World-type setting moé offers a much-needed theory of the media mix and contents tourism that accounts for practices where characters are not involved in fans' relationships to spaces. It accounts, in short, for the experiences of people such as a fan who describes his initial motivation for doing butaitanbō in terms of an attraction to the setting of the 2005 series *Air*: "the background was so beautiful—even after seeing one image, I felt the desire to see the place in reality."[55] In the case of butaitanbō, fans seek out the settings featured in their favorite works and take photos that match the background art not because of their relationship with characters per se, but because of their relationship with the world or setting *itself*. As Okamoto Ryōsuke writes, "To identify the places that have become settings is to unravel the mystery of the narrative world."[56] Identification, travel, and photography are ways of accessing the world, and photos further remediate the space into additional narrative fragments. As fragments, when the photographer looks back on them or shares them online, these photos provide further opportunities to access the world. World-type setting moé is the response to the "narrative quality" of places that is generated through the media mix (but not necessarily through characters).[57]

Another example of world-type setting moé is found in the contents tourism induced by the 2011 anime series *Hanasaku Iroha*, another case study popular in the literature. In addition to the Yuwaku Bonbori Festival, many fans make pilgrimages and engage in butaitanbō to Yuwaku Onsen and other featured locations at other times of the year. When one of the *ryokan* in Yuwaku closed its doors, *Hanasaku Iroha* fans gathered to say goodbye, demonstrating an attachment to Yuwaku that developed out of repeated pilgrimage.[58] *Hanasaku Iroha* was explicitly planned to promote contents tourism to the setting of Yuwaku, but Yamamura writes that the tourism planning for this series deliberately excluded promotional events centered around anime tie-ins, instead emphasizing a more "authentic" experience and providing room for fans to discover locations on their own.[59] Although promotional campaigns for Yuwaku have included character goods and images,[60] the character media mix has been limited to an extent in order to facilitate an experience with the setting where characters have a lighter touch. When attending the Bonbori Festival, some fans may have experienced embodied world consumption, imagining themselves as characters in the world of *Hanasaku Iroha*. However, as Yamamura writes, one goal of contents tourism is "to make the character fans into fans of the locality,"[61] and some fans' tourism was likely motivated by precisely this—an affective investment in the setting itself.

Indeed, this kind of investment can be found on the blogs of fans of the series. On a blog post dedicated to the setting of *Hanasaku Iroha*, the fan SnippitTee comments on screenshots depicting the lush background art of the series; characters are deemphasized, if present at all. The captions of these images emphasize the desire to visit and enter the world, for example, "This series is calling me to experience the onsen's purity of water, mineral richness, and heat" (Figure 3).[62] These sentiments express a desire to live in the world of *Hanasaku Iroha* and indicate an emotional investment in the setting. The importance of background art in sparking these feelings deserves highlighting: the studio P.A. Works is known for both beautiful backgrounds and for working with locales to inspire pilgrimages[63]—*Hanasaku Iroha* is an examplar of both. Another fan similarly writes, "This series just makes me want to step through my screen and end up at [the *ryokan*] Kissuisō."[64] These are not examples of tourism (though it may lead to tourism in the future), but the ways that world-type setting moé emerges from this fan's consumption of *Hanasaku Iroha* demonstrate the explanatory power of this concept to account for the affective investment of fans in the spaces and places of the media mix.

Setting moé sparked from viewing the anime is transformed and deepened when fans actually visit the setting in practices of pilgrimage and butaitanbō. The fan Shin, on a butaitanbō pilgrimage to the locations of the follow-up film *Hanasaku Iroha: Home Sweet Home* (2013) describes the landscape with passionate prose: "Overflowing emotions and kindness . . .

Figure 3. Onsen in *Hanasaku Iroha*.

the abundant nature and nostalgia contained in the scenery of the setting of Ishikawa Prefecture—all these were tenderly, beautifully, and delicately depicted on the big screen in *Hanasaku Iroha: Home Sweet Home.*"[65] In Shin's account, affection for the world of the anime and affection for real-life places bleed into each other: it is hard to delineate where one ends and the other begins. The scenery is mediatized through pilgrimage and semi-embodied world consumption, and affection for the world of the anime (world-type setting moé) is transformed and transferred onto real places.

Another fan, whose writing in a pilgrimage exchange book was transcribed by the scholar Yoshitani Hiroya, expresses their feelings after attending the Bonbori Festival in 2011: "The Bonbori Festival was the best. . . . As the deep reds are enveloped by the veil of darkness, the paper lanterns are lit throughout, and the flowery colors blossom [*hanasaki iromekidasu*, a pun on the title of the series], the atmosphere of the onsen town is the greatest! . . . I truly wish that this continues for 10 or 20 years—that's how much magic I feel this town and this festival have. . . . *Hanasaku Iroha* forever!"[66] Like Shin, this fan's love for *Hanasaku Iroha* and its world is transformed into a love for the real-world Yuwaku and festival: the "magic" of setting moé becomes the magic of the town. A consistent trend in the exchange notebook and in butaitanbō accounts that describe personal feelings alongside the technical details about photography is the desire to return again. The desire to return, and the return itself (including Waysdorf's "homecoming"), are the ultimate expressions of the transformation of setting moé. The investment in the world of anime becomes an investment in the real world, where the pleasures of accessing the fictional world and the pleasures of the real place become blurred and intensified.

Toward a Theory of Setting Moé: Characters, Spaces, and Worlds

Following from this discussion of setting moé, I would like to propose an open framework for understanding fans' relationships to characters, worlds, and spaces, especially relating to contents tourism. This framework is summarized in Table 1, which is organized around four different types or modes of fan relationships to characters and spaces. In the character media mix, fans consume character images in real-world spaces. In embodied world consumption, fans become characters as they access the narra-

Table 1. Types or modes of fan relationship to spaces and characters

NAME	RELATION BETWEEN CHARACTERS AND SETTING/SPACE	CASE STUDY	THEORETICAL LITERATURE
character media mix	seeing characters in space	*Lucky Star*	Steinberg
embodied world consumption	becoming characters in space	*Precure, Anne*	Benson, Bergstrom
setting moé— character type	space *as* character	*Aria*	Saitō
setting moé— world type, semi-embodied world consumption	no relation between characters and space (setting as setting)	butaitanbō, *Hanasaku Iroha*	Ōtsuka, Ocone

tive world through mediatized space. In character-type setting moé, the narrative setting is *itself* a kind of character, which engenders an affective response. And finally, in world-type setting moé, fans form affective investments in places themselves, without the involvement of characters. (However, this assertion is simplification, for in most cases, it is the characters and the events of the narrative that give the setting value.) It is important to emphasize that *these types are not mutually exclusive:* a fan's experience with contents tourism and the media mix may involve more than one—or even all four—of these types at once! Or a fan might start in one type and then move to another. This open framework thus allows media mix and contents tourism theory to adequately address a wide diversity of fans' experiences with places and characters.

There are still some theoretical kinks to work out. For example, world-type setting moé may sometimes be hard to extricate from embodied world consumption. When imagining oneself entering a world, is it also necessary to imagine oneself as a character in the world? If so, during pilgrimage, world-type setting moé may go hand-in-hand with embodied world consumption, where setting moé represents the spatial aspects of fan affect, and embodied consumption represents the character-embodiment aspects. An unaddressed fan experience is imagining characters (but not oneself) inhabiting the setting. This may fall under character media mix, even if it does not involve material representations of characters, or it may be another mode to add to the framework. Another problem is the elision of nontourist desire and tourist experience. That being said, contents tourism is always mediated—fans can never grasp the worldview in its entirety and so any tourist experience is of a fragment of this worldview—and because of this mediation, "setting moé" (an affective response to mediated/mediatized space) is still applicable to embodied experience. Additionally, as Waysdorf argues, there may be modes of fan engagement with space that are not related to accessing storyworlds, which would fall outside a world consumption framework entirely.[67] Finally, further research—particularly ethnographic research—would help ground the theorization of setting moé. Nevertheless, I believe this four-part theoretical framework offers the first steps toward a more complete, typological understanding of the ways in which mediatized space is a part of the contemporary media mix.

Conclusion

Contents tourism is part of the media mix, and its practice involves narrative consumption, but it is not always centered around characters. In order to access narrative worlds, fans may engage with character images in a space, but they can also embody characters in a space or even form affective attachments to mediatized space itself. Takeshi Okamoto highlights the "emotional connection" ("kanjōteki na tsunagari") between fans and places and writes that "for the development of contents tourism, the important question is how to create this 'emotional connection.'"[68] This "emotional connection" is what I am calling "setting moé." It is sparked when fans develop attachments to the worlds of the media mix when consuming source media, and it is transformed and deepened in the practice of fan pilgrimage. This transformation also involves other people—consistent in the literature on contents tourism and in many fan accounts is the importance of social relationships in fan connections to places. Ian Condry and Patrick W. Galbraith both assert the importance of sociality in character moé[69]; the likely importance of sociality in setting moé as well is another place for further research. Future research can also focus on the frictions caused by the commercialization of pilgrimage. Contents tourism may be part of the media mix, but the over-commoditization of place can work against setting moé.[70] It is clear that as contents tourism becomes an increasingly important part of the contemporary media mix, more attention will need to be paid to the diverse and multifarious ways that fans, characters, spaces, and worlds all interact.

....

Paul Ocone is an anthropologist and scholar of anime and manga, currently a Fulbright Fellow researching Japanese fan spaces at Meiji University's School of Global Japanese Studies. His research largely centers on four broad areas: the negotiation of cultural identities and values, especially in fan subcultures; space, both in terms of the online and offline spaces where people meet and in terms of the meanings people attribute to physical spaces; the political economy of anime and manga, such as the media mix; and aesthetics, especially the aesthetics of anime and manga. Paul previously published in *Mechademia: Second Arc* 13.2, and he has presented at the Mechademia, Fan Studies Network—North America, and Association for Interdisciplinary Studies conferences. He is also an amateur musician and composer. You can find him at https://www.paulocone.com/.

....

Notes

1. Wilhelm Donko, "'Hanasaku Iroha' Bonbori Festival Report—A Fictional Event Becomes Real Life Tradition," *Crunchyroll*, October 28, 2017, https://www.crunchyroll.com/anime-feature/2017/10/28-1/hanasaku-iroha-bonbori-festival-report-a-fictional-event-becomes-real-life-tradition (accessed July 15, 2022); Takayoshi Yamamura, "A Fictitious Festival as a Traditional Event: The Bonbori Festival at Yuwaku Onsen, Kanazawa City," in *The Theory and Practice of Contents Tourism*, ed. Nishikawa Katsuyuki, Philip Seaton, and Takayoshi Yamamura (Sapporo: Research Faculty of Media and Communication, Hokkaido University, 2015), 34–39, http://hdl.handle.net/2115/58300.
2. Philip A. Seaton et al., *Contents Tourism in Japan: Pilgrimages to "Sacred Sites" of Popular Culture* (Amherst, NY: Cambria Press, 2017).
3. Linda Lombardi, "Anime Is Turning Quiet Corners of the World into Major Tourist Attractions," *Polygon*, December 12, 2018, https://www.polygon.com/2018/12/12/18129103/anime-tourism-japan-your-name (accessed July 15, 2022); Takeshi Okamoto, "Otaku Tourism and the Anime Pilgrimage Phenomenon in Japan," *Japan Forum* 27, no. 1 (January 2, 2015): 12–36, https://doi.org/10.1080/09555803.2014.962565; Seaton et al., *Contents Tourism in Japan*.
4. Marc Steinberg, *Anime's Media Mix: Franchising Toys and Characters in Japan* (Minneapolis: University of Minnesota Press, 2012).

5. Matsuyama Shuichi, "Regional Revitalization, Contents Tourism, and the Representation of Place in Anime: The Seichi-Junrei of *Love Live! Sunshine!!* in Japan," *Journal of Cultural Geography* 39, no. 3 (September 2, 2022): 375–98, https://doi.org/10.1080/08873631.2022.2124062.

6. Steinberg, *Anime's Media Mix*.

7. Ōtsuka Eiji, "World and Variation: The Reproduction and Consumption of Narrative," trans. Marc Steinberg, *Mechademia* 5 (2010): 107.

8. Steinberg, *Anime's Media Mix*, 180.

9. Marc Steinberg, *Naze Nihon wa "media mikkusu suru kuni" nanoka* (Why is Japan a "media mixing nation"?), trans. Nakagawa Yuzuru (Tokyo: Kadokawa, 2015), 270–73.

10. Steinberg, *Anime's Media Mix*, 165.

11. Edmond Ernest dit Alban, "Pedestrian Media Mix: The Birth of Otaku Sanctuaries in Tokyo," *Mechademia: Second Arc* 12, no. 2 (2020): 140–63, https://doi.org/10.5749/mech.12.2.0140; Marc Steinberg and Edmond Ernest dit Alban, "Otaku Pedestrians," in *A Companion to Media Fandom and Fan Studies,* ed. Paul Booth (Hoboken, NJ: John Wiley & Sons, Inc., 2018), 289–304, https://doi.org/10.1002/9781119237211.ch18.

12. Anya C. Benson, "Becoming *Purikyua:* Building the Lifestyle-Text in Japanese Girls' Franchises," *Contemporary Japan* 31, no. 1 (January 2, 2019): 61–78, https://doi.org/10.1080/18692729.2018.1558023.

13. Seaton et al., *Contents Tourism in Japan,* 9.

14. Nelson Graburn and Takayoshi Yamamura, "Contents Tourism: Background, Context, and Future," *Journal of Tourism and Cultural Change* 18, no. 1 (January 2, 2020): 3, https://doi.org/10.1080/14766825.2020.1707460.

15. Marc Steinberg, *The Platform Economy: How Japan Transformed the Consumer Internet* (Minneapolis: University of Minnesota Press, 2019), 37–43; Seaton et al., *Contents Tourism in Japan,* 2.

16. Seaton et al., *Contents Tourism in Japan,* 5.

17. Seaton et al., *Contents Tourism in Japan,* 8.

18. Seaton et al., *Contents Tourism in Japan,* 267.

19. Graburn and Yamamura, "Contents Tourism," 5, 8; Abby Waysdorf, "'I Don't Think the Two Would Be the Same Without Each Other': Portmeirion as Unintentional Paratext," *JOMEC Journal,* no. 14 (November 12, 2019): 33–52, https://doi.org/10.18573/jomec.178.

20. Graburn and Yamamura, "Contents Tourism," 6.

21. Brian Bergstrom, "Avonlea as 'World': Japanese *Anne of Green Gables* Tourism as Embodied Fandom," *Japan Forum* 26, no. 2 (2014): 233, https://doi.org/10.1080/09555803.2014.900514.

22. Bergstrom, "Avonlea as 'World,'" 234.

23. Bergstrom, "Avonlea as 'World,'" 235.

24. Bergstrom, "Avonlea as 'World,'" 233, 239.

25. Graburn and Yamamura, "Contents Tourism," 5; Bergstrom, "Avonlea as 'World,'" 239.

26. Ōtsuka, "World and Variation," 109.

27. Bergstrom, "Avonlea as 'World,'" 234.

28. Benson, "Becoming *Purikyua*," 72.

29. Benson, "Becoming *Purikyua*."

30. Steinberg, *Anime's Media Mix*, 103, 109–10.

31. Benson, Becoming *Purikyua*," 76.

32. Bergstrom, "Avonlea as 'World,'" 237, emphasis in original.

33. Abby S. Waysdorf, *Fan Sites: Film Tourism and Contemporary Fandom* (Iowa City: University of Iowa Press, 2021), 38–40.

34. Lombardi, "Anime is Turning"; Okamoto, "Otaku Tourism," 22.

35. Seaton et al., *Contents Tourism in Japan*, 172–74, 213–14; Takayoshi Yamamura, "Contents Tourism and Local Community Response: *Lucky Star* and Collaborative Anime-Induced Tourism in Washimiya," *Japan Forum* 27, no. 1 (2015): 66, 68–69, 72–73, https://doi.org/10.1080/09555803.2014.962567.

36. Yamamura, "Contents Tourism and Local Community Response."

37. Yamamura, "Contents Tourism and Local Community Response," 64–66.

38. Yamamura, "Contents Tourism and Local Community Response," 79.

39. Patrick W. Galbraith, *Otaku and the Struggle for Imagination in Japan* (Durham: Duke University Press, 2019), 80.

40. Setha M. Low, "Symbolic Ties That Bind: Place Attachment in the Plaza," in *Place Attachment,* ed. Irwin Altman and Setha M. Low (Boston: Plenum Press, 1992), 173–75.

41. Ikuho Amano, "In Praise of Iron Grandeur: The Sensibility of *Kōjō Moe* and the Reinvention of Urban Technoscape," *Contemporary Japan* 28, no. 2 (2016): 145–64, https://doi.org/10.1515/cj-2016-0008.

42. Amano, "In Praise of Iron Grandeur," 149.

43. Saitō Tamaki, *Beautiful Fighting Girl,* trans. Keith Vincent and Dawn Lawson (Minneapolis: University of Minnesota Press, 2011), 20.

44. Patrick W. Galbraith, "Moe Talk: Affective Communication Among Female Fans of Yaoi in Japan," in *Boys Love Manga and Beyond,* ed. Mark McLelland et al. (Jackson: University Press of Mississippi, 2015), 162–63, https://doi.org/10.14325/mississippi/9781628461190.003.0008.

45. *Aria the Natural,* dir. Satō Jun'ichi (2006), available on Crunchyroll (accessed July 15, 2022).

46. Geoffrey H. Hartman, "Romantic Poetry and the Genius Loci," in *Beyond Formalism: Literary Essays, 1958–1970* (New Haven: Yale University Press, 1970), 311–36; Zuoming Jiang and Derong Lin, "Genius Loci of Ancient Village from the Perspective of Tourists Experience: Scale Development and Validation," *International Journal of Environmental Research and Public Health* 19, no. 8 (April 2022): 3, https://doi.org/10.3390/ijerph19084817.

47. Jiang and Lin, "Genius Loci of Ancient Village," 1–2.

48. Waysdorf, *Fan Sites*, 82.

49. Tachikichi, "Kanrinin kara no goaisatsu" (Greetings from the webmaster), ARIA the Navigation, 2010, http://aria-navigation.world.coocan.jp/information_hello.html.

50. Kagurazaka Tsumuri, "(Ōshū tabi) Chotto ARIA no seichi junrei shitekita (Venechia)" ([Europe trip] I did a bit of an Aria pilgrimage [Venice]), https://tsumuri5.com/blog-entry-405.html (accessed February 15, 2023).

51. Mizuya, "Arusenāru ~ kitarra no mise [Day3 genchi jikan 10:30~13:00]" (Arsenal ~ chitarra restaurant [Day 3 10:30–13:00 local time]), AQUA & ARIA seichi junreiki 2016, 2016, http://coolest.sakura.ne.jp/aquaria/day3-5.html.

52. Satō, *Aria the Natural*.

53. Mizuya, "Arusenāru."

54. Waysdorf, *Fan Sites*, 63–64.

55. NHK, "Fan ga tsutaeru 'seichi no miryoku'" (A fan conveys the appeal of "sacred places"), NHK, November 18, 2019, https://www3.nhk.or.jp/news/special/kyo-ani/article/article_08.html.

56. Okamoto Ryōsuke, "Zenkoku de seikyō no 'anime seichi junrei,' kado na bijinesu-ka ni furikiru risuku" (The national success of "anime pilgrimage," the risk of excessive commercialization), *Gendai Bijinesu*, November 22, 2016, http://gendai.media/articles/-/50249.

57. Seaton et al., *Contents Tourism in Japan*, 241.

58. Munōyaku kōcha dōkōkai, "Kō-chan to yukai na nakamatachi final" (Kō-chan and delightful comrades final), https://ameblo.jp/munouyaku-k/entry-12361679161.html (accessed April 3, 2023).

59. Yamamura, "A Fictitious Festival as a Traditional Event," 37–38.

60. Daryl Harding, "Help Yuwaku Onsen Recover from Lack of Tourists with Hanasaku Iroha Campaign," Crunchyroll, July 4, 2020, https://www.crunchyroll.com/anime-news/2020/07/04-1/help-yuwaku-onsen-recover-from-lack-of-tourists-with-hanasaku-iroha-campaign.

61. Yamamura, "Contents Tourism and Local Community Response," 79.

62. SnippetTee, "Journey to Kissuiso: Sightseeing Hanasaku Iroha," https://snippettee.wordpress.com/2011/06/04/journey-to-kissuiso-siteseeing-hanasaku-iroha/ (accessed July 15, 2022).

63. Michael Vito, "Weekly Review of Transit, Place and Culture in Anime 97," https://likeafishinwater.com/2014/07/06/weekly-review-of-transit-place-and-culture-in-anime-97/ (accessed January 27, 2023); Donko, "'Hanasaku Iroha' Bonbori Festival Report."

64. Chris Joynson, "Anime Corner: Hanasaku Iroha Blossoms for Tomorrow Review," https://neverarguewithafish.wordpress.com/2020/10/09/anime-corner-hanasaku-iroha-blossoms-for-tomorrow-review/ (accessed January 27, 2023).

65. Shin, "Hanasaku Iroha HOME SWEET HOME butai meguri" (*Hanasaku Iroha: Home Sweet Home* scene pilgrimage), http://626shin.blog.fc2.com/blog-entry -132.html (accessed January 27, 2023).

66. Yoshitani Hiroya, "Anime 'Hanasaku Iroha' no seichi junrei to Yuwaku Bonbori Matsuri: Seichi junrei nōto ni chūmoku shite" (Pilgrimage for *Hanasaku Iroha* and the Yuwaku Bonbori Festival: focusing on the pilgrimage notes), *Komatsu Tankidaigaku Chīki Sōzō Kenkyūsho Nenpō* 3 (2012): 26–36, https://web.archive .org/web/20151112195037/http://www2.komatsu-c.ac.jp/~yositani/2012bon bori.htm.

67. Waysdorf, *Fan Sites*, 141.

68. Takeshi Okamoto, "Anime ga kankō sangyō o kakushin suru buki ni naru wake: Raki suta no seichi de okiru koto" (Why anime is becoming a weapon to revolutionize the tourist industry: what happened at the sacred place of *Lucky Star*), *Tokyo Keizai Shinbun*, October 19, 2018, https://toyokeizai.net/articles/-/242733.

69. Galbraith, "Moe Talk; Ian Condry, *The Soul of Anime: Collaborative Creativity and Japan's Media Success Story* (Durham: Duke University Press, 2013).

70. Okamoto, "Zenkoku."

Drawing Works Together

Anime Media Mix and Graphic Style
as a Shared Cultural Resource

OLGA KOPYLOVA

Media mix lies at the heart of the otaku market; indeed, one can say that it shapes, supports, and organizes both the market in a broad sense—as a conglomeration of media, genres, and industries—and each of its segments. Currently, most stories, worlds, and characters (or *contents*, in the industry jargon) are created under the premise that they will spread across multiple works and material forms, usually in the form of transmedia adaptation, transtextual expansion (in the shape of sequels, serialization, etc.), or the combination of both. All of these fall under the general term media mix.

If manga (closely followed by text-based media forms such as light novels and visual novels) serves as an ideal low-budget testing ground for the future franchise, then anime usually becomes its central hub.[1] It is easy for producers to branch out from anime in various directions, because there are so many elements that can be repurposed, repackaged, and recast in other forms.[2] Visuals perpetuate this centrifugal drive because most of the primary media involved have historically utilized hand-drawn images rooted in the same stylistic traditions. At the same time, the visual affinity between heterogeneous constituents of the media mix implies that centripetal drive for their visual integration should also be possible.

Of course, any kind of affinity based on shared imagery is modified and limited by material differences between media, their current conventions, and the specifics of production processes.[3] Despite shared codes, aesthetics, and more recently production tools, any direct correspondence between anime, manga and other related media is unachievable. In fact, both anime producers and their target audiences are well aware of these limitations: when they talk about following or reproducing the visuals of the source work, they mean primarily characters. Defined as "a particular combination of name and visual design that is in some sense independent from any particular medium," the character remains both recognizable and modifiable. It therefore travels without much difficulty between various contexts and material supports.[4]

190

In other words, it is perfectly suited for transmedia development. A typical anime media mix is therefore character-driven, but under the condition of visual consistency, or fidelity, between all character incarnations.[5]

With that said, the relationship between character image and visual fidelity as conceived here is not that straightforward: one must distinguish between design as a composition of certain elements and the category of graphic style, which includes the level of iconic abstraction (where the image fits on the scale from photorealistic to cartoonish) and the drawing manner. In other words, graphic style determines *how* the character is drawn. Most contemporary accounts of characters that inhabit the otaku market downplay this last parameter to underscore their adaptability and malleability.[6] Arguably, the most pertinent and clearest model explaining the use of characters in otaku-oriented visual media comes from manga researcher Iwashita Hōsei.[7] Iwashita proposes the tripartite model of character that includes a particular story-bound incarnation (*tōjō jinbutsu*), a visual image (*kyara zuzō*), and "personality" (*jinkaku*)—the most abstract entity that unites all transtextual and transmedial variants of the character. Iwashita describes character image as "constructed through a particular arrangement of conventional elements," a code that, if properly executed, makes the character recognizable across media.[8] The issue of visual semblance is thus disentangled from any particular drawing style, allowing for a plethora of character manifestations in various forms.

Anime media mixes starting with adaptation from other visual media have repeatedly exploited this feature. Often the result is a slight tweaking of the source drawings, but some such projects undertake a full-scale visual overhaul of the adapted source. Furthermore, graphic style and character designs tend to diversify the more the media mix grows and the wider it spreads. In fact, old, sprawling franchises may adopt distinct looks over time, and "the challenge becomes one of differentiation from earlier franchise production cycles."[9] This alteration, both during the initial adaptation and at latter stages of media mix development, does not necessarily draw ire or resignation from fans; some changes are widely successful, while others remain unnoticed. Between the inherent malleability of character image described by Iwashita, and the tendency toward divergence, rather than strict consistency of contents in the media mix, one is compelled to ask whether visual fidelity is a relevant concept when discussing adaptations.

The most substantial evidence for the adaptability of character visuals comes from fans, or participatory consumers who recreate and share countless renditions of their favorite characters on a global scale in the form of fan art, cosplay photo shoots, etc. Paradoxically, it is also consumers who have repeatedly and pointedly demonstrated a commitment to consistent graphic style and visual fidelity in media mixes. For decades in manga, the drawing manner (known as *tatchi*, or touch) has been perceived as the signature of a particular author or movement but additionally as a means of communication and community-building, as well as a selling point, since readers tend to gravitate to particular graphic styles. The great advantage of adapting a successful manga title into anime is that it can bring along a preexisting fanbase.[10] Consequently, producers often feel pressured to follow what Bryan Hartzheim calls the "stylistic blueprint" of the source work.[11] Attempts to appease the fans are not the only factor at play: graphic style allows a creator, a work, and a franchise to stand out in an oversaturated media market, where new contents are generated through endless rearrangements of familiar "database elements."[12] While a new combination might itself be highly appealing, graphic style enhances visibility, a point of particular importance in media mixes originating from original anime series. However, graphic style as a mark of distinction is not limited to transmedia projects: iconic studios and auteur directors develop a consistent and memorable template for drawing characters. In such cases, stylistic idiosyncrasy becomes the sign of quality, as well as an expression of artistic vision, as evidenced by Studio Ghibli and directors such as Yuasa Masaaki.

This last point foregrounds the relation between graphic style and individual creative pursuits, which is by no means limited to the work of directors and character designers. Some concrete examples of drawing-as-signature below the line have been documented by the former anime producer and fandom theorist Okada Toshio. According to Okada, already in the 1970s early anime enthusiasts, the so-called proto-otaku (*gen'otaku*), spared no effort to identify the unique touch of animation directors and key animators.[13] Notably, such distinctions were sought—and found—in both original and adapted titles. Likewise, complex negotiations of creative identity based on the drawing manner happen at the upper levels of the production hierarchy, as well as between workers involved with distinct media. In the otaku market, the graphic style of character drawings thus serves not only as a marketing tool or a locus of fan affection, but also as the means of self-actualization, the way to determine and demonstrate one's position vis-à-vis a specific franchise and other creators. As a consequence, visual fidelity gets enmeshed in hierarchical relationships between various media mix producers and between the production side and the participatory audiences.

This article aims to elaborate on and illustrate the aforementioned socio-logical, artistic, and cultural facets of the graphic style. To this end, it examines how the anime industry treats visual fidelity, and how this understanding affects both the creative workers and anime fans. In a typical media mix, most of the officially produced character manifestations conform to the look established and fixed in the anime (regardless of its originating point), making the anime's rendering of characters representative of the entire title. Anime magazines with their long-cultivated ties to the production provide a valuable source in this regard, as they reveal the "discursive context" of the anime industry, that is, "meanings, messages, and values" it cultivates and communicates.[14] My two-part demonstration first engages a qualitative analysis of published interviews with creative professionals and, second, undertakes a case study of *Psycho-Pass*, a media mix originating in an original animated series. The transmedia development of *Psycho-Pass* demonstrates how visual fidelity can reflect—and shape—creative hierarchies between above-the-line laborers, including those working in different media. The graphic style of character drawings is, I argue, a tangible, distinct parameter playing an important role in media mix development and warranting continued critical attention, alongside emerging industrial and interdisciplinary approaches.

Anime Magazines and the Tiered Model of Visual Fidelity

Most anime media mixes start with an adaptation from other media, absorbing the graphic style of source works if possible. As already mentioned, anime producers often depart from the source visuals, both out of necessity and by choice. We have witnessed, however, that for some fans, the drawing manner of their favorite manga artists and illustrators is crucial, and the failure to preserve a graphic style may end up in a big controversy. What is the role of the anime industry in the visual fidelity discourse?

Specialized periodicals for anime viewers provide a partial answer. Anime magazines played an integral part in the formation of the anime fandom in Japan during the pre-internet era,[15] and continue to persevere despite the wave of rival digital media. Survival strategies include either increased specialization or, on the contrary, diversification and tiering of contents. For instance, monthly magazines *Animage* and *Newtype* (running since 1978 and 1985, respectively) offer basic information on anime titles, broadcast schedules, behind-the-scenes production anecdotes, and, of course, countless advertisements for otaku-oriented goods. While some columns, feature articles, and interviews may include in-depth information and trivia aimed at the type of fan described by Okada,[16] most editorial content targets a wider readership with varying levels of commitment. It is precisely this broad reach of contemporary anime magazines that makes them a promising source of research data. Therefore, in this study, I conducted a quantitative and qualitative analysis of some 250 issues of *Animage* and *Newtype* in order to discover what stances the industry assumes in relation to visual fidelity of character drawings.

Media scholar John T. Caldwell rightfully cautions researchers to stay skeptical of infotainment promising glimpses into the inner workings of the industry.[17] Such texts often amount to little more than glamorized press releases intended to serve marketing goals, not to inform or to educate. This warning certainly applies to anime magazines, entangled as they are with the anime industry. However, their dependent position presumably turns the same publications into one of the platforms where producers can directly address consumers. This makes any discussion of fidelity in the pages of these magazines particularly relevant, since fidelity in commercial adaptation does not have self-evident value—it is meant to appeal to, and be judged by, the audiences. Through published interviews, producers reflect upon and react to perceived fans' needs, as well as advocate their vision and priorities. In other words, they both engage in and shape the fidelity discourse.

The important first step in the current study was to confirm whether said discourse incorporated the issue of visual fidelity. I therefore started by scanning for interviews and feature articles mentioning the visuals of the discussed works, regardless of their origins. Particular attention was paid to interviews with character designers, because this is the creative position with the most direct and significant input into the graphic style of character images. This quantitative filtering of magazine contents focused upon the creative-worker type produced a data set for the qualitative analysis of the main topics and approaches that emerge in the discussions of graphic style, visual fidelity, and concomitant creative labor (Table 1). The inquiry was supplemented with a number of articles (34 from *Newtype* and 17 from *Animage*) that featured other industry workers such as producers, directors, and series composers. This additional corpus was limited to the discussions of anime based on preexisting visual materials, including sequels, remakes, or spin-offs that incorporated character designs from previous installments. Notably, all the interviews under analysis involve above-the-line staff. This limitation

Table 1. Number of interviews with character designers in *Newtype* magazine (2010–19) and *Animage* magazine (2010–20).

	NEWTYPE (KADOKAWA)	ANIMAGE (TOKUMA SHOTEN)	TOTAL INTERVIEWS
	2010–19 (115 issues)	2010–20 (132 issues)	
Interview w/ character designer (original)	18	14	32
Interview w/ character designer (adaptation)	29	24	53
Interview w/ character designer (style not mentioned) (original)	19	16	35
Interview w/ character designer (style not mentioned) (adaptation)	5	5	10
Interviews w/ character designers (all)	71	59	130
Special section "Free Space" in *Animage*		130	

follows from the premise that the main contributors to the visual fidelity discourse are the same creative figures and executives that have the final say in major stylistic choices. At the same time, it reflects the bias evident in the magazines themselves: artists in charge of developing or adapting the graphic style of the work receive considerably less attention than other creative personnel in both *Newtype* and *Animage*. Across 247 issues, I found less than 150 interviews with character designers or concept artists, an average of less than one interview per issue. In contrast, the January 2020 issue of *Newtype* included 15 interviews with voice actors and 12 with anime directors; the July 2013 issue of *Animage* had 9 and 10, respectively. Even when one adds regular columns like *Newtype*'s "Creation Archive," or *Animage*'s "Free Space," which are dedicated to character designers, the disproportion is glaring. There is a noticeable imbalance related to the prestige of the source work, too: older, sometimes legendary, titles get more extensive coverage, and issues of style are raised more often. Additionally, character designers and concept artists involved in original productions tend to receive more attention than those tasked with adaptation from other media. This distortion reflects promotional strategies emphasizing the artistic and aesthetic appeal of the new work to compensate for the lack of familiarity. At any rate, the absence of source work does not preclude discussion of adaptation practices.

In this regard, one must distinguish between the positions of character concept artist (*kyarakutā gen'an*) and character designer (*kyarakutā dezainā*) in the anime production. A character concept artist's work is limited to creating a collection of comparably rough but detailed drawings that need to be polished and completed by someone else. This extra step makes issues of visual fidelity pertinent even to original anime productions. It became common in the 2010s to commission character concept art from popular illustrators and manga artists. Involving big names is good for publicity (and often essential in securing sponsorship for an original anime title)[18] and extends the initial reach of the series by bringing in the artist's personal fans. Many famous creators have a well-developed and unique graphic style—which must be adequately adapted by the character designer. The responsibilities of the character designer are quite extensive: they revise and modify the existing character visuals, such as manga illustrations or character concept art, or develop them from scratch to fulfill the needs of the adapting medium, whether anime or game. Most important for this discussion, the character designer working on someone else's source drawings must break down and distill their idiosyncratic style and streamline it for transmedia uses. The result must be easy to animate, instantly recognizable, and readily reproducible in other material forms, so some primary tasks are reducing the number of lines required for the character form, fixing the line quality, and developing distinctive silhouettes. Furthermore, the character designer must set an acting style as a range of possible expressions for each character, and organize the corresponding drawings into a character model sheet. Often the character designer doubles as chief animation director to maintain the consistency of character appearances and acting styles throughout the production sequence. These directorial activities ultimately mean that the character designer becomes the principal symbolic guarantor of visual fidelity in anime adaptation, which explains why the topic emerges so often in connection with this creative position.

However, while conversations with character designers typically touch upon visual fidelity and graphic style, they tend to do it only in passing, even in specialized magazine columns like "Creation Archive." Interviews follow a similar pattern in both magazines: there are inquiries about the interviewee's attitude toward the adapted material, their opinions on fellow creative workers, and their history within projects. Some questions appear standard: "What were your first impressions when you first read [the adapted title]?" "What can you tell us about the upcoming episodes?" "Who is your favorite character?" In other words, the general direction of interviews with character designers and concept artists is similar to other creative personnel such as voice actors. While they are often asked to share what character is the easiest or the most difficult to draw, they rarely describe the adaptation process itself in much detail.

The same tendency is noticeable in illustrative materials. Despite the infrequency of interviews dedicated to character designers, the concrete product of their labor, character model sheets, features prominently on pages of both magazines as visual supplements for both in-depth features and short promotional announcements—especially in *Newtype*'s column "Newtype Express." Additionally, columns like *Newtype*'s "Creation Archive" or *Animage*'s "Character Model Sheets FILE" (*Settei shiryō FILE*) are dedicated to the representation of character designs and assets. While these materials tease an upcoming show and offer fans a glimpse behind the scenes, they do not convey the actual working process of the character designer, which starts very early in the production, sometimes even before script writing. Developing parallel to the story, character images initially go through multiple early iterations, leaving behind considerable material evidence. Fragments of this preliminary, discarded artwork sometimes appear in officially released production and art books. But magazines tend to forego such early drafts, which means that a crucial stage of visual adaptation—from manga image or concept art to the cleaned-up character sheet—remains mostly "black-boxed." The focus shifts instead toward the evolution of production materials from the approved version into the final product.

This production-material emphasis on the afterlife, rather than genesis, runs parallel to descriptions of the actual production process as an exercise in visual infidelity. On one hand, producers, directors, and character designers proclaim their determination to maintain the unique looks of the source works or concept art. Conversely, at the same time, character designers emphasize that the style of the anime image is the result of collective effort. At the preproduction level, the character designer usually works closely with the director and the producers. Down the line, creative workers at every stage of animation production contribute to changes in the approved character model. Absolute consistency of the visuals across the series is not always a priority. Some chief animation directors loosen control over other people's key animation in order to allow for richer expression (it is worth mentioning though that most such claims refer to original animations, hinting that adaptations tend to take a more restrained approach). In an extreme case, the position of chief animation director may get eliminated altogether, and the final look of each episode is largely determined by its individual director. Basic designs may be altered at a later stage to better suit the needs of production or as creative workers develop a more nuanced understanding of a character. The common defense is that the initial character design is just a starting point. Anime magazines thus present visual fidelity as an important, but flexible quality, black-boxed at the initial stage of production, foregrounded at the next, and downplayed at the last.

This account, however, would be incomplete without touching on yet another type of cultural production that constitutes the intrinsic part of the otaku market—the unofficial one. The issue of visual fidelity surfaces regularly not only in the formalized, top-down accounts of anime production, but also at those sites where official producers and fans meet as fellow creators. One such site is the long-running column in *Animage* called "Free Space" (see Table 1). The column consists of several pages of fan art dedicated to a particular title. The guest columnist selecting and commenting upon the contributions is usually the character designer affiliated with said title (sometimes joined by other studio representatives). The final page is reserved as a special space for their hand-drawn message to fans. While referred to as a "One-point lesson," it typically presents a bonus illustration or a joke, instead of addressing common mistakes in the reviewed fan art or providing basic drawing cues. Regardless of their visual content, messages often include some words of encouragement, and they also tend to minimize the importance of strict visual fidelity. Rather, the recurring sentiment is that the character will be recognizable if drawn with love.

Together the three types of textual spaces in anime magazines—the interviews, the character model sheet collections, and the fan art corner—construct a special set of relations between the fan-readers, their beloved titles, and official producers. Character sheets are not just promotional content or insider information—glimpses into production—they are also reference materials intended for fans wishing to make a drawing of their own. At the same time, creators encourage fans to improvise, experiment, and quite possibly break the predefined character model, that is, to exercise creative visual infidelity very much like professional animators are reported to do. Even typical questions to the creative workers appear in a new light in this context: after all, are not they the same ones that fan artists direct at themselves and each other? The parallels, of course, do not reflect the realities of the production scene, where one's creativity is held in check by other parties. The initial character design may be just a starting point, but there are limits to how far one can stray from it. Comments and criticisms key animators hear from animation directors are probably much less lenient than the comments published in "Free Space." Still, at least in the pages of *Animage*, unofficial fan producers can enjoy the illusion that they occupy the same position as the official ones.

To summarize, voices from the production side put a different emphasis on visual fidelity at different stages of adaptation. One can imagine the resulting structure as a set of concentric circles. At the center, the character designer and chief animation director strive(s) to stay as close to the source images as possible. At the wider orbit are key animators and episode animation directors, who often enjoy a degree of creative freedom in visually interpreting characters and their acting manner. The outer expanse is the domain of fans, who can but need not maintain strict fidelity in graphic style to either the original or the adapted work. This multitiered framework in fact duplicates the perspective of the fandom, which generally allows for stylistic variety in fan works, but tends to become vigilant when it comes to official productions. The framework appears to favor and cater to fans as both viewers and amateur creators. However, in practice it is more balanced. Fans enjoy greater freedom regarding drawing style and skill because their creations reach an extremely limited audience and are easily ignored or rejected. The work of the character designer, on the other hand, affects the entire franchise and sets up a touchstone to adhere to, for official and non-official producers alike.

As a mouthpiece of the industry, anime magazines promote a set of evaluative criteria and standards for future adaptations through the discourse on visual fidelity that stems from power dynamics between creative workers and dedicated audiences. The magazines do not simply reproduce this discourse, they also reinforce and legitimize it with direct references to the authority of official producers. However, as the next section demonstrates, in a media mix both the concern with graphic style and the concomitant hierarchies extend beyond the relationship between the two media or a single production site.

Graphic Style and Negotiated Creativity in the Media Mix Development

Within anime magazines one finds a recurring concern with graphic style in the anime industry. Character drawings are also represented as one of the sites of struggle—with technology, production exigencies, or apprehensive viewers—in transmedia adaptations. Adaptation of character drawings is thus indeed a "process of negotiation between material and human actors."[19] But it is important to remember that graphic style also provides another creative outlet for the cultural producers, albeit unequally shared, so negotiation of style can also be framed as negotiation of creative identity. In media mixes, this negotiation becomes much more multifaceted.

When several industries get involved in the transmedia development, the creative freedom of a particular artist or a group of artists is often determined by a number of factors, including their professional clout and intended role in the project, the popularity of the source text and the significance attributed to its graphic style, the amount and variety of other iterations of the same content, and the overall position of the work in the franchise. Consider, for instance, those comparatively rare occasions when anime is comicalized, that is, adapted into manga. While it is definitely easier to imitate the anime image on the manga page, many comicalizations forego the effort. For the most part, this visual inconsistency remains unaddressed, even though controversies around stylistic changes in manga-to-anime adaptations crop up on a regular basis. The relative freedom of expression enjoyed by the manga artists may be explained by the overall attitude to comicalizations, which often amount to abridged anime retellings or changed fictional worlds, narrative events, or characterization in ways that break continuity with works in other media. As such, they are deemed fringe, or even illegitimate parts of the franchise network, and are often disregarded by fans even before visual fidelity becomes an issue.[20] At the same time, a combination of a relatively obscure source work and an illustrious anime production team affords much more leeway to the character designer, who may introduce a complete stylistic reinterpretation of the adapted drawings without incurring significant fan displeasure.

These shifting standards of evaluation, however, rarely surface in discussions of media mix practices. The tendency among researchers to emphasize horizontal, equitable relations between components of a media mix obscures inter- and intra-institutional hierarchies that regulate transmedia development of contents and the resulting webs of works and commodities. The same applies to the issue of authorship. If early research on anime and manga focused upon isolated, auteur-like creators, today, the focus has shifted to participatory cultures and the collaborative nature of media production, where the attribution of singular authorship is both impossible and undesirable. This inherent ambiguity, however, does not negate the concept's discursive power. Crucial in the promotion of media works and in consumers' corresponding interpretative practices, the authority associated with authorship serves creative workers at all levels and to various ends. Underplaying the inequality of media mix participants and the power of attributed authorship means that the motivations, priorities, and strategies of the creative personnel and participatory audiences entangled in these power relations remain largely unaddressed.

The following study of the *Psycho-Pass* media mix provides an illustrative example of such enmeshed interests and coexisting strategies. More specifically, *Psycho-Pass* demonstrates subordination and negotiation of creative agency in the course of franchise development hinging upon graphic style and the attribution of authorship. *Psycho-Pass* also demonstrates an interplay of visual semblance between works within and outside the franchise, facilitated and sustained by both professional creative decisions and fan imagination.

The *Psycho-Pass* media mix launched in 2012 with the broadcast of an original animated TV series.[21] As mentioned earlier, it has become customary for such projects to outsource character concept art to professionals from outside the industry, typically popular manga artists. This is how Amano Akira got involved with the *Psycho-Pass* media mix. At the time, Amano was at the peak of her fame as her top-selling manga series *Reborn!* (2004–12, *Katekyō hittoman Ribōn!*) was approaching its end. As is typical of many *Shōnen Jump* series, *Reborn!* was popular among both male and female readerships, so Fuji TV producer Yamamoto Kōji deduced that Amano's drawings would appeal to a broader audience.[22] The decision to include Amano proved successful and *Psycho-Pass* gained its distinctive look (Figure 1). As is often the case, this distinctiveness resides first and foremost in characters' facial features and head proportions: full lips, elongated eyes, stubby noses, and voluminous, tousled hair. As the project continued to develop in the following years, with additional TV seasons, serialized animated films, manga, and a visual novel, it continued to maintain an extremely high level of visual consistency, always staying close to Amano's aesthetic.

Figure 1. *Psycho-Pass* character concepts by Amano Akira, *Amano Akira: Kyarakutāzu bijuaru bukku: Rebo to Dlive* (Tokyo: Shueisha, 2014), 146–47.

However, Amano is only one of the "big names" in charge of the *Psycho-Pass* visuals. As the media mix continued to expand, character drawings were increasingly shaped by the graphic style of another established creator, Onda Naoyuki. Onda has been consistently involved with all animated installments of the franchise (except the second season of the TV anime)[23] as the chief animation director and, after *Psycho-Pass: The Movie* (2015),[24] the character designer (Figure 2). His hand is easily recognizable in the more recent animated features due to his preference for more balanced facial proportions, including smaller eyes and longer noses. Onda also likes to emphasize forms rather than mere shapes, so his faces approach a more 3D look. Altogether, the *Psycho-Pass* visuals have arguably gained more weight and volume and become slightly less cartoonish under Onda's influence. Nevertheless, Onda has maintained a somewhat deferential stance toward the author of original character concepts: for instance, in a short interview included in the production book for the first movie, he talks about his struggle to preserve Amano's drawing manner under the tight production schedules.[25]

Figure 2. Character sheet by Onda Naoyuki from *PSYCHO-PASS Saikopasu OFFICIAL PROFILING 2* (Tokyo: Kadokawa, 2015), 111.

This recollection, however, downplays the input of the third creator who helped to determine the appearance of the characters, and indeed, might have played the key role in doing so. It was Asano Kyōji, a distinguished animator himself, who converted Amano's drawings into character model sheets to create the main reference point for all other producers, starting with animators (Figure 3). Asano also designed new characters for the TV anime *Psycho-Pass 2* (2014) and for the visual novel *Psycho-Pass: Mandatory Happiness* (2015, *Saikopasu: Sentaku naki kōfuku*),[26] some of which carried over to the succeeding works. Apparently, other professionals value and respect Asano's input. Tatsunoko Pro producer Kanae Masahiro describes the decisive factor that convinced him to join the production of *Psycho-Pass 2*: a strong team that included director Shiotani Naoyoshi, screenwriter Ubukata Tow, the chief writer for the first series Urobuchi Gen (now in the role of a supervisor), and Asano.[27] Nevertheless, Asano's name rarely comes up in interviews or fan talk, especially compared to Amano.

Figure 3. Character sheet by Asano Kyōji from *PSYCHO-PASS Saikopasu OFFICIAL PROFILING* (Tokyo: Kadokawa, 2013), 24.

Despite continuous and substantial contributions from other professionals, then, the character concept artist remains the linchpin of the *Psycho-Pass* franchise. This is immediately evident from the newest set of novelizations of *Psycho-Pass 3* (2019) released in 2019 and 2020.[28] Their covers, drawn by Amano, presumably serve a double purpose: they legitimize the characters designed by Onda as an authentic part of the franchise even as they reconnect Amano with the property and reinforce her creative authority (Figure 4).

This authority extends beyond animated works, the primary locus of the franchise. Each *Psycho-Pass* animated TV series has received a manga adaptation, and all three artists responsible—Miyoshi Hikaru, Takano Saru, and Sai Natsuo—maintained visual fidelity to the anime source almost to the line. Such uniformity implies that the decision was most likely made by those in charge of the overall media mix development, rather than the artists themselves. Indeed, the shared graphic style between manga and the anime ensured greater consistency between the two parallel threads in the

Figure 4. Cover image by Amano Akira for from Yoshigami Ryō's *Saikopasu 3.C* (Psycho-Pass 3.C) (Tokyo: Shueisha, 2020).

Psycho-Pass media mix, which have also remained very close content-wise, defending against fan bias against comicalizations. Interestingly, whenever fan reviews draw direct comparisons (admittedly, such occasions are rare), they refer to Amano. Herein lies the paradox: the three artists did not directly imitate Amano's drawing manner, despite working in the same medium, but could not escape comparisons with her anyway. The authority of the celebrated concept artist thus exceeded its intended reach.

At the same time, Asano's graphic style passed the borders of the media mix itself, exported by Miyoshi Hikaru, whose manga adaptation of the very first *Psycho-Pass* anime, *Inspector Akane Tsunemori* (2013–14, *Kanshikan Tsunemori Akane*), [29] received so much praise from fans. In 2016, Miyoshi moved to another project, *Moriarty the Patriot* (2016–present, *Yūkoku no Moriāti*),[30] loosely based on Sherlock Holmes stories by Sir Arthur Conan Doyle. Despite this new start, Miyoshi retained the previously established drawing manner with only slight alterations (Figures 5–7). The most obvious difference lies in the linework: Miyoshi utilizes crisper and more even lines in *Moriarty the Patriot* and switches to a lighter tone for hair outlines. However, face proportions, the shape of characters' eyes, and the way of drawing mouths remain largely similar to those in *Inspector Akane Tsunemori*. Of course, the continuity with the *Psycho-Pass* style might be simply a matter of habit: after all, the comicalization was Miyoshi's first full-scale serialization. However, it is equally possible that Miyoshi maintained the style deliberately, especially since the artist made the central character, William Moriarty, a virtual copy of the iconic *Psycho-Pass* antagonist, Makishima Shōgo (Figure 5).

The resemblance extends beyond the visual representation: the two characters share common personality traits, as well as common intertextual roots (Makishima himself is loosely based on Conan Doyle's famous criminal mastermind). Still, it is the character design and drawing manner that ensured the popularity of Miyoshi's new series among *Psycho-Pass* fans and inspired many happy comparisons online. The intertextual visual connections came almost full circle when *Moriarty the Patriot* (2020–21)[31] was put on screen by Production I.G, the same studio that had worked on the majority of the *Psycho-Pass* anime. Importantly, fans' reaction cannot be explained away as a simple example of database consumption described by cultural critic Azuma Hiroki.[32] The visual similarity between Makishima and Moriarty stems from the shared graphic style rather than a combination of conventionalized elements (Figures 6 and 7). When reinforced by similarities in their respective stories, this visual semblance inspired fans to reframe the relationship

Figure 5. Miyoshi Hikaru's drawings of Makishima Shōgo from *Inspector Akane Tsunemori* 2 (Tokyo: Shueisha, 2013), 96 (left) and William Moriarty from *Moriarty the Patriot* 1 (Tokyo: Shueisha, 2016–present), 149 (right).

Figure 6 (left). Miyoshi Hikaru's drawings of Makishima Shōgo from *Inspector Akane Tsunemori* 3 (Tokyo: Shueisha, 2013), 141 (top) and William Moriarty from *Moriarty the Patriot* 1, 82 (bottom).

Figure 7 (right). Miyoshi Hikaru's drawings of Makishima Shōgo from *Inspector Akane Tsunemori* 6 (Tokyo: Shueisha, 2015), 182 (top) and William Moriarty from *Moriarty the Patriot* 1, 70 (bottom).

between the two titles. A number of online posts jokingly identify *Moriarty the Patriot* as a derivative work, a piece of *Psycho-Pass* fan fiction. Miyoshi's stylistic and designer choices were therefore instrumental in the success of the new manga series, because they called forth favorable associations and offered readers the pleasure of intertextual play.

In summary, homogenous graphic styles bound to the single authorial figure of Amano Akira serve to reinforce the thematic and narrative consistency of the *Psycho-Pass* franchise. Creators like Onda Naoyuki, who occupy higher positions in the production hierarchy, may modify the character image to both establish and express their creative vision, but the figure of the character concept artist dominates both official and fan discourse, to the point that any likeness of the *Psycho-Pass* visuals is traced back to Amano. Media workers in charge of less privileged parts of the franchise (such as comicalizations) must defer to this authority, keeping character designs consistent; but they can also internalize, rework, and utilize the prescribed manner of drawing for their own purposes, as demonstrated by Miyoshi Hikaru. Finally, fans and casual readers seek familiar visuals to reconnect with their beloved property, to engage in intertextual games, or to discover some new object of attachment.

Conclusion

Despite the blossoming of research on the media mix and its contents in the last two decades, little attention has been paid to the specifics of media mixed images that are hand-drawn in a specific style, by particular artists. Such accounts that exist are dedicated not to images per se, but to the ontology of fictional characters. The predominant focus on the changeability and divergence of media mix contents and the spread of full 3DCG animation in recent years may have also diverted the scholarly attention away from media mixed drawings and graphic style as their core characteristic.

This article demonstrates, however, that the visuals or, more specifically, the graphic style, takes an important part in the discourse of anime producers, in the exchange between cultural industries of the otaku market and their dedicated audiences, and in the creative endeavors of all the participants in the transmedia franchise development. In the anime media mix, the graphic style of character drawings clearly becomes a vehicle for what cultural anthropologist Ian Condry calls "anime creativity," or "collaborative creativity, which operates across media industries and connects official producers to unofficial fan production."[33] It may serve as a sign of quality and legitimacy, a trademark and a promotional tool, an expression of commitment or ingenuity and distinction; it also highlights "unequal industrial and cultural status between production communities" and individual creators.[34] Media scholar Derek Johnson describes how in contemporary media franchises creative laborers, along with participatory consumers, "have become stakeholders that, even when lacking ownership of a shared property, develop vested interests in its ongoing productive use."[35] Graphic style is precisely such shared property, a cultural resource in its own right, which mediates and serves a variety of personal and interpersonal agendas as it is reproduced, altered, and appropriated across interconnected sites of production and consumption that constitute the otaku market.

It comes as no surprise then, that reflections on the graphic style released to this day emphasize its sociological aspects, either in terms of the labors of cultural production or in the practices of grassroots community-building.[36] These findings have not exhausted the subject, however: it is possible to explore further how this resource is generated, shared, and employed in the transmedia expansion of intellectual properties in the contemporary media environment. It would be also instructive to investigate how publications aimed at the professionals inside the industry, or so-called deep texts,[37] address these issues (if they address them at all). Graphic style in Japanese media mix and the concomitant notion of visual fidelity bear investigation from the viewpoint of multiple disciplines, including media and industry studies, fan studies, and adaptation studies. If style is a multipurpose tool, it can surely be used as a key to exploring the otaku market and its various phenomena.

....

Olga Kopylova received her PhD in Manga Studies at Seika University, Kyoto, with a thesis exploring the role of adaptation in a story-based Japanese media mix. Her main research interests still lie in the sphere of adaptations, but now they have come to include issues of visual style, material connections between media, and the labor of creative workers involved in production of transmedia franchises in Japan. She also holds interest in transmedia development of narratives and fictional worlds, as well as in activities of fan audiences that pursue their favorite stories and characters across multiple reincarnations.

....

Notes

1. Woojeong Joo, Rayna Denison, and Furukawa Hiroko, "Manga Movies Project Report 1: Transmedia Japanese Franchising," UK Arts and Humanities Research Council Research Project *Manga Movies: Contemporary Japanese Cinema, Media Franchising and Adaptation*, 16–23, https://www.academia.edu/3693690/Manga _Movies_Project_Report_1_-_Transmedia_Japanese_Franchising.

2. Nakayama Atsuo, *Otaku seisanken sōseiki: GAFA no tsugi wa 2.5 jigen komyuniti ga sekai no shuyaku ni naru ken* (Genesis of the otaku economic sphere: How the 2.5D community will rule the world after GAFA) (Tokyo: Nikkei BP, 2019), 60–63.

3. Olga Kopylova, "Style Negotiated: Transformations of the Visuals in Manga-to-Anime Adaptations," in *Images, Philosophy, Communication: Aesthetics and Thought in Japan and the World*, ed. Christopher Craig et al. (Milan: Mimesis International, 2021), 201–19.

4. Marc Steinberg, *Anime's Media Mix: Franchising Toys and Characters in Japan* (Minneapolis: Minnesota University Press, 2012), 83–84.

5. Ian Condry, *The Soul of Anime: Collaborative Creativity and Japan's Media Success Story* (Durham: Duke University Press, 2013), 71, 83; Steinberg, *Anime's Media Mix*, 196.

6. Itō Gō, *Tezuka izu deddo: Hirakareta manga hyōgenron e* (Tezuka is dead: Toward an open manga stylistics) (Tokyo: NTT, 2005).

7. Iwashita Hōsei, "Kyarakutā o miru, kyarakutā o yomu" (Seeing characters, reading characters), in *Manga Kenkyū 13 Kō* (Manga research 13 lectures), ed. Koyama Masahiro, Tamagawa Hiroaki, Koike Ryūta (Tokyo: Suiseisha, 2016), 166–67.

8. Iwashita, "Kyarakutā o miru, kyarakutā o yomu," 166. All in-text translations in this essay are my own.

9. Joo, "Manga Movies Project Report 1," 26.

10. Joo, "Manga Movies Project Report 1," 16.

11. Bryan Hikari Hartzheim, "Inside the Media Mix: Collective Creation in Contemporary Manga and Anime" (PhD diss., UCLA, 2015), 185.

12. Azuma Hiroki, *Dōbutsukasuru posutomodan: Otaku kara mita nihon shakai* (Tokyo: Kōdansha, 2001); trans. Jonathan E. Abel and Shion Kono as *Otaku: Japan's Database Animals* (Minneapolis: University of Minnesota Press, 2009).

13. Okada Toshio, *Otakugaku nyūmon* (Introduction to otakuology) (Tokyo: Ōta Shuppan, 1996), 11–13.

14. Matthew Freeman, *Industrial Approaches to Media: A Methodological Gateway to Industry Studies* (London: Palgrave Macmillan, 2016), 67.

15. Okada, *Otakugaku nyūmon*, 19–20, 23.

16. Okada, *Otakugaku nyūmon*, 20.

17. John Thornton Caldwell, *Production Culture: Industrial Reflexivity and Critical Practice in Film and Television* (Durham: Duke University Press, 2008), 252–53.

18. Ishiguro Tatsuya (Pony Canyon), "Mayoiga: Kuraudofandingu wa 'kōenkai' . . . Sakuhin to fan o yori chikazukeru tame no shuhō" (Mayoiga: Crowdfunding group is a 'fan club' . . . How to bring fans closer), Otacul website (2016), https://web.archive.org/web/20160416043728/http://www.sanspo.com/otacul/news/20160404/otc16040412180004-n3.html.

19. Stevie Suan, "Consuming Production: Anime's Layers of Transnationality and Dispersal of Agency as Seen in *Shirobako* and Sakuga-Fan Practices," *Arts* 7, no. 3 (2018): 27, https://doi.org/10.3390/arts7030027.

20. Derek Johnson, *Media Franchising: Creative License and Collaboration in The Culture Industries* (New York: New York University Press, 2013), 140–51.

21. *Saikopasu* (Psycho-Pass), dir. Shiotani Naoyoshi and Motohiro Katsuyuki (FUNimation Productions, 2012–13); available on Netflix (accessed July 9, 2022).

22. "Newtype's Archive: Psycho-Pass," *Newtype* 3 (2019) (Tokyo: Kadokawa, 2019), 2–3.

23. *Saikopasu 2* (Psycho-Pass 2), dir. Shiotani Naoyoshi and Suzuki Kiyotaka (Tatsunoko Productions, 2014); available on Amazon Prime (accessed July 9, 2022).

24. *Gekijōban Saikopasu* (Psycho-Pass: The Movie), dir. Shiotani Naoyoshi and Motohiro Katsuyuki (Production I.G, 2015).

25. *Gekijōban Psycho-Pass: Saikopasu gengashū* (Psycho-Pass the Movie: Key frame collection), ed. Shiotani Naoyoshi (Tokyo: Kadokawa, 2016), 293.

26. *Saikopasu: Sentaku naki kōfuku* (Psycho-Pass: Mandatory Happiness), dir. Makoto Asada and Rumie Higashinaka (5pb, NIS America, Inc., 2015).

27. "Newtype's Archive," 18.

28. *Saikopasu 3* (Psycho-Pass 3), dir. Shiotani Naoyoshi (Production I.G, 2019), available on Amazon Prime (accessed July 9, 2022); Yoshigami Ryō, *Saikopasu 3* (Psycho-Pass 3), 3 vols. (Tokyo: Shueisha, 2019–20).

29. Miyoshi Hikaru, *Kanshikan Tsunemori Akane* (Inspector Akane Tsunemori), 6 vols. (Tokyo: Shueisha, 2013–14).

30. Miyoshi Hikaru (art) and Takeuchi Ryōsuke (script), *Yūkoku no Moriāti* (Moriarty the Patriot), 18 vols. (Tokyo: Shueisha, 2016–present).

31. *Yūkoku no Moriāti* (Moriarty the Patriot), dir. Nomura Kazuya (Production I.G, 2020–21), available on Netflix (accessed July 9, 2022).

32. Azuma, *Otaku*, 47.

33. Condry, *The Soul of Anime*, 56, 2.

34. Johnson, *Media Franchising*, 131.

35. Johnson, *Media Franchising*, 7.

36. Takeuchi Miho, "Biteki tōya to shite no manga: Bijutsu kyōiku, hyōgenron, tekusuto bunseki" (Manga as aesthetic Bildung: Art education, manga expression, textual analysis) (PhD diss., Kyoto Seika University, 2017).

37. Caldwell, *Production Culture*, 26.

Terms, Histories, and Methods

ŌTSUKA EIJI, TRANS. BRIAN BERGSTROM AND MARC STEINBERG

The Wartime Media Mix and Participatory Fascism as the Internalization of an Information Space

Thinking Through The Imperial Assistance Family *and* Momotarō: Sacred Sailors

Translator's Introduction

While *Mechademia* usually includes translators' introductions, manga writer, critic, and researcher Ōtsuka Eiji likely requires no introduction for most readers of the journal. Indeed, *Mechademia* has been translating his work since 2008.[1] His early work on narrative consumption is a reference for many articles in this issue, as well as a key theoretical pillar for much work on the media mix—including the special issue editor's own work on the topic.[2] If in his early career he worked as a freelance editor, writer, and theorist for the Kadokawa media mix factory, in more recent years he had what we might term a political conversion to being its staunchest critic. In the past two decades, from the mid-2000s through the 2020s, Ōtsuka has dedicated his research, time, and writing to tracing first otaku culture and more recently the media mix back to the wartime period, showing how the very things we assumed to be postwar or post-1980s phenomena—the media mix, media synergies between works, the mobilization of multiple media forms within a single franchise, fan cooperation, otaku practices, even postwar manga styles—all started in the wartime period.[3] What follows is a previously unpublished article that Ōtsuka wrote, at the invitation of special issue editor Marc Steinberg, to introduce his recent research and writing to English language readers. As such, this article offers something of an overview of Ōtsuka's research trajectory over the past decade, most notably his groundbreaking 2018 book, *Taisei yokusankai no media mikkusu: "Yokusan Ikka" to sanka suru fashizumu* (The Imperial Rule Assistance Association's media mix: Participatory fascism and *The Imperial Assistance Family*).[4] Rejecting the premise that the media mix is a postwar phenomenon, Ōtsuka builds the case (in the book and in this article) that we should look to the wartime period as a moment of consolidation of the advertising theories and media practices that would become the basis for postwar and contemporary media mix practices. Dialoguing with existing accounts of the media mix, media convergence, and fan studies, he develops a theory of the media mix as the production of an externalized "information space" (coordinated sounds, images, words) as well as an internalized information space that forms the basis for subsequent artistic production. As such, here and elsewhere, Ōtsuka strikes a fine balance between careful, archival, historical research that unearths some forgotten truths *and* his big-picture critique of nationalism and state-based interventionism, which he finds at work in both wartime fascism and contemporary "Cool Japan" policies. In doing so, he reminds us that all political histories are histories of the present.

The Wartime Media Mix and Participatory Fascism as the Internalization of an Information Space: Thinking Through *The Imperial Assistance Family* and *Momotarō: Sacred Sailors*

ŌTSUKA EIJI

1. "Collaboration" in The Imperial Assistance Family

In Japan, the inauguration of the fascist order—that is, the codification of "assisting" Imperial Rule—came about as the goal of the Imperial Rule Assistance Association (*taisei yokusan-kai*) that first met in November 12, 1940. Also referred to as the New Order (*shintaisei*), it represented the beginning of a government policy explicitly aiming to renovate not only the political economy but culture and lifestyle as well—a transformation of everyday life.[5] Much hope was placed in popular culture as a key piece of infrastructure for promoting and enlightening the populace about this new policy to transform the everyday life of each citizen. This included not only media forms like popular films, manga, pop songs, and the like, but also the political use of "new" forms of expression like anime, drama, photography, *kamishibai*, puppet theater, and movies that had been reorganized around left-wing movements while appearing to be merely popular. The state of affairs whereby marginal forms of media are mobilized by the state despite their subversive lineages differs little from that of today—one cannot look at this wartime phenomenon without being reminded of contemporary Japan, in which the need for approval displayed by manga and anime as typical forms of otaku culture is actively drawn upon as a form of political power. I am someone who was formed by the aesthetics and methods of postwar otaku culture myself, but at the same time, I can see that the origin of phenomena like the "media mix" and "derivative works," usually thought of as unique to the media culture of post-1980s Japan, can in fact be found during wartime.

A major mode of popular mobilization at that time was what was called "collaboration"—the communal, participatory creation of writings, performances, and the like. This means that the methods described by theorists like Henry Jenkins as examples of political engagement within fan cultures were in fact established in Japan as propaganda techniques during the period of fascist rule. The term *kyōdō* (協働)—collaboration or collaborative work—is frequently used in present-day Japan to describe the creation of fan-made derivative works published in dōjinshi, but looking at how political mobilization through "amateur" creative expression was orchestrated during wartime by the "new theater" pioneer Kishida Kunio in his capacity as the Cultural Director of the Imperial Rule Assistance Association, one cannot escape a sense of profound slippage, as a concept that was associated with left-wing theater during the Taisho and early Showa periods—namely, the idea of "collaborative" or "amateur" theater, by which the masses become creators and therefore active participants in a movement—became a model of *governmental* collaboration, in other words, the Imperial Assistance System. "Collaborative theater" corresponded well with the "cooperativism" that lay at the heart of the New Order promulgated by the Konoe government in 1938. In simple terms, cooperativism urges participation in collaborative activities by which everyone can pool their strengths and create something together. Such collaboration becomes problematic when it becomes the propagandistic promotion of assisting Imperial rule (or a means toward doing so); that is, when the partner in this collaborative work is the State.

An example of an experiment in just such "collaborative" creation is the multimedia development of *The Imperial Assistance Family* by the Imperial Rule Assistance Association's Propaganda Bureau. The characters, "world," and "copyright" were all prepared beforehand by this Propaganda Bureau, paving the way for the simultaneous release of materials across media in a variety of forms by a variety of creators. This method of development, by which characters and worlds are created in advance and then managed as a matter of copyright guiding transmedia storytelling, bears more than a passing resemblance to the media mix strategy that served as the business model for Kadokawa

Publishing in the 1990s. That this media mix strategy was first refined as part of wartime propaganda strategy forces us to consider its political meaning as we recall this largely forgotten historical case.

In the manga world, the New Cartoonists Association of Japan, which included most of the key mangaka at the time, emerged from the "merger" of various manga artists' groups in August 31, 1940—in other words, just before the formation of the Imperial Rule Assistance Association. These groups of mangaka served as mutual aid organizations for cartoonists, much like production companies formed by professional mangaka do today. The New Cartoonists Association of Japan subsequently received a demand from the Imperial Rule Assistance Association's Propaganda Bureau that was passed along to its members on November 26 of the same year. The demand was extremely concrete. Discussions of "serialized manga" and "manga submissions" can be found in the records from that time, as can the title *The Imperial Assistance Family*. This means that the rough outline of the proposed project had already been hammered out a mere month and a half after the Imperial Rule Assistance Association's formation.[6]

The Imperial Assistance Family was thus, from the very start, meant to be produced as a "collaborative work" (*gassaku*) to which various creators contributed material with shared characters and premises. The authors of such collaborative works had previously been the mangaka groups mentioned earlier. While some were part of the proletarian arts movement and thus considered themselves part of a political movement, most were essentially production companies that included various mangaka. Such groups frequently attempted to secure space in magazines and newspapers using the term gassaku to refer to these collaboratively created works. It is reasonable to think that *The Imperial Assistance Family* was seen as an opportunity to expand the possibilities of publication and creation under the auspices of the Imperial Rule Assistance Association, and that this was the main intention behind the consolidation of the various mangaka groups into the New Cartoonists Association of Japan following the promulgation of the New Order. However, once production on *The Imperial Assistance Family* was underway, its copyright was "contributed to"—that is, confiscated by—the Imperial Rule Assistance Association and the right to create collaborative works was opened up to artists outside the New Cartoonists Association, including those in the colonies.

The proposed project, including its media mix component, was concretized quickly. The articles announcing *The Imperial Assistance Family*'s serialization and introducing the characters and the premise appeared in almost all major newspapers in both Osaka and Tokyo, including *Asahi Shinbun, Yomiuri Shinbun, Osaka Mainichi Shinbun,* etc., on December 5, 1940. The "world" of Imperial Assistance included not only the Yamato family—the main characters of *The Imperial Assistance Family*—but also members of the Neighborhood Association (*tonarigumi*) around them; these Associations were the smallest units of national mobilization under the New Order (Figure 1). This world picture (*sekai-zō*) was a means of elucidating the "everyday" within a world portrayed as a series of nesting boxes with "Family" at the center and expanding outward to include "Neighborhood Association," "Municipality," "Japan," and finally, "Co-Prosperity Sphere." After this introduction, serialization began with cartoons by different mangaka appearing every other day or in "relay" fashion. This was only nine days after the Imperial Rule Assistance Association first contacted the cartoonists' union. The popular understanding of postwar manga history states that Japanese newspaper comics took as their model Murat Bernard "Chic" Young's comic strip *Blondie*, which was serialized in *Asahi Shinbun* following the end of World War II, but now we can see that the "nuclear family" plus "neighborhood" set-up characteristic of postwar Japanese comics finds its precedent in *The Imperial Assistance Family* comic created during wartime.

In December of 1940, notices announcing audio recordings and film adaptations of *The Imperial Assistance Family* were already appearing in newspapers, and the comedian Furukawa Roppa writes in his diary about rising from his sickbed and rushing to the recording studio by the end of the year to contribute to the audio version.[7] The colophon of a book-length *Imperial Assistance Family* manga by Yamamoto Ryūichi shows that it was first released on December 30 of that year. Starting in 1941 and continuing through 1943, with 1942 as the most active period, an incredible variety of versions of the manga appeared, not only in newspapers but in weekly magazines and even women's magazines, until it was hard to even get a sense of *The Imperial Assistance Family* universe as a whole; not only that, but versions also appeared in almost all forms of media being produced at the time—radio dramas, picture books, dance, theatrical scripts, modern rakugo scripts, ryōkoku narrative singing, *kamishibai* paper plays, novels—as well as in the form of "goods" like hina dolls, Pog-like menko games, and even patterned kimono cloth. This was clearly a media mix development plan that included the participation of a wide variety of creators making products that all referred to the same characters and world.[8]

Of particular interest is the fact that after an announcement appeared in the December 12, 1940 edition of *Asahi Shinbun* stating that Tōhō "was

Figure 1. A notice about *The Imperial Assistance Family* in *Tokyo Asahi Shinbun*, December 5, 1940, p. 7.

embarking on" a film version of *The Imperial Assistance Family*, another, more detailed notice appeared in the *Manshū Nichi-Nichi Shinbun* (*Manchurian Daily News*) on December 20. It was a small article, but it included very concrete details: the producer would be Yamashita Ryōzō, the director would be Saitō Torajirō, and the screenwriter would be Yamazaki Kenta. Yamashita had previously produced the film *Tonarigumi no Gashō* (*The Neighborhood Chorus*), directed by Kondo Katsuhiko, which came out October 16, 1940—around the same time that the Imperial Rule Assistance Association was formed. The film was best known for the song "Tonarigumi (Neighborhood Association)" (with lyrics by Okamoto Ippei and music by Iida Nobuo) that appeared in it, especially the onomatopoetic opening line sung by Tokugawa Shusei that went *"Ton-ton-ton-karari!"* Saito Torajirō, after he moved to Tōhō, was known as the "God of Comedy" for directing a string of films starring the most popular comedians of the time, including Enomoto Ken'ichi, Furukawa Roppa, and the comedy duo Entatsu-Achako. Yamazaki Kenta had teamed up with Saitō in 1939 to make the Furukawa Roppa vehicle *Furukawa Roppa's Okubo Hikozaemon*, and went on to be a screenwriter on 1943's *The War at Sea from Hawaii to Malay* (*Hawai Marē Okikaisen*, 1942), a film made at the behest of the Imperial General Headquarters Naval Press Office. This was a formidable lineup, as suited a planned production starring Furukawa Roppa, but despite a notice appearing in the "On Location News" column in the March 1, 1943 edition of *Eiga Shūhō* (*Movie News Weekly*) that stated that Saitō Torajirō was "currently in full mobilization along with all the comedians at Tōhō, [and] committed to spreading the spirit of imperial assistance far and wide," there appears to be no evidence that filming ever started, and the project ends up disappearing from the historical record without a trace.

As for the animation version, *Yomiuri Shinbun* had announced that the Imperial Rule Assistance Association's Propaganda Bureau solicited scripts and selected the works that would be included in the adaptation, paving the way for *Yomiuri*'s film production department to produce it, but this project was also apparently cancelled midway. However, the family did appear in *Defeat of the Spies*, which was written and produced by Yamamoto Sanae and released by Sankō Shōkai in March of 1942 (Figure 2). This was a propaganda anime about counterintelligence perpetrated by neighborhood associations.

The mangaka who contributed work to the project included not only known artists belonging to cartoonists' associations but also then-unknown creators like Sakai Shichima (who came up with the original idea and script for Tezuka Osamu's breakthrough manga *New Treasure Island*) and Hasegawa Machiko (creator of *Sazae-san*, one of the most well-known and longest-running manga serializations and anime TV shows of the postwar period). Tezuka himself debuted not during the postwar period, but rather during wartime, revealing in roundtable discussions and the like that he had written a work related to *The Imperial Assistance Family* universe.[9]

Figure 2. *The Imperial Assistance Family* characters appear in the animation film, *Supai gekijo* (dir. Yamamoto Sanae, March 1942). Frame capture from the film.

What deserves particular notice here is that it was not only professional creators participating in this media mix but, as the public call for anime scripts demonstrates, amateur creators (called "*shirōto*" at the time) as well. In other words, this was "collaboration." In the realm of theater, we can see scripts being published for use not only by professional entertainers like Furukawa Roppa, but also by "citizens" to direct and star in *The Imperial Assistance Family* "collaborative theater" productions. Nazi Germany had experimented with participatory mobilization using puppet theater, and, based on this model, three versions of a manual for puppet theater productions of *The Imperial Assistance Family* were published, and classes were also held to teach people how to put these manuals into practice.

We can see similar experiments in "collaborative work" related to manga as well. *Asahi Shinbun*, as the most enthusiastic of the promoters of the New Order, swiftly used its Tokyo Headquarters to solicit submissions from readers, publishing and serializing these submissions in its pages. They intentionally designed *The Imperial Assistance Family*'s characters with easy-to-imitate shapes like circles and crescents (Figure 3). This opened up production to unknown amateurs so they could create what today would be referred to as "derivative works." I have never seen Tezuka's legendary *The Imperial Assistance Family* debut, but the fact that his youthful sketch *Till the Day of Victory*, a piece of self-published propaganda manga he drew in his university notebook, includes not only characters from *The Imperial Assistance Family* but also the same "neighborhood" premise amply demonstrates how widely this amateur participation had spread.[10]

The form of amateur-mobilizing media mix intentionally created through *The Imperial Assistance Family* is clearly responding to the participatory fascism called *collaboration* as put forth under the New Order. This system of mobilization via participatory fascism was itself premised on the broad mobilization of "amateurs who express themselves" that first arose under the Taishō democracy and its civil society of the 1920s.

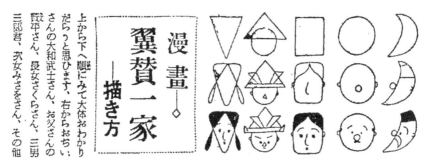

Figure 3. *The Imperial Assistance Family* characters' easy-to-imitate shapes like circles and crescents. Explained in *Asahi Shinbun*, December 8, 1940.

2. The Imperial Assistance Family in Overseas Territories

The Imperial Assistance Family, particularly its manga iterations, also expanded outside the main islands of Japan to parts of East Asia under Japanese Imperial rule (known as its "overseas territories"), especially Taiwan, Korea, Manchuria, North China (華北), and Shanghai. Although never as straightforward as the example from *Asahi Shinbun*, we still see some calls for public contributions to *The Imperial Assistance Family* in these areas. The amateur manga artists of the overseas territories were trained and organized to be local propaganda workers. The issue of media education during the wartime period—including Japanese film and other forms of media expression—requires further research and debate.

Among the various developments in the overseas territories that deserve focus is the Korean version of *The Imperial Assistance Family*. The decisive difference in the Korean development of the work from that of other regions is that the characters of the family were given a new set-up. Moreover, this was a political "localization" in step with Japan's colonization of Korea. Here, *The Imperial Assistance Family* focuses on two families: one a Korean family forced to change their names to Japanese ones, the other a Japanese family living in the overseas territory of Korea.

In April 24, 1941, an article titled "The Birth of the Imperial Rule Families: The Shikishima Family and the Kanayama Family" ran in the pages of three of *Asahi Shinbun's* overseas editions: Seisen (西鮮), Chūsen (中鮮), and Hokusen (北鮮) (Figure 4). The article reads:

> Across from the mainland Yamato Family, the Shikishima Family (Japanese mainland citizens) and the Kanayama family (Koreans) are born.
>
> Created by the Korean Federation of Nationalist Associations and the Korean Cartoonists Association, this comic will soon appear in various publications, including in the printed materials of stores and associations. Amidst its laughter and satire, the comic will play a cheerful role in the development of the Federation of Nationalist Associations of the Peninsula.

Insofar as this portrayal of two families in Korea took the fascist system of "love of country" as its basis, it differed little from the Japanese *The Imperial Assistance Family* in telling stories about "family" and "neighborhood." However, the Korean version of *The Imperial Assistance Family* was also a tool of indoctrination around the Japanese language, operating in sync with the mandate to force Korean people to learn Japanese. One example of this was Hori Mantarō's *Tsuzuki manguwa wa yūkai na kazoku* (Tsuzuki Manhwa is a Happy Family), a serial manga published in *Kōmin nippō* (皇民日報) from its founding edition on June 25, 1942, through its 159th serialization in the December 13, 1942, edition (Figure 5). The aim of both the manga serialization and the newspaper itself was to educate readers in the Japanese language. It is important to acknowledge in this regard that in the Korean peninsula, Japanese language education was also employed to prepare Koreans for conscription into the Japanese army. Additionally, we also find the Korean Cartoonists Association creating character settings, developing amateur artists through the running of workshops and manga-drawing contests, and seeking contributions to *The Imperial Assistance Family* project.

Figure 4. Article titled "The Birth of the Imperial Rule Families: The Shikishima Family and the Kinzan Family," in the *Asahi Shinbun*, Chūsen Edition, April 24, 1941, p. 7.

Figure 5. Hori Mantaro, *Tsuzuki Manguwa wa yūkai na kazoku* (Tsuzuki Manhwa is a Happy Family), a serial manga published in *Kōmin nippō* (皇民日報). The first issue of the *Kōmin Nippo*, June 25, 1942, p. 2.

Once again, what we find here around *The Imperial Assistance Family* lines up precisely with the kind of media mix scheme that I outlined in my earlier work, *A Theory of Narrative Consumption*: the use of copyright to centrally control and manage a media mix while mobilizing audiences into the production of derivative fan works around it.[11] For this reason, given the fascist uses of this media mix method outlined above, I cannot feel particularly positive about theories that discover so-called democratic possibilities of civic engagement in the "collaboration" around "fan participation."

3. The Ubiquitous Media Mix and Its Weaving of Quotations

What I would like us to take away from the example of *The Imperial Assistance Family* and the political nature of the media mix is that the media mix itself is something that developed during the wartime era. Now, Marc Steinberg argues that the Japanized English term "media mix" (media mikkusu) was first established around the year 1960.[12] But there are two supplementary points I would like to make about this.

First, there is the profile of the advocates of the media mix in the 1960s, who fall into two groups. One the one hand, there are those like Kobayashi Tasaburō and Kawakatsu Shō who were proponents of postwar North American advertising theory. On the other hand, there were those like Arai Shin'ichirō and Kuriya Yoshizumi who had worked under the wartime regime, first as corporate advertising practitioners and later as part of those who established the theoretical architecture of wartime propaganda under the banner of so-called "national advertising" (*kokka kōkoku* 国家広告). While Arai is credited with establishing the idea of the North American-style art director within the advertising world of the postwar period, his career as an adman started in 1932 within the advertising division of confectioner Morinaga Seika. Kuriya, in turn, entered the Morinaga advertising division even earlier than Arai, in 1925, and by 1930 had become a lecturer on advertising theory at Meiji University. Arai worked as an ad copywriter at Morinaga where the designer Imaizumi Takeji also worked, the latter having joined the company a year prior to Arai.

In 1940, partly at the behest of the Cabinet Intelligence Bureau, Arai, Imaizumi, and others set up what they termed the "News Technology Research Group" (*hōdō gijutsu kenkyūkai*) to undertake the theory and practice of so-called national advertising (i.e., wartime propaganda). Along with refining wartime film, photography, and other areas of media theory into theories of "advertising" (that is, propaganda), the News Technology Research Group worked alongside groups including the Imperial Rule Assistance Association Propaganda Bureau to put this theory into practice. This was the organization that created the foundations for postwar advertising agencies, corporate advertising theory and practice, as well as human resources. On the other hand, Kuriya was a researcher who was present at the dawn of advertising theory, helping formalize it into an academic discipline concerned with the psychological dimensions of department store displays and advertising. Yet Kuriya is also known for his work on wartime propaganda, notably his influential 1939 book, *War and Propaganda*, that examines wartime propaganda and argues that Germany's defeat in World War I was in part due to its defeat in the "advertising war."[13] In short, the narrative that postwar advertising is the product of the introduction of North American advertising theory to Japan obscures the development of advertising theory during the wartime period and its subsequent continuities in the postwar period. We must be particularly attentive to the political significance of the people who engaged with media mix theory in the 1960s, as some of them were also involved in the production and theorization of wartime propaganda.

The second point to add to Steinberg's argument is that at this moment in the 1960s, what was called the "media mix" referred specifically to the effective use of different media forms for the same advertising message. In other words, it was limited to the meaning of the "advertising mix" or "admixture."[14] When Steinberg examines the television anime *Tetsuwan Atomu* (*Astro Boy*, 1963–66), he gives insufficient attention to the diverging interests and motivations of its creator Tezuka Osamu and the series' chocolate-maker sponsor Meiji Seika. To be sure, for Tezuka, the development of the animated version of *Tetsuwan Atomu* and its expansion into character merchandising constituted a multimedia expansion of the original work. But for Meiji Seika, the sponsor of the TV show, *Tetsuwan Atomu* as an animated work and Atomu as character were both simply *advertisements* or icons that reminded viewers of Meiji Seika and its Marble Chocolates. That said, Steinberg does rightly note that the Marble Chocolates product is in fact depicted on the TV anime version of *Atomu*, and that this is a form of reflexive acknowledgment that the anime itself is a form of advertising.[15]

In the period of early TV anime that started with *Atomu*, animated television programs for children basically consisted of a single sponsor whose name was often included in the lyrics of the opening song of the TV series, as was the case with *Tetsujin 28-gō* (Iron Man Number 28, 1963–65) and *Shōnen Ninja Kaze no Fujimaru* (Child Ninja Fujimaru of the Wind, 1964–65), among others. Indeed, many of these had the very name of the sponsor in the title of the show or as character's names, from *Kaze no Fujimaru* (sponsored by **Fuji**sawa Pharmaceuticals), to live action effects dramas like *National Kid* (sponsored by Panasonic, known by its brand name **National**), to puppet animation like *Shisukon Ōji* (sponsored by the homophonic **Cisco** brand [pronounced Shisuko], 1963–64). In short, in the early days of children's television, the characters in children's television shows were used as "corporate characters" by their sponsors. For this reason, the development of the advertising media mix of this era extended beyond just television ads, and included program titles, their opening songs, the shows themselves, the ads placed on the covers of the magazines these shows were serialized in as manga, as well as, of course, the various freebies or "premiums" used as advertising tools by these very sponsors. All of these should be considered part of the advertising media mix.

Considered in this light, the wartime media mix example of *The Imperial Assistance Family* should be rethought, in my view, as a set of characters created for the political advertisement of both the Imperial Assistance System and the Neighborhood Association. While the Imperial Rule Assistance Association did not pay for ads, and did not much concern itself about reader popularity or demand, it undertook a simultaneous, multimedia development wherein each part of the media mix was not a "commodity," but rather an "advertisement."

The manner of thinking behind the multimedia development of national advertising was essentially the media mix *avant la lettre*. Indeed, there was already a form of wartime media mix theory being developed within the publications of the News Technology Research Group led by Arai and others. This is proved in part by the following description by Imaizumi Takeji:

> All news media outlets must be controlled to keep out disorderly elements. This is what we can call the interconnection of media functions. The true unification [of media] does not simply allow radio to be radio, film to be film, or print to be print as if each functions autonomously in its own domain. The idea is to combine the capabilities of each medium so that they might complement each other, and to bring to light a single idea or policy. We should allow the different functions of the sounds we hear, and the shapes, colors, and letters we see to cooperatively come together so that they express something in common. For instance, the day after a radio lecture we should publish a study lesson in the newspaper to repeat the message. Another example is to put the notices from the circulation boards into films so as to visualize these notices. Or, use posters to repeat and stimulate memories of the messages around public debt cancellation policies that were first explained on the radio and in film. In addition to this parallel cooperation of mediums, the relations between media forms must be consciously ordered, and the expressive spheres of each must be allocated, streamlined, and controlled in a planned manner. The temporal linkage between radio and newspapers were established in the past, wherein the environmental relationships between locations—from the house, to the workplace, to the streets—were put into mutual relation with each other in order to form an internal news system. An uncontrolled reporting system only makes us feel like there is confusion in the policy, whereas it is only by systematizing the relations between visual, sensory, and linguistic news can one begin to express a complete existence.[16]

This problem of multimedia "relations" was inextricable from the planning and creation of an information space that could efficiently disseminate state propaganda. This information space had two axes—time and space, or more specifically the temporally mediated "theoretical relation" between different regions, and the actual space where these existed in reality—with the aim of, in the end, creating within the audience an "internal news system." In other words, the defining feature of the strategy for creating the wartime information space was its aim to foster the *internalization* of that space. My use of the word *internalization* comes from the stated aim of Konoe's New Order: "mobilization from the inside." This refers to the creation of a news system that is internalized by each and every citizen within a media mix context.

The media strategies used to bring this about include (1) making representations ubiquitous and (2) transforming media expression into a "weaving of quotations" or "weaving of voices" (*in'yō no orimono* 引用の織物).[17] What Steinberg points out as characteristic of the contemporary Japanese media mix—the literal and physical ubiquity of images, as well as their paradoxical invisibility—is fundamentally true of wartime propaganda, too.[18] His insight on this point is vital for understanding the issue.

Let us look at the wartime anime *Momotarō: Sacred Sailors* (*Momotarō: Umi no shinpei*) as an example of what I mean.[19] This is an animated film that was characterized as seeming "more like a documentary than a cartoon" and using "elements of culture films"—referring to a form of filmmaking developed as a documentary mode by the Soviet and Nazi regimes—by none other than Tezuka Osamu himself, who had seen it at the time of its release as a young boy in wartime Japan.[20] Tezuka is using the term "culture film" (*bunka eiga*) in a methodological sense here, but the film itself "quotes" directly from culture films, documentary films, and newsreels at the level of image, incorporating these quotations into its shots and scenes, which means it may well have impressed even viewers at the time as being a type of "culture film." What is important to note here, though, is that these quoted images were repeated continuously all over the media already—not just in culture films, but in news photos, wartime picture books, newspaper and magazine articles, posters, and so on.

An example of one such ubiquitous image quoted by *Momotarō: Sacred Sailors* can be found in the scene where Momotarō forces the "demon" to unconditionally surrender (Figures 6.1, 6.2, 6.3, and 6.4). This scene quotes the famous tableau of Arthur Percival, the British Commanding Officer in Malay, surrendering to Japanese Imperial Army Lieutenant-General Yamashita Tomoyuki after the Fall of Singapore on February 15, 1942, a consequence

Figure 6.1. Momotarō presses for unconditional surrender. Frame grab from the animated film *Momotarō: Umi no shinpei* / *Momotarō: Sacred Sailors* (dir. Seo Mitsuyo, 1945).

Figure 6.2. Photograph of news of the meeting between Yamashita Tomoyuki and Arthur Percival (*Dōmei shashin news*, No. 1688, February 24, 1942).

Figure 6.3. Frame capture from newsreel film of the meeting between Yamashita and Percival (*Nihon News*, no. 90, February 23, 1942).

Figure 6.4. Miyamoto Saburō's war picture "Yamashita and Percival Meeting," from Asahi Shinbun ed., *Greater East Asia War Art* (Tokyo: Asahi Shinbun Tokyo Head Office, 1943).

of the Malay Operation, the initial stage of the Imperial Japanese Dutch East Indies Campaign that began on November 6, 1941, just before the start of the Pacific War with the United States. This tableau was one found not only in news photos, newsreels, and battle paintings and prints, but also in prose, described repeatedly in war reporting at the time. *Sacred Sailors*—whose Japanese title translates to "sacred soldiers of the sea"—was produced at the behest of the Ministry of the Navy, and it portrays the Battle of Menado, a paratrooper attack on the island of Celebes that was orchestrated by the Japanese Imperial Navy on January 11, 1942. But as a news item, this event was displaced by the Battle of Palembang on the island of Sumatra, which had been orchestrated by the Imperial Army on February 14, 1942. The success of this paratrooper attack was announced by the Imperial General Headquarters and portrayed in the documentary film *Sacred Soldiers of the Air,* leading to a media mix environment in which music of the same name was also released. The anime thus quotes the tableau with Lieutenant-General Yamashita, but this quotation is coupled with a chain of associated images linking paratroopers to the Army and therefore to the "sacred soldiers of the air." *Momotarō: Sacred Sailors* (that is, "soldiers of the sea") corrects this representation so that the paratroopers are *naval* soldiers commanded by Momotarō, and it is to him that the "demon" unconditionally surrenders. In other words, the quotation of omnipresent, ubiquitous images paves the way for the commander of the naval paratroopers to become Momotarō and the "sacred soldiers of the air" to become the "sacred soldiers of the sea."

The quotations woven into *Momotarō: Sacred Sailors* do not stop there. Another example is its incorporation of numerous details from the scenes in the documentary film *Sea Eagles* (*Geijutsu Eiga-sha*, 1942) that show the Naval Air Force swinging into action, from preparing for battle to actually dropping bombs. Shots of weapons being distributed amongst the soldiers at the naval base, of the soldiers' downtime, of the flight of a reconnaissance plane and its return, of the line-up of soldiers and their launch into battle, of the soldiers in charge of servicing the airplanes waving their hats as the soldiers take off, of the multilayered formation of airborne fighter planes as seen from within one of the planes, of the brightness outside the aircraft as seen from the dark interior—all these images, in both their sequence and their flow, are common between *Sea Eagles* and *Momotarō: Sacred Sailors,* save for the shots of paratroopers riding in and jumping from the aircraft. The famous shot of a doll from a care package hanging from the ceiling in one of the aircraft is also a quotation from *Sea Eagles* (Figures 7.1 and 7.2). The scene transition using a

Figure 7.1. A doll on board the military aircraft in the animation *Momotarō: Sacred Sailors*. Frame capture.

Figure 7.2. A doll on board a military plane in the documentary film *Umiwashi* (dir. Inoue Kan, 1942). Frame capture.

birdcage is reminiscent of Ozu Yasujirō, while the way the monkey soldiers' bodies transform into fighter planes is taken straight from Disney.

Further, the paratrooper scenes from the film were published over and over in propaganda magazines like FRONT, meaning that those in the colonies, including in Southeast Asia, may very well have encountered *Momotarō: Sacred Sailors* images. Motifs well-known from battle paintings and prints were echoed in the compositions of the anime (Figures 8.1, 8.2, and 8.3).

In this way, even for a modern spectator such as myself, with only a smattering of experience with the wartime image vocabulary, the film is filled with elements evoking a distinct sense of déjà vu. It feels like watching an exhaustive repetition of overly familiar images, sequences, and catchphrases.

It might seem abrupt to bring up Roland Barthes at this point, but watching the film, I was struck by how *Momotarō: Sacred Sailors* brings images that had become ubiquitous in wartime Japan together into a large-scale "weaving of voices."[21] Further, this "intertextuality"—this "weaving of voices"—was itself the ultimate goal of wartime media expression, as exemplified by this anime. This clarified for me for the first time exactly what the News Technology Research Group meant when it theorized the wartime media mix as "systematizing relations between visual, sensory, and linguistic news" into a "complete existence." Isn't this systematizing of relations into a "complete existence" the very definition of a media space or media environment? This realization allowed me to finally properly understand the nature of Tezuka Osamu's youthful manga *Till the Day of Victory* for the first time as well—a manga I have written about repeatedly.[22] Didn't Tezuka's manga and *Momotarō: Sacred Sailors* both weave in voices taken from the archive of ubiquitous media images circulating in wartime Japan?

Restrictions on publication prevent me from showing you the images themselves, but Tezuka's *Till the Day of Victory* incorporates elements from at least three sources: the Information Ministry-commissioned documentary film *Till the Day of Victory* (Nihon Eiga-sha, 1943), Naruse Mikio's comedy *Till the Day of Victory* (1945), and *Momotarō: Sacred Sailors*. Naruse's *Till the Day of Victory*, the comedy film, was a product of the overall mobilization of comic actors, and there is high likelihood that Tezuka's "mobilization" of characters from both American and Japanese manga and anime in his work was a nod to this example. I have already pointed out how Tezuka's critical stance can be detected in his realistic portrayal of the power of firebombing, a sharp contrast to the "laugh bombs" in the Naruse film from which comedians explode to the delight of the audience. We can also see direct quotations of scenes and

Figure 8.1. Frame capture from *Momotarō: Sacred Sailors* Mitsuyo Seo (dir. Seo Mitsuyo, 1945).

critical remarks about *Momotarō: Sacred Sailors* in Tezuka's unfinished *South Seas Military Base Edition* of *Till the Day of Victory*. The death of the reconnaissance plane pilot is only referred to verbally in *Momotarō: Sacred Soldiers*, but Tezuka shows the corpse directly in the pages of his manga. Moreover, as pointed out previously, *Momotarō: Sacred Sailors*'s quotations of images from *Sea Eagles* is remarkable, but the images Tezuka incorporates into the *South Seas Military Base Edition* give the impression that Tezuka was probably also looking at collections of stills from *Sea Eagles* as well. Evidence that images from the documentary film *Till the Day of Victory*, which concerns wartime labor service, were also on Tezuka's mind can be seen in the form of the old bearded laborer in the factory who appears in the trailer for that film, while the portrayal of the firebombing and the like seems to echo any number of so-called air raid films made by the government to warn the populace about the dangers of firebombing.

Further, Tezuka's portrayal of how to defend oneself from air raids quotes not only from these air raid films, but also the illustrated steps for protecting oneself during firebombing found in air raid pamphlets at the time. It is also

Figure 8.2. Miyamoto Saburō, "The Navy Paratroopers' Menado Raid" (1943).

Figure 8.3. Tsuruta Gorō, "Sacred Soldiers Descend on Palembang" (1942).

highly possible that the portrayal of how to identify a US aircraft from its silhouette (and Tezuka's realistic depiction of this aircraft) was taken from a manual distributed to children for how to identify enemy war machines. The theme of defending oneself from aerial bombing and the insertion of intertitles between each sequence both echo the format of culture and documentary films of the time. We can also see the influence of the culture film in the manga's sheer lack of story.

I have already touched on the way Tezuka's *Till the Day of Victory* mobilizes characters circulating during the Fifteen Year War, but in addition to that, the subject matter is air raids, the setting is the "neighborhood," and Yamato Sanpei, a character from *The Imperial Assistance Family*, appears as the commander of the neighborhood's air raid preparedness activities. From this, we can conclude that the worldview of Tezuka's *Till the Day of Victory* is in fact drawn from the very neighborhood found in *The Imperial Assistance Family*—the Imperial Rule Assistance Association's media mix property. Parenthetically, I might add that though the documentary film named after the *Till the Day of Victory* slogan was produced in 1943, wartime songs and film comedies were part of multimedia development from the end of 1934 through the beginning of 1945, with the record of the same name receiving the "Audio Culture Prize," and even advertising copy taking up the slogan.

In this sense, we can see that Tezuka's *Till the Day of Victory* is the embodiment of the wartime intertextual information space itself, as it is a "weaving of voices" and quotations drawn from all these sources that in turn draw material from each other. Therefore, I propose as a hypothesis that both young Tezuka and *Momotarō: Sacred Sailors* are simply works made up of elements "cut-and-pasted" from the weaving of voices formed from the ubiquitous images of wartime Japan—that is, from the "internal news system" proposed by the News Technology Research Group, which was formed from the archive of various interlinked pieces of "national advertising." At the same time, Tezuka's interiority, as an amateur creator, had itself melded completely with this wartime "news system." It becomes all too easy for an amateur to willingly produce propaganda in such an environment, naively seeing it as a pure form of self-expression.

The News Technology Research Group theorized the creation of this sort of information space not only among various media and news outlets, but also in the interiorities of each and every individual citizen, as well as across the entire East Asian Co-prosperity Sphere. Yet this was not just a theory or hypothesis, but something that actually came into being during wartime. For proof of the existence of this interiorized information space, we need look no further than Tezuka Osamu's *Till the Day of Victory*, which we can say is a "cut-and-paste" taken from the "weave of voices" making up the wartime media environment.

....

Brian Bergstrom is a lecturer and translator who has lived in Chicago, Kyoto, and Yokohama. His writing and translations have appeared in publications including *Granta, Aperture, Lit Hub, Mechademia, Japan Forum, positions: asia critique,* and *The Penguin Book of Japanese Short Stories.* His translation of *Trinity, Trinity, Trinity* by Kobayashi Erika (2022) won the 2022 Japan–U.S. Friendship Commission (JUSFC) Prize for the Translation of Japanese Literature. He is currently based in Montréal, Canada.

Marc Steinberg is Professor of Film Studies at Concordia University, Montreal, and director of The Platform Lab. He is the author of *Anime's Media Mix: Franchising Toys and Characters in Japan* (2012) and *The Platform Economy: How Japan Transformed the Commercial Internet* (2019), as well as co-author of *Media* *and Management* (2021). He co-edited *Media Theory in Japan* (2017), as well as special issues of *Asiascape: Digital Asia* on "Regional Platforms," and *Media, Culture & Society* on "Media Power in Digital Asia: Super Apps and Megacorps."

Notes

1. Ōtsuka Eiji, "Disarming Atom: Tezuka Osamu's Manga at War and Peace," trans. Thomas Lamarre, *Mechademia* 3 (2008): 111–25.
2. Marc Steinberg, *Anime's Media Mix: Franchising Toys and Characters in Japan* (Minneapolis: University of Minnesota Press, 2012).
3. Ōtsuka Eiji, "An Unholy Alliance of Eisenstein and Disney: The Fascist Origins of Otaku Culture," *Mechademia* 8 (2013): 251–77.
4. Ōtsuka Eiji, *Taisei yokusankai no media mikkusu: "Yokusan Ikka" to sanka suru fashizumu* (The Imperial Rule Assistance Association's media mix: Participatory fascism and *The Imperial Assistance Family*) (Tokyo: Heibonsha, 2018).
5. Ōtsuka Eiji, *"Kurashi" no fashizumu: Sensō wa "atarashii seikatsu yōshiki" no kao wo shite yattekita* ("Living" fascism: War came in the form of a "new kind of life") (Tokyo: Chikuma Shobo, 2021).
6. Ogawa Takeshi, *Shin Nihon mangaka kyōkai kiroku* (A record of the New Cartoonists Association of Japan) (Saitama: Saitama Public Library Archives, 1940).
7. Furukata Roppa, *Furukawa Roppa no Shōwa nikki* (The Showa diary of Furukawa Roppa) (Tokyo: Shobunsha, 1987).
8. Translators' note: For Ōtsuka's earlier theorization of the relationship between character and world, see Ōtsuka Eiji, "World and Variation: The Reproduction and Consumption of Narrative," trans. Marc Steinberg, *Mechademia* 5, no. 1 (2010): 99–116.
9. Tezuka Osamu, Baba Noboru, Takeuchi Toshiharu, and Tomita Hiroyuki, "Manga hakken" (The discovery of manga), in *Minwa* (Folktales) (May 1960).
10. Translators' note: For an analysis of this work, see Ōtsuka, "Disarming Atom."
11. Translators' note: Ōtsuka first published *Teihon monogatari shōhiron* (A theory of narrative consumption) as a book in 1989; he has published iterations and rewrites of the book since then, each one more critical than the last, including the 2008 revised edition (Tokyo: Kadokawa shoten). For an English translation of a section of the original work, see Ōtsuka, "World and Variation."
12. Marc Steinberg, *Naze Nihon wa "media mikkusu suru kuni" nanoka* (Why is Japan a "media mixing nation"?), trans. Nakagawa Yuzuru, supervised by Ōtsuka Eiji (Tokyo: Kadokawa, 2015). Translators' note: this book is a revised and expanded translation of Steinberg, *Anime's Media Mix*.
13. Kuriya Yoshizumi, *Sensō to senden* (War and advertising) (Tokyo: Jidaisha, 1939).
14. Kobayashi Tasaburō, "Media mikkusu" (Media mix) in Fukami Yoshikazu, ed., *Māketingu kōza dai 4: Kōkoku seisaku* (Marketing lectures volume 4: Advertising policy) (Tokyo: Yuhihaku, 1966).

15. Steinberg, *Naze Nihon wa "media mikkusu suru kuni" nanoka.*

16. Imaizumi Takeji, "Insatsu hōdō ni okeru gijutsu kōseitai" (The technological system of print news), in *Hōdō gijutsu kenkyū* (Studies of news technologies) 5 (1942).

17. Translators' note: the Japanese *in'yō no orimono* (引用の織物) can literally be translated as the "weaving of quotations," and in this piece we frequently translate *in'yō* in its more literal translation, namely, quotation. In the media mix, one form of media "quotes," mimics, or reproduces representations from another media form or text. However, Ōtsuka is also drawing on Roland Barthes's phrasing, which becomes the "weaving of voices" in English, but is translated into Japanese as *in'yō no orimono*. So, we alternate between quote, quotation, and voices, using voices almost exclusively only when the phrase "weaving of voices" appears in full as an explicit nod to Barthes.

18. Steinberg, *Naze Nihon wa "media mikkusu suru kuni" nanoka.* Translators' note: in the Japanese edition of Steinberg's media mix book, he opens with a discussion of how the media mix is both omnipresent and ubiquitous in Japan and also how this ubiquity allows both the images and the media mix itself to disappear into the perceptual background of everyday life.

19. *Momotarō: Umi no Shinpei*, dir. Seo Mitsuyo, 1945. Translators' note: The film title is often translated as either *Momotarō: Sacred Sailors* or *Momotarō: Divine Sea Warriors*. We choose the former title both since it is a standard translation and for its clearer resonances with the title of the earlier documentary film *Sacred Soldiers of the Air*, to which its Japanese title refers.

20. Tezuka Osamu, "Omoide no nikki" (A diary of memories), in *Tezuka Osamu daizen 1* (Tezuka Osamu collected works 1) (Tokyo: Magazine House, 1992).

21. Roland Barthes, *Monogatari no kōzō bunseki* (A structuralist analysis of narrative), trans. Hanawa Hikaru (Tokyo: Mizusu shobō, 1979).

22. Translators' note: See, for instance, *Tezuka Osamu to senjika mediaron: Bunka kōsaku, kiroku eiga, kikai geijutsu* (Tezuka Osamu and wartime media theory: Cultural crafts, documentary films, mechanical arts) (Tokyo: Seikasha, 2018) and *Atomu no meidai: Tezuka Osamu to sengo manga no shudai* (The Atomu Thesis: Tezuka Osamu and the main theme of postwar manga) (Tokyo: Kadokawa shoten, 2009). In English, see Ōtsuka, "Disarming Atom."

Disney Meets Anime

Twisted Wonderland *and the Limits of*
Media Mix Methodologies

EDMOND ERNEST DIT ALBAN

On a long, sleepless night in the summer of 2020, a friend tweeted about a newly trending game application in her fanzine circle: Disney's *Twisted Wonderland*. Disney trending in Tokyo's homoerotic fanzine communities was a surprising novelty that I felt merited further inquiry. Now, after two years and hundreds of hours of gameplay, I face a methodological dilemma. *Twisted Wonderland* (known in Japan as *Tsuisute*) is a property of Disney Japan, supervised by the talented manga artist Toboso Yana, developed by the famous anime studio Aniplex and its media conglomerate, with connections to national anime retail store leader Animate and to legendary manga and game publisher Square Enix. The concept is simple: Toboso took the trendy villain characters of canonical Disney films and transformed them into young, handsome male characters. The game's scenario remixes the themes of Disney movies to fit the setting of a high school for sorcerers. This convergence of Disney storylines and characters with the audience, format, and industry typical of current women's game applications in Japan forces me to address a rather pedestrian yet hopefully productive question: what happens if we treat *Tsuisute* as a case of "transmedia" or "media mix"? This article aims to explain how considering *Tsuisute* as an object of academic study reveals deep methodological questions in the current field of media mix studies.

Analyzing *Tsuisute* through the subfield of media mix studies raises a critical discussion about the ideological and methodological divisions between the academic study of "Western" transmedia storytelling and "Japanese" media mix. Far from simply feeding orientalist and essentialist oppositions, such binary imaginaries of participatory cultures reflect upon larger processes of knowledge production that historicize, spatialize, and categorize global transmedia cultures as specific objects, if not cultural areas, with their separate methodologies and epistemologies. *Tsuisute* represents the opportunity to look back at the currently available academic tools for analyzing and situating Japanese transmedia in order to ask: where do media mix studies stand intellectually in the age of global transmedia studies? Comparing, if not combining, transmedia and media mix epistemologies invites us to reflexively find understudied perspectives in both fields. This potentially includes new methods and objects of study as well as a deeper understanding of both fields' original historical contingency to specific conceptualizations of serialization, storytelling, and participation. To that end, this article will ask: what is the history behind our methods? What kinds of assumptions do they contain? And how can we extend them to new horizons?

Until recently, it has been quite rare for academic literature to actively bind the epistemologies and methods of both Western transmedia and Japanese media mix studies. Even occasional crossovers, including Lawrence Lessig's description of the Comic Market convention in *Free Culture*, often reinforce the otherness of Japanese (or American) media systems.[1] Both academic and industrial research on transmedia storytelling and media mix originally shared common grounds in communication, folklore, television, and at times, religion studies. As Japan's first transmedia manifesto, Ōtsuka Eiji's pioneering theory linked Western and Japanese frameworks, including Disney's recent interest in anthropological discourses about fairy tales, *Star Wars*' blockbuster serialization, and Japanese folk studies.[2] While transmedia and media mix scholars often share film and television as primary media complexes, they frequently diverge on technology's degree of involvement in designing serialization and participation. In addition, media mix studies' proximity to Asian and global Japanese studies departments means it has inherited Arjun Appadurai's theorization of media circulation as a cultural construct binding the geographies of the globalized world.[3] Thomas Lamarre's focus on media specificity and the material preconditions of anime's moving image technologies also became a key factor in envisioning image circulation as a framework, bridging film studies' subfields of animation, audience, world cinema, and industry studies.[4] Meanwhile, transmedia studies focused on North American industries, such as Derek Johnson's work on media franchising and Paul Booth's study of digital fandom, generally take a narrative approach to the multimedia expansion of, for instance, *The Lord of the Rings* or *The Matrix* franchises' crossing of video games with movies, the corporate organization of creative labor, and later the convergence of fandoms, social media, and social justice.[5]

For these reasons, I argue that academic approaches to transmedia storytelling and media mix can be seen as two similar strategies with divergent philosophies of serialization: one focused on the story and its diffusion across various media products, and the other transforming the animation of characters in and across media products as a mode of dissemination. Because transmedia and media mix emerged from specific media forms, their academic analysis envisioned intertextuality and intermediality based on their original content. The very idea of what counts as such content furthermore depends on the material and social conditions binding production and reception. While anime fandoms originally had access to the content (images) used in the making of anime to create zines, at least to my knowledge, soap opera fans did not interact with the content of their favorite series through the collection of *Dynasty*'s original filmstrips. Academic and popular notions of transmedia, participation, or serialization therefore revolve around the definition of "what travels in between media." In sum, media mix studies' simplified answer to a cultural divide in global participatory cultures therefore relies on a double equation: transmedia = story-based, and media mix = image-based. Some even oppose a converging American model (the story acts as unifying logic) with a diverging Japanese model (images create multiple stories).[6]

Such perspectives are nevertheless tied to Cool Japan's consumerist revisions of Japaneseness for global audiences or Hollywood's self-proclaimed role as the center of global entertainment. Nationalist marketing and media imperialism aside, are transmedia and media mix essentially or ontologically different? Probably not. The academic approaches that have surveyed said strategies, however, articulate the technologies, imaginaries, and spaces supporting media serialization and audience participation in different ways, and within a globalized capitalist and neoliberal world, their subsequent consumption patterns are furthermore used to justify cultural differences and imagine geographical areas like "America" or "Japan." As such, treating transmedia and media mix as industrial strategies emerging from specific cultural contexts unravels a wide spectrum of issues and solutions, notably the narrative of a global world solely divided between American and Japanese transmedia legacies. We need more frameworks that take into consideration the transcultural complexity of converging or diverging transmedia histories. As such, here, I refer to *transmedia storytelling* and *media mix* as academic epistemologies and methodologies, and to transmedia as a general term encompassing multiple histories of serialization.

Throughout his career, Ōtsuka has noted how most media mix studies tend to erase the colonial past of Japanese participatory cultures while praising the history of Japanese fine arts. Just like bland takes on transmedia storytelling as a universal act tend to serve Disney's American imperialism, media mix studies are not exempted from ideological inclinations and revisionist histories.[7] How, then, can we use the tools provided by these distinct models critically? The comparison of strategies, and not essences of cultural industries, could support our exploration of the origins, stakes, and transformation of so-called transmedia cultures worldwide, from adaptation or intertextuality studies to fan and media studies. Ideally, such inquiry would also look at the historical development of the academic field of transmedia studies to understand how intellectual frameworks came to be in interaction with transcultural industries and fandoms. Transmedia history, just like film and animation history, is often an account of bootleg and pirated media, holding the potential to expose the ideological, cultural, and spatial construction of our societies around specific notions of authorship, creativity, and democracy via the idea of participation.[8] As such, hybrid franchises like *Tsuisute* actively support current scholarship that aims to expand the narrow definitions of so-called national transmedia and audiences, as in the work on transcultural fandom done by Lori Hitchcock Morimoto and Bertha Chin.[9]

While such reflections prompted me to investigate Disney's infiltration within women otaku cultures, here, my contribution will be less grand and will instead stick to questioning key methods and frameworks dealing with the construction of media mix as an academic object of study. Because *Tsuisute* assembles traits usually associated with "Western" and "Japanese" transmedia, I use this opportunity to productively test the tensions created by the close interaction of these supposedly estranged analytical models. Far from reinforcing the monolithic definitions of each approach, I provide a critical inquiry into the fusion of Disney's fictional universe with women's otaku cultures. In doing so, my goal is not only to highlight a couple of ongoing discussions in Japanese and transcultural transmedia studies but also to illustrate the very real struggles we all face when studying transmedia. Our theoretical frameworks are never perfect, and neither are our methods. Despite my critique of popular discourses about media convergence in Japan, my goal is to invite future work to actively open canonical frameworks to new perspectives by integrating new objects and transdisciplinary literatures. In sum, my study of *Tsuisute*'s media mix in the first years of its launch questions the approaches created by certain definitions of what counts as media mix. Whose voice is included? What becomes an object of transmedia study? What discourses about cultural industries are we feeding? After presenting the basic methodological starting point of media mix chronology, the following sections cover three intertwined perspectives that I find useful to study

Tsuisute and discuss some of the current challenges of media mix studies: gender, space, and fan labor.

Welcome to the Villain's World: Mapping the Object(s), Mapping the Field(s)

A popular method to research media mix is to map the structural backbone supporting a given franchise: the industrial model. One can map the main industrial actors through official releases or press coverage, and even include fan responses to understand the development of a given media mix project. As used in the works of transmedia linguists such as Senko K. Maynard, chronological methods start from the original medium to chase down all the iterations preceding and following the franchise release.[10] Determining what counts as the original medium already represents a potential methodological bias. As Kawasaki Takuhito and Ikura Yoshiyuki's inquiry of Kadokawa's multimedia pointed out, after the 1990s, anime is rarely "the original."[11] Careful chronologies may also look at the various cycles of media mix that arise as works are rebooted in different eras or acquired by different publishers, studios, or rights-holders. Indeed, while historically central to the field, industry-based methods support specific narratives; some, such as Ian Condry, look at national creativity, while others such as Bryan Hartzheim look at the convergence of transmedia form with content, or at the collaborative economies sustaining transmedia franchises, as in Marc Steinberg's work.[12] Here, while providing a basic mapping of media mix chronology, my goal is to reach beyond the potential biases of industrial perspectives. Despite the rich stimulation provided by intellectual ties of industry studies with animation, folklore, and Japanese studies, academic research on media mix still lacks in epistemological reflexivity: description of media chronology or content is not objectivity, but a tool of power often used by publishers to justify, if not normalize, transmedia models. In sum, revisiting methods to describe media mix development may transform into a critical tool to map out the various interventions that exist in the field. In the following pages, I demonstrate how this can be done using the case study of *Tsuisute*.

Announced during Anime Summer Fest 2019 as a Japan-only release, *Tsuisute* reached a million subscribers a few months after it debuted in March of 2020, supported by a 95 percent female fanbase.[13] The game was developed by F4samurai for Aniplex, an anime studio that has recently expanded its expertise to social games based on renowned anime IPs like *Fate Stay Night*. In *Tsuisute*'s case, promotional setups involve girl's anime and game magazines, online radio shows or talk shows featuring voice actors (AbemaTV), and music events by Sony Music's idol group Night Ravens. Adaptations of the game's scenario in Square Enix's 2021 manga and 2022 novels came later, as the focus was originally given to amateur manga throughout 2020 and 2021. Since March 2020, *Tsuisute*'s main media mix apparatus has been the monthly release of accessories in national anime retail stores. Despite the chaos propagated by the COVID-19 crisis, *Tsuisute* has grown a stable pattern, reusing the images of its characters to produce limited editions of key holders, badges, clear files, and other accessories, both in shops (Animate, Tora no Ana) and online (Movic, Disney Store, Bambrest). But *Tsuisute*'s media mix development mostly made history as the second game franchise to officially join Disneyland Tokyo's Halloween cosplay party in October of 2021, following the inclusion of *Kingdom Hearts* in 2019. Current expansions of the franchise include hotel rooms, pop-up museums, cafés, and an upcoming Disney+ original anime series.

Academic media mix studies have historically been dominated by top-down perspectives investigating anime's production models like *seisaku iinkai* (production committees) to understand the distribution of funding, roles in development, hierarchies in industrial collaboration, and intellectual property of a given anime franchise. By top-down, I signal a tendency of media mix studies to rely on industrial insider knowledge and/or high media theory to describe everyday experiences of transmedia. This usage of knowledge and theory is usually associated with male authors writing in the field of "otaku-ology." As a result, the established discourse in media mix studies tends toward a model of knowledge production that discusses fan experiences without including fan voices (or at least, voices besides those of male otaku).

The evolution of Ōtsuka's and Steinberg's works over the past decade nevertheless illustrates productive transformations in scholarship from top-down methods toward newer socioeconomic analyses of media mix's entanglement with platforms, as mobile gaming and user-generated content are slowly replacing manga and light novels as a main source for anime adaptation.[14] As media mix networks become one with platform economies, the field is reducing its reliance on television and satellite, along with partners in toy, music, or food industries, and moving toward digital platforms and currencies, such as online games and NFTs. Media mix's current reliance on both physical and digital channels of serialization means that future scholars will also have to engage with game studies and retail studies. This includes my recent urban explorations of women gaming's media mix as a strategy based on limited-time events gathering audiences in specific geographies of retail, musicals, cafés, and museums, as well as the work of Joleen Blom.[15]

Turning to the current dialectics of online platforms and urban space, however, does not erase industrial discourses' objectification of female consumption, as well as the imagined hierarchies that reduce women participation to the mere consumption of media mix's urban ecology. In simpler terms, while providing useful tools to visualize and analyze the industrial development of media mix, descriptions of media chronologies often assert industrial dominance over less visible phenomena, namely, women otaku's amateur transmedia cultures, which focus on developing characters over worlds.[16] As such, analyzing *Tsuisute* requires us to develop methods that actively bridge and criticize the lines separating women amateurs from industrials. As the author of the best-selling *Black Butler* franchise and *Tsuisute*'s main contributor, Toboso's aura is well established in women's 2.5-dimensional cultures and voice fandoms, two underrated forces of media mix history that have existed since at least the 1980s.[17] Female cosplayers, dance groups, and voice actor fandoms for *Tsuisute* quickly emerged following the game's release. Women Youtubers and Vtubers also played a crucial role in the game's hype through the pandemic in gacha videos, while women amateur novelists and manga artists flooded websites like Pixiv with tens of thousands of illustrations and fan fictions. How, then, can we redress the apparent lack of media mix studies' engagement with women's participation?

World vs. Character: On the Gender Divide of Media Mix Methods

While women's media mix is at the heart of many transmedia industrial innovations, our field could further explore the methods of otaku women's scholarship. From the scholarship of Kotani Mari to Mizoguchi Akiko and Hori Akiko, works dealing with the social power harnessed by women's transmedia cultures have been published in Japan since the 1980s.[18] Their erasure from the top-down discourse of media mix described above is usually justified as a "methodological" incompatibility: focusing on gender studies or sociological perspectives did not fit the mercantile discourses supporting the media mix industry, or the avant-garde techno-philosophical narrative of male otaku scholarship. Japan's first acclaimed media mix manifesto, Ōtsuka

Eiji's *A Theory of Narrative Consumption* (*Teihon monogatari shōhiron*), framed the industrial process of transmedia serialization as a narrative experience located in fictional worlds or IPs: his world-variant model arguably erased any gender divide as *Captain Tsubasa* yaoi fanzines were discussed as variants.[19] This affiliation of women's fanzine cultures as a part of the world, held by the industry, and variants, produced by fans, eventually supported the institutionalization of amateur authors during women's fanzine industrialization in the 1990s. The graphic liberation of female desires advocated by women's erotica nevertheless sat badly with publishers, who often exercised censorship over yaoi.[20] For these reasons, and while the industry has incorporated women's transmedia storytelling into its marketing, transmedia relationships, that is to say a transmedia storytelling driven by the development of interpersonal relationships within a cosmogonic worldview, has been dismissed as an amateurish enterprise or a subcategory beneath the neoliberal imagination of worlds typical of male otaku fandoms.[21] Aside from Kathryn Hemman's recent intervention, little to no work has been done to discuss the power structures hidden by the complicit writing of media mix theory and history by male critics and industry actors.[22]

While in anglophone scholarship the world-vs.-character debate's gender divide has been ignored in favor of discussions about Japan's allegedly unique notion of character, as in Itō Gō's model of kyara and kyarakutā, in East Asian queer studies, this opposition has indirectly supported the emergence of transnational boys love (BL) research.[23] Transmedia relationships represent a chance to open media mix studies to a more inclusive historical dimension extending from women's media mix herstory toward transcultural fandoms and global queer transmedia. As such, transmedia relationships may structure future research on *Tsuisute* and other transcultural media mix as it reveals important passages between industrial and amateur transmedia practices within various local, regional, and (trans)national scales. For example, Thomas Baudinette's work on Thai BL's recent addition to the media mix ecology invokes transcultural translation, localization, and piracy as entangled global transmedia forces evading simplistic top-down or bottom-up frameworks.[24] As the generalization of frameworks based on male otaku cultures like moé, sekaikei, or world theory, continues to monopolize the discussions on media convergence in Japan, we need to address how industrial discourses have relegated other transmedia legacies to subsequent, derivative, and subjugated subcategories, and work to bring discussions of women or queer fandom into the forefront of media mix research.

Tsuisute's usage of world theory exemplifies such dynamics by using the shipping logics as an entry point for female consumers to participate in Disney's worldbuilding. *Tsuisute* features a story mode accompanied by two types of mini games: combat and rhythm. The interface is reminiscent of visual novels, with an emphasis on character animations and voices. Playing *Tsuisute* requires the user to read the main story and use the gacha system, which randomly distributes character cards. Users then train the cards to win battles in the story mode and unlock new episodes, voice lines, and illustrations. Looking at *Tsuisute's* narrative structure may help us to contextualize the current media mix expansion of mobile games from world theory's roots in Bikkuriman chocolates.[25] Just like Bikkuriman chocolates gave some background on the Bikkuriman world, each of *Tsuisute's* character cards comes with specific episodes that progressively recreate the backstories behind the main story. When Ōtsuka originally developed world theory, the idea was to have consumers pursue fragments of an imaginary large cosmology that does not exist per se but comes alive through fan participation. *Tsuisute's* full story-world is only attainable with all virtual cards in hands, and hours of card-training in magic classes. The practice of framing media mix serialization as the access to a world has been often present in the light novel industry, but is less common in women's gaming. *Tsuisute's* storytelling therefore puts the player in a strangely familiar world where one literally experiences flashbacks from Disney films at the beginning of each chapter

Tsuisute's Disney mystery comes with a plethora of aesthetic and gameplay elements taken from women's fanzine cultures and transmedia relationships, including "shipping" (supporting particular couples) and the *bishōnen* archetype.[26] The male character designs crafted by Toboso are heavily reminiscent of both yaoi homoerotic cultures and *otome* or *yumejo* (romance-based transmedia) works, two legacies with common roots in shōjo manga, musicals, and boy bands. *Tsuisute's* gameplay is heavily passive. Users spend hours to train their characters by sending them to class, which simply requires the user to press one button and leave their smartphone run. The (absence of) gameplay in classes nevertheless serves as an in-game cinematic, producing stories from character images, voices, and relationships: among other stats to raise, each card has a buddy level that grows during Alchemy classes. Growing the literal chemistry between characters attributes "hit points" (HP) or attack bonuses during combat, and even unlocks dialogues and animations between shipped characters. As such, by mobilizing the relationship-based logics of women's otaku cultures, *Tsuisute's* core mechanic, the buddy system, supports world building on both narrative and gameplay levels. While the fanbase is divided on how to read said relationships, *Tsuiste* effectively binds the generalizing view of Disney's franchising with interpersonal shipping mechanics exploring the scenario's episodic structure and cosmological lore. The struggle against patriarchal structures inherent in the invention of handsome male characters' transmedia relationships becomes a tool binding the overarching logic of the Disney worlds' crossover with women's otaku cultures.

Far from North American transmedia scholarship's recurrent focus on daily inequalities, power structures, and social movements, media mix industries and studies have often naturalized and de-problematized participatory cultures.[27] Mixing industrial and sociological methods contributes to complex investigations of transmedia phenomenon and fan identities as codependent constructions articulating daily interaction, commutation, and transformation of serialized media ecologies. For a long time, women's scholarship was not recognized as part of media mix studies because they focused on amateur manga. Media mix studies, while advocating for an intermedial perspective, chose anime as its main center, and male-focused media epistemologies as the "right" methodological choice. For these reasons, Toboso's systematic jumps between manga, anime, games, musicals, and now Disney properties through the means of transmedia relationships urges us to confront the potential limits of the field, and the systematic ostracization of gendered perspectives as an "outside" of the main object of study. This eventually leads us to the bigger debate of how minorities have often been labelled as beneath authorship and intellectual property. As such, the current turn in fan studies toward fandoms of color and diasporas may help us to build richer and more inclusive methodological approaches to media mix research.[28]

Tokyo Disneyland's Pedestrian Invasion: Worlds as Transmedia Objects, Space as a Method

From the early stages of the game's development, Disney's theme parks have been an inspiration in organizing *Tsuisute*'s crossover world.[29] The opening movie and title screen showcase the famous Disney castle, as well as the statues of seven great villains from *Alice in Wonderland*, *The Lion King*, *The Little Mermaid*, *Aladdin*, *Snow White*, *Hercules*, and *Sleeping Beauty*. *Tsuisute*'s high school, Night Raven College, is in the castle, and its entrance, Main Street, refers to the central promenade in the real-world theme parks. Spatial imaginaries play a cosmological role in the games' interface. In story mode, chapters are visually located on a virtual world map. Within the game, locations from Disney's many films and theme parks form a harmoniously combined territorial patchwork that reinforces Disney's overall brand image, conflating their intellectual and physical "properties." However, there have been debates over who can interact with those properties and what kinds of interventions they can make, especially when it came to the real-world theme parks. For instance, a short-lived yet profound "territorial panic" sprang up among Japanese Disney fans when young female cosplayer groups appeared at Disney Tokyo Resort in the summer of 2020 to visit the places resembling in-game locations. Online rage was heaped on the cosplayers for ignoring social distancing, mask policies, and basic manners, but their main offense was appearing in costume, thus ignoring the rules created by Disney to visually separate cast members from guests. *Tsuisute*'s imaginary mapping of space unwittingly invited unexpected guests to interact with the physical territories of their favorite IPs. This controversy brings to the surface two divergent spatial organizations that echo the participatory specificities of the transmedia-media mix divide: one based on parks enclosing the transmedia narrative experience emerging from film and TV franchises, and the other revolving around the management of fan pilgrimages spontaneously emerging across public spaces where anime images circulate.

The 2020 pedestrian invasion of Tokyo Disneyland reveals the tensions created between world imaginaries, such as the fictional world of *Tsuisute*, and the disciplinary enclosure of the subaltern practices of womenfandoms at a spatial level, as the cosplayers' behaviors in the Tokyo Resort park spaces were policed by fellow fans. Media mixes have historically relied on strategies of capturing the mobility of otaku pedestrians taking strolls between their favorite local anime shops, notably Animate, Tora no Ana, and Oh My Café in *Tsuisute*'s case.[30] The secluded magic of Disney's experience was upset by the pedestrian chaos resulting from the intrusion of media mix practices, such as improvised cosplay Tiktoks and unorganized merchandise exchanges of the sort found in nearby otaku sanctuaries. This collision of physical and mediated practices is a consequence of *Tsuisute*'s development, which was premised on the convergence of Disney transmedia worlds with otaku cultures' urban networks of image dissemination. While supposedly operating within Disney's worldviews, *Tsuisute* acted as an uncontrolled passage between guests who were following the social and spatial rules set by Disney Tokyo Resort and fans who acted out of a different transmedia habitus based on otaku pedestrian culture. This unforeseen confrontation reveals how transmedia serialization moves from virtual world imaginaries to urbanism and physical spaces, a movement that has been discussed by scholars of fan and anime studies since the 2010s who have explored transmedia's manifestations in museums, national memorial sites, and cities.[31] Future research may comparatively reevaluate the implications of transmedia worlds and media mix's spatial materialization within and beyond their role as a policing agent shaping the practice, imagination, and structures of serialized media participation.

Ōtsuka's world-variant theory was born amidst Tokyo Disneyland's construction, the global diffusion of VHS, and 1980s Cold War worldviews. As such, early anime media mix relied on a bank of recycled images used week after week to produce episodes. These same images were then shared with local bookstores, before being transformed by fans into new zines and fan goods.[32] For these reasons, media mix models have historically integrated fan places, networks of local bookshops, and fanzine conventions into the production process of transmedia products, to the point that multimedia publishers like Kadokawa have grown a business of exploiting amateur works after the late 1980s. If world-variant theory's hidden agenda was to bring amateur modes of storytelling back into the industry, and therefore take down the author-publisher cultural hierarchies operating against creative crowds, world imaginaries ended up locking fan participation into specific relations to IPs, such as sponsored fanzines.[33] *Tsuisute's* pedestrian invasion may help us to look back critically at how media mix models have been historically inspired by transcultural transmedia, but also how they have implemented spatial top-down hierarchies when industrializing already existing grassroots modes of amateur transmedia. In sum, within media mix history, worldviews have transformed from democratic imaginaries to territorial production structures capturing pedestrian networks and regulating daily fan activities.

The spatial dilemma exposed by the opposition in Disney's transmedia and media mix relationship to public space, fan places, or conventions should compel us to further explore transmedia as situated knowledge. *Tsuisute's* impromptu confrontation of serialization models both highlights and transcends the simple opposition of worldviews and ideologies by inducing a method already fleshed out by research on transcultural multifandoms.[34] As pedestrians, fans may become guests in certain situations. The coexistence of different models of serialization entangled in various material and digital spaces reveals fluctuations between various regimes of fan subjectification dispatched across wide territories, institutions, and online networks. As corporations try to legally, mentally, and physically separate franchises, while asking consumers to be proactive, space becomes a method to envision the daily stakes and tensions emerging from local, regional, and global iterations of specific philosophies of transmedia.

Bottom-up Platforms and Democratic Discourses: Fan Labor as a Method

A solid groundwork has been laid for research on fan labor in studies on prosumers, cosplay, fanzines, gaming, and a host of other fan- and industry-generated practices. However more work remains to be done as fan labor continues to evolve. Future research may look at media mix history as successive regimes of participation reflective of Japan's sociocultural transformations. Such inquiries may combine the growing academic literature of game and platforms studies in and out of Japan. Since the 2000s, game studies have coined popular terms such as playbor to discuss the evolution of players' involvement in gaming industries, including the turn to casual and mobile gaming.[35] *Tsuisute*'s notorious gameplay style of *ikusei*, or "nurturing" characters by sending them to class and developing their relationship with each other, converges with current discussion of playbor as the commodification of fan's time investment in East Asian girls' gaming cultures.[36] *Tsuisute*'s gaming involves a daily nurturing labor based on time management in so-called magic classes, including potential shortcuts such as paying to skip class waiting times and obtain item drops. While fans are virtually in charge of discovering the world, understanding the narrative, and raising the characters, *Tsuisute*'s media mix emerged around the planning of seasonal events in and out of the game with one unifying logic: scarcity and limited availability. In-game collecting cards and physical merchandise are both randomly distributed through a gacha mechanic or random lottery system. While quite banal in the current landscape of Japanese transmedia cultures, the convergence between virtual and physical gacha mechanics places fans in specific regimes of transmedia participation.

Kadokawa's merger with Niconico video owner Dwango in 2014 inspired incisive reactions from some media mix scholars, who took this event as an opportunity to discuss media mix's historical role in Japanese propaganda and amateur exploitation, a phenomenon that Ōtsuka called mobilization when excavating World War II media mixes including the *Yokusan Ikka* amateur manga series.[37] When faced with unprecedent transmedia fan markets, Kadokawa's world theory progressively faded away in the late 1990s to be replaced by strategies that would reinforce the barriers between professionals and amateurs in the anime and manga industry. As an example, light novel character Suzumiya Haruhi became her own manager and invited fan participation strictly in dances, a model that the *Yo-kai Watch* franchise would later repeat.[38] Indeed, the development of Niconico video and YouTube in the 2000s gave a new life to world imaginaries, but this time supported by the web's philosophy of global world views and free speech. In this context, media mix started to shift from state propaganda or participatory models including fans in the very creation of franchised transmedia texts toward the curation of online user-generated content like *odotte mita* (dance) or *utatte mita* (song cover) videos. For Ōtsuka, this skillful twist hides an invisible confiscation of the free right to be a transmedia storyteller, a right that publishing industries had previously confiscated during Japan's modernization with pure literature's authorial model.[39] In sum, platforms have become an apparatus to regulate and produce (in the sense of becoming executive producers of) transmedia fan-made content in Japan. In so doing, platforms focused on transmedia often try to present themselves as bottom-up, democratic, and empowering.

Tsuisute's platformed media mix complicates such enthusiastic narratives. Fan participation in the official text has been currently limited to two sponsored fanzine anthologies by a dozen carefully handpicked authors. The franchise's first platform, its game application, nevertheless invites other forms of participation, and mostly what fans have called "the magic of money" (*kakin no mahō*), or paying for stickers on LINE, for premium viewership on Ameba TV to access live events, for more in-game currency to spend in live stream gacha videos on Youtube, or for lottery items sold randomly on Ichibankuji .com for "unboxing" Tiktok videos. The final frontier of *Tsuisute*'s fan online participation extends to accessing Disney's classic films on Disney+, another paywalled platform. Free speech, democratic access, and amateur storytelling are clearly not part of *Tsuisute*'s worldview and official platforms. Instead, the fan labor of discovering the world of Disney crossovers is governed by the restricted interactions with content related to the game's worldview dispatched on each platform. *Tsuisute*'s platform economy-ecology extends to platforms specifically designed for user generated content, but the official channels are largely used for promotional purposes and are subject to moderation and censorship, which only reinforces the separation between official content and unmoderated amateur online content.

Since the 2010s, media mix industries have struggled to keep pedestrian fan activities on board with their expectations of a tamed, yet useful participation. In light of Simon Gough and Annie Lee's analysis of game franchises close to *Tsuisute*,[40] I would argue that it is the media mix product's very capacity to create various paths of transmedia storytelling that pushed the enclosure of official content within virtual gacha platforms: only there can the access to content, the exchanges between players, and the monitoring of fan participation be removed from the impromptu and convoluted iterations of pedestrian practices. Platforms nevertheless bring a twist to the territorial opposition of official spaces and amateur places of urban media mix: while pedestrian flows are more difficult to capitalize on, online activity can be separately mobilized by each platform into content, product, and data.

In sum, the recent introduction of digital platforms in media mix studies points toward a potential opening of the field to historical reconstructions of participatory cultures. The historical use of transmedia franchises to promote nationalist and militarist ideologies among fans indeed invites us to reflexively question the past, present, and future of transmedia in Japan. Worldviews have been politically and industrially used to manifest specific reactions from audiences, and during World War II, fanzine projects like *Yokusan Ikka* may have formed the roots of current media mix models: audiences were given maps, characters, and episodes to formulate their own story chapters based on racist and imperialist views of Asia. Looking at *Tsuisute*'s very similar structure (map, character, episodes), we may have to further decolonize media mix studies. Doing so may require following animation studies' tendency to seek global media forms or regional histories, supporting transcultural inquiries on media mix. *Tsuisute*'s transcultural fandom has had illegal access to the game in various regions, transcending narrow definitions of transmedia as American or media mix as Japanese. If done in a critical perspective, studying such hybrid circulation may help us build more global perspectives on transmedia.

Conclusion

In recent years, industrial discourses in Japan have presented transmedia and media mix as two completely different phenomenon that may converge in the future with Japan's adoption of transmedia as a brand-new strategy.

Funnily enough, Henry Jenkins's *Textual Poachers* was translated soon after such claims, supporting the idea that American and Japanese transmedia histories had somehow never met before. This strange discourse may partly be attributed to Japanese transmedia's recent invasion of Hollywood, a success story that all too easily justifies looking at transmedia through an industrial lens. Despite the actual diversity of fan and academic contributions dealing with the transcultural or global dimensions of transmedia, media mix studies' historical reliance on such industrial worldviews may dangerously influence our perception of disciplinary boundaries, limiting at the same time the growth of new theoretical and methodological tools.

While critical to future developments, it may not be practical to focus solely on meta-theoretical criticism of how media mix theory has been made. Investigating cases like Disney's *Twisted Wonderland*, or even more obscure phenomena may help future scholars to actively search for the new delimitations of media mix studies and productively expand their theoretical and methodological tools. Despite this article's critical position toward top-down, industrial male media-centered texts that have supported the emergence of the field, the overall intent of this piece is not to condemn existing media mix scholarship. Rather, it aims to raise the stakes and provoke future inquiries. What methods do we choose? How can we amplify diverse voices in media mix scholarship, including those of fans and independent scholars working outside of established academic institutions? If choosing methods implies perpetuating or institutionalizing certain images and imaginations of media mix and its fandoms, how are we to deal with the subsequent ethical issues and potential ideological inclinations that are tied to certain approaches? Only by considering such questions can the field of media mix studies progress along with the changing transmedia ecology we are witnessing now, in cases like *Tsuisute* and many others yet to be explored.

....

Edmond (Edo) Ernest dit Alban is an assistant professor of Communication and Asian Studies at Tulane University where they teach Japanese and Asian animation and transmedia cultures. Their research examines the role of fan's quotidian pedestrian mobility in the construction of transmedia environments, industries, and products. Edo is interested in the reconstruction of inclusive transmedia histories, looking at city space as point of convergence between diverse perspectives on animated media, storytelling, media production, and even activism. Their current book project discusses the recent evolution of Japanese transmedia, media mix, in dialogue with the creative transmedia tensions emerging from the urban crossroads where women's otaku cultures meet with LGBTQ+ media. The manuscript explores the potential and limits of grassroots social movements' inscription in transmedia industries.

....

Notes

1. Lawrence Lessig, *Free Culture* (London: Penguin Press, 2004).
2. Ōtsuka Eiji, *Teihon monogatari shōhiron* (A theory of narrative consumption) (Tokyo: Kadokawa, 2001).
3. Arjun Appadurai, *Modernity at Large: Cultural Dimensions of Globalisation* (Minneapolis: University of Minnesota, 1996).
4. Thomas Lamarre, "Introduction to Otaku Movement," *EnterText* 4, no. 1 (Winter 2004/2005): 151–87; Marc Steinberg, *Anime's Media Mix: Franchising Toys and Characters in Japan* (Minneapolis: University of Minnesota Press, 2012).
5. Derek Johnson, *Media Franchising: Creative License and Collaboration in the Culture Industries* (New York: New York University Press, 2013); Paul Booth, *Digital Fandom: New Media Studies* (Bern: Peter Lang, 2010).
6. Nakamura Akinori and Susana Tosca, "The Mobile Suit Gundam Franchise: A Case Study of Transmedia Storytelling Practices and Ludo Mix in Japan," *Transactions of the Digital Game Research Association* 5, no. 2 (2021): 1–32.
7. Ōtsuka Eiji, *Media mikkusuka suru nihon* (The media mixification of Japan) (Tokyo: East Press, 2014).
8. Pang Laikwan, *Creativity and Its Discontent: China's Creative Industries and Intellectual Property Rights Offenses* (Durham: Duke University Press, 2012).
9. Lori Hitchcock Morimoto, "Trans-cult-ural Fandom: Desire, Technology and the Transformation of Fan Subjectivities in the Japanese Female Fandom of Hong Kong Stars," *Transformative Works and Cultures.* no. 14 (2013); Bertha Chin and Lori Morimoto, "Reimagining the Imagined Community: Online Media Fandoms in the Age of Media Convergence," in *Fandom: Identities and Communities in a Mediated World,* ed. Jonathan Gray, Cornel Sandvoss, and C. Lee Harrington, 2nd ed. (New York: NYU Press, 2017), 174–88.
10. Senko K. Maynard, *Raitonoberu hyōgenron: Kaiwa sōzō asobi no disukōsu no kōsatsu* (Expression in light novels: An evaluation of the ludic discourse of dialogical imagination) (Tokyo: Meijishoin, 2012).
11. Kawasaki Takuhito and Iikura Yoshiyuki, "Ranobe kyara ha tachōsakuhin sekai no yume wo miruka" (Are characters dreaming of multiple worlds?), in *Raitonoberu kenkyūjosetsu* (An introduction to light novel studies), ed. Ichiyanagi Hirotaka and Kume Yoriko, 18–32 (Tokyo: Seikyūsha, 2009).
12. Ian Condry, *The Soul of Anime: Collaborative Creativity and Japan's Media Success Story* (Durham: Duke University Press, 2013); Bryan Hikari Hartzheim, "Pretty

Cure and the Magical Girl Media Mix," *Journal of Popular Culture* 49 no. 5 (2016): 1059–85; Steinberg, *Anime's Media Mix.*

13. "Māketigu riisachi de hanmei dizuni tsuisute pureiyā hachi wari ijō ga," *Dengeki Online,* August 8, 2020, https://dengekionline.com/articles/47416/.

14. Ōtsuka, *Media mikkusuka suru nihon*; Marc Steinberg, *The Platform Economy: How Japan Transformed the Consumer Internet* (Minneapolis: University of Minnesota Press, 2019).

15. Joleen Blom, "The Manifestations of Game Characters in Media Mix Strategy," in *Comics and Videogames* (London: Routledge, 2020), 201–21; Edmond Ernest dit Alban, "Pedestrian Media Mix: The Birth of Otaku Sanctuaries in Tokyo," *Mechademia* 12, no. 2 (Spring 2020): 140–63. See also Blom's "The Geshin Impact Media Mix," this volume.

16. Azuma Sonoko, *Takarazuka yaoi: Ai no yomikae josei to popyū rakaruchā no shakaigaku* (Takarazuka yaoi: The double reading of love: A sociology of women and popular culture) (Tokyo: Shinyōsha, 2015).

17. Sugawa-Shimada Akiko, *Nitengojigen bunkaron: Butai, kyarakuta, fandomu* (A cultural approach to 2.5 dimension: Musicals, characters, fandoms) (Tokyo: Seikyūsha, 2021); Ishida Minori, *Anime to seiyū no mediashi, onna wa naze shōnen wo enjiru no ka* (The media history of anime and voice actresses; why do women play young boys?) (Tokyo: Seikyūsha, 2020).

18. Mizoguchi Akiko, *BL shinkaron: Bōizurabu ga shakai o ugokasu* (BL as a transformative genre: Boys' love moves the world forward) (Tokyo: Ōta Shuppan 2005). Mari Kotani, "Otakuin wa otakuia no yume o mitawa" (Otaqueen dreamed of otaqueer), in *Amijo genron F-kai: Posutomodan, otaku, sekushuariti* (Netlike discourse F, revised: Postmodern, otaku, sexuality), ed. Hiroki Azuma (Tokyo: Seidoshoa, 2003), 119–20. Hori Akiko, "Yaoi wa gei sabetsu ka?: Manga hyōgen to tashaka" (Is Yaoi discrimination? Manga expression and othering) in *Sabetsu to haijo no ima 6: Sekushuariti no tayōsei to haijo* (Discrimination and exclusion today 6: Sexual diversity and exclusion) ed. Yoshii Hiroaki (Tokyo: Akashi Shoten, 2010), 21–54.

19. Ōtsuka, *Teihon monogatari shōhiron,* 15–16.

20. Misaki Naoto, *Shōgyōansorojii to okosamatachi: Gakeppuchi de sukippu suru ojōsama-tachi* (Commercial anthologies and children: Young girls a step ahead the cliff), (self-published, 1996), retrieved from http://www.st.rim .or.jp/~nmisaki /works2/repo_book.html#FLAG7.

21. Komori Kentarō, *Kamisamonakuba zan'nen* (God, if not a lasting notion) (Tokyo: Nan'undo, 2013).

22. Kathryn Hemman, "Queering the Media Mix: The Female Faze in Japanese Fan Comics," *Transformative Works and Cultures* 20 (2015), https://doi.org/10.3983 /twc.2015.0628.

23. Itō Gō, *Tezuka izu deddo: Hirakareta manga hyōgenron he* (Tezuka is dead: Toward an opened manga expression) (Tokyo: NTT, 2005); James Welker, ed., *BL ga*

hiraku tobira: Hen'yo suru Ajia no sekushuariti to jendā (BL opening doors: Sexuality and gender transfigured in Asia) (Tokyo: Seidosha, 2019).

24. Thomas Baudinette, *Boy's Love Media in Thailand* (London: Bloomsbury, 2023).
25. Ōtsuka, *Teihon monogatari shōhiron*, 7–54.
26. Nishimura Mari, *Yaoi to Aniparo* (Yaoi and Aniparo) (Tokyo: Ōta, 2002).
27. Henry Jenkins, "'Cultural Acupuncture': Fan Activism and the Harry Potter Alliance," in *Popular Media Cultures*, ed. L. Geraghty (London: Palgrave Macmilan, 2015), 206–29.
28. Rukmini Pande, *Squee from the Margins: Fandom and Race* (Iowa City: University of Iowa Press, 2018).
29. Disney fan editors, *Twisted Wonderland Fanbook* (Tokyo: Kōdansha, 2020), 15.
30. Marc Steinberg and Edmond Ernest dit Alban, "Otaku Pedestrians," *A Companion to Media Fandom and Fan Studies*, ed. Paul Booth (Hoboken, NJ: Wiley-Blackwell, 2018), 289–304.
31. Kathryn Phillips and Thomas Baudinette, "Shin-Ōkubo as a Feminine 'K-pop Space': Gendering the Geography of Consumption of K-pop," *Japan, Gender, Place & Culture* 29, no. 1 (2020): 80–103.
32. Ōtsuka Eiji, Inoue Shin'ichiro, and Takahashi Yutaka, "Kadokawashoten no hada kankaku to animeito no tetsugaku," *Neppu sutajio jiburi no kōkishin* 9, no. 12 (Tokyo: Studio Ghibli, 2011): 31–48.
33. Ōtsuka, *Media mikkusuka nihon*, 17–56.
34. Sandra Annett, *Anime Fan Communities: Transcultural Flows and Frictions* (New York: Palgrave Macmillan, 2014).
35. Julian Kücklich, "Precarious Playbour: Modders and the Digital Game Industry," *The Fibreculture Journal* (2005), https://five.fibreculturejournal.org/fcj-025-precarious-playbour-modders-and-the-digital-games-industry/.
36. Sarah Cristina Ganzon, "Investing Time for Your In-Game Boyfriends and BFFs: Time as Commodity and the Simulation of Emotional Labor in Mystic Messenger," *Games and Culture* 14, no. 2 (2018), https://journals.sagepub.com/doi/abs/10.1177/1555412018793068.
37. Ōtsuka, *Media mikkusuka nihon*, 17–56.
38. Marc Steinberg, "Media Mix Mobilization: Social Mobilization and *Yo-kai Watch*," *Animation* 12, no. 3 (2017): 244–58.
39. Ōtsuka, *Teibon monogatari shōhiron*.
40. Simon Gough and Annie Lee, "Material Multiplicities and Sanrio Danshi: The Evolution of Sanrio's Media Mix," *Electronic Journal of Contemporary Japanese Studies* 20, no. 1 (2020), https://www.japanesestudies.osrg.uk/ejcjs/vol20/iss1/gough_lee.html.

Between Media Mix and Franchising Theory

A Workshop on the Theoretical Worlds of Transmedia Production

DEAN BOWMAN AND JAMES McLEAN

On August 6, 2019, the authors of this article organized an academic workshop to explore the issue of transnational media franchises and transmedia narratives at the Digital Games Research Association (DiGRA) conference at Ritsumeikan University in Kyoto, Japan. At the same conference, the authors also organized a panel of academic papers utilizing the long-running Disney/ Square Enix collaboration *Kingdom Hearts* as an exemplar of transmedia, transnational storytelling. The papers were written up as a special journal edition of the Canadian Game Studies Journal, *Loading . . .* , and provide a case-study-driven counterpoint to this discussion.[1] The workshop was organized with support from Dr. Tarnia Mears and Professor Rayna Denison (who acted as chair) and was funded by the Great Britain Sasakawa Foundation. It addressed that year's conference theme: "Game, Play and the Emerging Ludo Mix," with the latter term referencing the Japanese concept of the "media mix" only refocused around video games and play. Media mix is considered by many to be a specifically Japanese version of what, in the Western context, is typically referred to as transmedia storytelling: a concept that explores how narratives flow through complex arrangements of media products. Our feeling was that before exploring the changing role of games in the media mix formula, as the conference intended to do, it was first necessary to explore these key terms and how they functioned in relation to one another as well as in their specific cultural contexts.

To that end, we were able to draw together some of the leading voices in the field from Japan, the United States, and Europe. These included Marc Steinberg of Concordia University, the author of one of the defining English-language books on the media mix, *Anime's Media Mix: Franchising Toys and Characters in Japan*; Henry Jenkins (who kindly provided a video address), Provost Professor at the University of Southern California, who has been one of the leading architects of transmedia theory through his career; Bryan

Hikari Hartzheim (Waseda University), who undertakes production studies research on the media mix in anime production companies and game developers; Akiko Sugawa-Shimada (Yokohama National University), whose work has been instrumental in theoretically developing the now influential concept of "2.5-dimensional" culture (2.5D) and its associated fandoms[2]; and early-career researchers Luca Bruno (then with Leipzig University), whose work explores the extension of the media mix into the cultures and spaces of Akihabara; and Dean Bowman, who was interested in exploring shifting models of fan consumption within the mix. All quotations from these participants refer to the workshop unless stated otherwise.

Henry Jenkins has argued that contemporary media, developed in an era of what he calls "convergence culture," is fundamentally designed to spread.[3] In this workshop we were interested in exploring whether media might spread differently under the cultural logics of media mix and transmedia. Were the two terms interchangeable or did they have their own rules? As we (James McLean and Dean Bowman) have argued in a special issue of the journal *Loading . . .* on the *Kingdom Hearts* franchise, these modes of production, distribution, and consumption cannot simply be isolated to their geographical locales but engage with each other in the entire process of textual creation and adaptation.[4]

This article synthesizes some of the key discussions of the workshop, providing a snapshot of the event that may be useful to ongoing conversations about transmediality. However, since the write-up of the event was disrupted by the COVID-19 pandemic we have sought to return to some of the speakers in order to further reflect on their thoughts and experiences in the four years since the 2019 panel. This hopefully places their positions into conversation with our current moment, potentially shedding some light on the accelerated changes to our media landscape wrought by the pandemic, such as the increasing role of digital on-demand streaming platforms.

Our approach to the data has been guided by thematic analysis, as developed by Virginia Braun and Victoria Clarke, which has helped us to identify "repeated patterns of meaning" in order to reconstruct some of the more insightful moments into a narrative within the more constrained space of an article.[5] Following the method, points made were grouped for relevancy, then sorted thematically, ultimately structuring the report around three key areas. Much of the workshop was dedicated to defining and unpacking key terms as a prerequisite to developing them further, and so the first section, "Conceptualizing Transmedia Storytelling," covers the frameworks of what Steinberg referred to here as "transmedia Hollywood" and "Japan's media mix." The emphasis on culture in this section (and throughout) emphasizes how the panel spoke to broader understandings of cultural storytelling rather than merely seeing these phenomena as wholly determined by industry frameworks. Cultural storytelling, in the context of transmedia, builds on John Caldwell's research into the social dynamics of production cultures.[6] However, we wish to expand on this approach to incorporate and acknowledge that similar social dynamics can be seen at play not only through the interlinked circuits of production but also in acts of consumption. The importance of cultural specificity to these terms was another point frequently made by all panelists, with Steinberg noting that the Japanese "media mix" is a reminder that we must "pay attention to how and where discourses happen, as well as to [the] histories of a concept." He concluded that "while media mix might be similar to transmedia in principle, it has a crucially distinct history that requires its own treatment."

The second area, "Understanding Transmedia Cultures," considers the relevance of production committees, official lines of distribution, and the geography of media distribution. However, discussions go beyond the traditional circulation of texts through the production-distribution chain, acknowledging how the cultures of consumers and fans respond to media texts and organize their own spread of them. The final section, "Research, Methodology and Mutation," explores how we contend with transmedia as researchers, how we organize research into these phenomena, and (crucially) where we research it. The section reflects on some of the problems and barriers raised by the panel, including issues of access, industry secrecy, and the parochial attitude that exists in Western scholarship, prioritizing Hollywood as the prime mover and the norm against which all else is measured.

Key Theme 1: Conceptualizing Transmedia Storytelling

The panel began with an opening video contribution from Jenkins to set out some of the key concerns, whereupon each panelist gave a short address as to their interest and theories on the topic. In the video, Jenkins set the tone of the discussion by returning to the example of *The Animatrix*, a case study that loomed large in his book *Convergence Culture* as a kind of benchmark of transmedia storytelling.[7] Elsewhere, he defines this practice as one in which a range of media organized as a network each contributes something unique towards building an integrated narrative whole that transcends its individual parts.[8] In his opening video address at the transmedia workshop, Jenkins drew on this previously published work, saying it was significant that the Wachowskis had developed their creative strategy for *The Matrix* franchise on the way back from the Tokyo premiere of the film, where they had "been inspired by what they had seen of the media mix in Japan," as the example demonstrated a mechanism by which "transmedia in the United States is seeded by developments in the Japanese media system." This suggests a shift from the more linear franchise model that dominated Hollywood for much of the twentieth century, toward a more complex arrangement.

Continuing his address, Jenkins claimed this makes *The Animatrix* not only a key historical moment of "intersection between the media mix and transmedia" but also something of a "failed experiment" for Hollywood in that it differs from the dominant example of transmedia we see in America today, best embodied in the form of Disney's Marvel Cinematic Universe (MCU). Jenkins observed that Hollywood seemed to have "retreated from the systematic integration of story elements across all of the segments [of the mix] towards a mothership model with central franchise pieces driving everything else," which seems like a more comfortable and traditional hierarchical model of franchising. In his own address Steinberg agreed, calling these offshoots from the centralized mothership text "extensions" and stressing that "this 'brand extension' model of transmedia is the most common way it is used at present," further noting that this format is much closer to what the Japanese marketing agency Dentsu has "called cross-media marketing—a way to sell a single product by mobilizing multiple media to create a buzz." For Jenkins, "transmedia has been boxed in by the Hollywood studio system of the United States" and is no longer "central to the storytelling system," while in Japan there is usually a greater level of partnership between different media companies, in what has been called a production committee approach.[9]

This overview allows us to start cataloging the elements that make up transmedia and the media mix and to start exploring what distinguishes them from one another. One element is that Hollywood transmediality, as suggested by *The Matrix* example, is a very ordered and planned process. In the workshop, Steinberg claimed that while in Hollywood a transmedia policy is "often planned and formalized from the beginning," the media mix by contrast is "more organic and informal (at least at first)." Furthermore, he pointed out that more cultural entities get rolled into the media mix in Japan: "the sheer number of media mix developments in Japan is astounding. Everywhere you look in a bookstore, or in a media shop, something is tied into something else. Media mix 'tie-ins' or 'tie-ups' are ubiquitous." While we may think of the MCU as all encompassing, the media mix appears even more pervasive, fully and unavoidably penetrating the spaces of culture from top to bottom in Japan. In short, while Western media franchise history has a hierarchical sensibility to how it manages media texts and intellectual property, media mix theory emphasizes the horizontal movement of IP through an ongoing cultural dispersal within a more complex network.

As pointed out by Sugawa-Shimada in her presentation, the character also plays a greater role in the Japanese media mix, acting as a flexible stylistic device that functions differently in the realms of production, consumption, and adaptation. Meanwhile, as Jenkins observed in his opening address, transmedia tends to emphasize worlds and world building over individual characters, as attested to by Mark Wolf's impressive historical survey of transmedia worlds and what Tolkien famously called the "subcreation" of fictional worlds.[10] That said, a consideration of recent trends in the MCU toward TV tie-ins does suggest that corporations are beginning to emphasize the character's role much more. Jenkins elaborated on this point in his follow-up conversations with the authors, reflecting back on the workshop: "Consider the case of *Doctor Strange and the Multiverse of Madness*. The film builds directly on character conflicts that were initiated on *Wanda/Vision* for television. One of the parallel universes involved was introduced on *What If?* and our current understanding of the multiverse is shaped by what we learned in *Loki*." As Steinberg has pointed out previously, it is the character rather than story that is easier to claim ownership over under copyright law.[11] This is something that James McLean also drew attention to in the workshop by inquiring about the complexity of IP relations in the agreement between Marvel and Sony over Spiderman. In the context of that agreement, Marvel needs to hit a certain threshold of film releases to continue using the character before it defaults back to Sony. In this sense we can note that transmedia is not always smooth but can include some antagonistic elements including, but not limited to, battles over IP rights.

At this point, a useful comment from the audience noted how the media mix is a messy thing, with little specific regulation, but that it started to change after Ōtsuka began to theorize it, ushering in a new set of relations between fans and users. This is a reference to Ōtsuka Eiji's influential 1989 work *Monogatari shōhiron* (A theory of narrative consumption, 1989), which presented a significant early attempt for a practitioner to deeply theorize the implications of changes to the media landscape that was later to be termed the media mix.[12] Unlike theorists of the postmodern such as Hiroki Azuma, who saw fan consumption in the media mix negatively as a kind of atomized "grazing" over the surface of endless signifiers with nothing substantial behind them,[13] Ōtsuka still believed there was a coherent metanarrative (*sekai*, or worldview, a term he derived from Kabuki theatre) to be found behind individual works, and that fans (or *otaku*) acted like detectives attempting to access the greater whole through its parts.[14] As it was impossible to sell the grand system *in toto*, he deduced that it had to be broken up and sold in cross-sections, but that fans would then inevitably produce their own small narratives (like fan fictions) from the meta form. This ultimately threatened copyright holders because, as Ōtsuka speculated, it might lead to a "final stage of narrative consumption" in which "there will no longer be manufacturers. There will merely be countless consumers who make commodities with their own hands and consume them with their own hands."[15] Continuing this language of fan appropriation and embodiment, Sugawa-Shimada noted in her presentation how the idea of the medium inevitably includes the human body itself, and how it adapts to and interfaces with culture and technology. The fan's body thus becomes an important component in the media mix, a semiotic system that expresses itself through elements like tattoos or T-shirts or through the cultural practice of cosplay.[16] Such embodied practices of consumption are so often dismissed, although fan studies scholars such as Jenkins have done much to reclaim them as valuable.

Sugawa-Shimada uses the theory of 2.5D culture to frame this embodiment, which she defines as any "cultural practices which reproduce the fictional space of contemporary popular cultural products (such as manga, anime, and videogames) along with the fans' interplay between the real and fictional spaces."[17] In the context of the panel she emphasized how the interplay of fan practices, from toys, to cosplay, to consumables, are also contingent to the media mix. She noted how such meta-practices can act to draw together the fictional world of the transmedia text and the real world of fandom, a discussion she has continued in a recent issue of this journal.[18]

The Japanese and American industries seem to have a different relationship toward these newly active fandoms, and Luca Bruno observed how the system in Japan tends to highlight a more cooperative framework between production and fandom, compartmentalizing profits and losses, while the American model sees radical fan interactions as a more straightforward threat. This is not a universal rule, however, and seems to vary from company to company, with Nintendo, for instance, being perceived as a litigious company, similar to Disney, due to their tendency to close down fan adaptations.[19] The academic attitude to fans in both contexts also seems to differ, with Jenkins suggesting in his presentation that in Japan, otaku studies tends to be antagonistic to fans while Western fan studies appears to be more aligned to the interests and desires of fan communities, even sometimes growing out of them. For instance, in his book *Textual Poachers* (New York: Routledge, 1992) Jenkins coined the term "aca-fan" to name the kind of scholar that had one foot in the academy and the other one in the fan community they were studying.[20] In this context scholars tend to be more critical of producers and their attitudes towards fans. The attitudes of fans themselves toward the corporations that control their objects of fandom may also differ in the two geographic spheres. In the same conversation, Steinberg suggested how North American fans will often reject transmedia narratives if deemed unacceptable to their idea of canon, emphasizing further rigidity in Western transmedia culture. He concluded that in North America, fidelity to narrative and character is key.

Clearly there are nuanced differences between transmedia and the media mix at the levels of production and consumption, some of which are embedded in the cultural milieu of their context, but what makes the translation of one term to the other so difficult is that both seem to be in a permanent state of flux. Steinberg argued that with media mix we need to understand the cultural production contexts themselves and ask, "What is the model governing this particular media mix? Is it generalizable into a schema? And is this schema different from what we've seen before?" Steinberg emphasized the formality of Hollywood transmedia as opposed to the media mix, however he was keen to note that media mix is not any less systematic. In fact, he posited that the reason the media mix can be informal at the beginning is precisely because it is so formalized and systematized overall. He referred to the system of Japanese media, which begins as manga, novels, or games, thus establishing a common pattern of production. This he compared to the heavy capital investments of Hollywood where the spread must be preplanned, with the proviso that preplanned "doesn't necessarily lead to greater success."

Steinberg noted that in general terms the media mix is often seen as going further or being more "elastic" than its North American counterpart. While the latter "emphasizes unitary and continuous worlds" the former "doesn't require continuous stories, and it often embraces contradictions." Indeed, all this suggests to Steinberg that the media mix is more indicative of a "divergence culture" rather than Henry Jenkins's famous model of convergence culture, a term that, roughly, denotes a process by which multiple media forms (old and new) combine and coexist in complex hybrid platforms. Such a distinction demonstrates how the panel conceptualized Hollywood transmedia and Japan's media mix not only through their different production frameworks, but also emphasized the impact of the specific cultural foundations to the spread of media. Transmedia must be considered through a cultural lens, and it is through that lens that the scholar must ultimately acknowledge the deep complexity of the field. We explore the implications of this in the next section.

Key Theme 2: Understanding Transmedia Culture

While the above observations provide a useful foundation to build from, they in no way exhaust or completely pin down these concepts as they continue to evolve and are put to a variety of uses in actual production contexts. Consequently, the panel discussed the nature of franchises, scale of operations, and the importance of geography to transmedia. As Steinberg was keen to emphasize, the genealogy of the media mix and its ongoing mobility is built on a distinct history that requires its own understanding, as well as the discourses and histories that bind them. Through this cultural awareness, the exploration of transmedia extended beyond production cultures and into its entrenchment in culture itself. Continuing the theme of divergence, Steinberg noted the ubiquity in the geography of Japan's media compared to North America, where there are comparatively fewer bookstores and fairs. Steinberg's ongoing work focuses on the importance of Japanese convenience stores that spread media at local levels, providing pathways into the media mix. As he summarized it during the workshop:

> From bookstores to train "chirashi" ads, to convenience stores, and large public billboards, to the magazines in which many of these media mixes are first serialized as manga, ads are everywhere. And so "entryways" to the media mix are also everywhere. As a result, the media mix (or ads for it) infiltrates daily life in a way that is quantitatively and qualitatively incomparable to what goes on in North America.

The importance of locality and access to the media mix is supported by Sugawa-Shimada, who argues that Japan has seen a flourishing of anime tourism that has reenergized local communities. This continued her discussion of embodied fandom and 2.5D culture as an essential cultural ingredient to the media mix. It is the media mix's pervasiveness within Japanese culture that ensures these practices are transfused through the daily life of audiences from childhood. She also explored the gendered aspect of the mix, considering how boys and girls are inculcated into different genres of manga and anime in Japan, and how anime in turn acts as advertising for wider products like toys that are also gendered. Additionally, Bruno brings up the notion of *moé*, which describes the extreme affective attachment (usually male) otaku can develop with (often female) characters, which suggests a gendered power relation based on the objectification and atomization of female forms, as critiqued by Azuma.[21]

Fan practices are key to the spread and impact of a media mix, but the nature of this relationship on the production context needs further theorization, as Bowman argued in the workshop, there is a feedback loop between fan engagement and the production of texts that ultimately forces the theories we produce to be more dynamic, shifting with the object of analysis meaning that "these models change in recursive and iterative ways." This raises other important questions about where, precisely, fans have the most material impact on the mix, in terms of how they consume, spread, and engage with the media. Additionally, what is the result of their impact on media production and media franchises, and can these impacts be read in the very texts made in response to these interactions? The iterative relationship of fan interaction within transmedia is further explored by Bowman and McLean elsewhere.[22] These were all questions that well suited the conference's idea of the ludo mix and the manner in which game studies theorizes games as recursive, interactive systems. In short, there is much that transmedia studies can learn from game studies and its long-standing interest in interaction and immersion. For instance, see Joleen Blom's article on the free-to-play gaming model in the *Genshin Impact* media mix in this volume of *Mechademia*.

Speaking on franchises, the synergetic engagement Japan's media franchises have in Japan's local community led Steinberg to argue that it is important to "put the McDonalds and the 7-Eleven back into studies of media mix and franchising." He noted the standpoint differs from the conceptualization of media franchises by franchise scholar Derek Johnson that drew a sharp distinction between franchised retail (a license fee to conduct business under a shared corporate trademark) and of media franchise "the multiplied replication of culture from intellectual property resources." [23] While the study of merchandising has been a central component to studies such as Janet Wasko's famous research on Disney, it has had a lesser role in transmedia studies.[24] Still, Steinberg argued that franchise retail and media content synergize and that our knowledge of these can be enhanced through an understanding of the media mix.

Sugawa-Shimada then shifted the audience's attention to Japanese anime production committees (collaborations between studios operating in different media), which are quite temporary and when a series loses popularity, they become hard to approach. She suggested that in the context of Japanese production committees, there is no singular framework, and they can be quite complicated. Big companies are more powerful and have control of the market, and in other cases, anime companies can have smaller scale agreements with sponsors. She argued for a case-by-case study, and Steinberg reflected that neglected or entrenched industry artifacts such as legal documentation (contracts or shareholder releases, records of court proceedings, or what John Caldwell conceptualizes as industry embedded "deep texts"[25]) could serve as useful sources of information but presented what Steinberg described as a kind of "final frontier for media studies." Expanding this thought, Bowman noted that although the deep texts that drive such studies may be difficult to access (though court records and the earnings calls of publicly traded companies are usually accessible in some form), perhaps a more fundamental issue is that such approaches are less attractive to scholars than more popular formats such as textual analysis or ethnographic inquiries that dominate the field. However, fandoms were noted to be a key part in the media mix, and Sugawa-Shimada has since argued that their impact should be ignored by producers (and, we would argue, academics) at their own peril.[26] These debates on how the deep texts of the media mix can be traced and accessed raises important methodological questions for researchers as to how we can better understand and engage with the complexities of transmedia in a meaningful way, which leads us into our third theme.

Key Theme 3: Research, Methodology and Mutation

A question from the floor on methodology queried how we go about disaggregating these terms in the kinds of practical ways that will help us to conduct research. Hartzheim responded that we must do so carefully, since the terms have overlapping definitions with multiple assumptions. Sugawa-Shimada also noted that the "mix" is not the only concern for research, and that considering what the term "media" means to different cultures can also be crucial, for instance noting that in Japan it carries more connotations of news and journalism than entertainment. Steinberg asked whether there is an argument that we should move from thinking about media to platforms, since this is what a lot of industries are now talking about. However, he warned that platforms are different from the media that is built upon them, so this isn't a simple substitution. The authors consider the role of platforms theoretically in their introduction to the *Loading . . .* special issue.[27] He also argued that we must pay attention to how and where discourses happen, as well the histories behind any prescribed concept. This is how, for Steinberg, media mix can be like transmedia in principle, but still possesses a distinct cultural history that demands its own treatment. Steinberg suggested that with a more robust definition and understanding of transmedia we can look for different historical precedents (although a too robust definition alternatively risks imposing our own precedents *a priori*). He argued that we need to gather and timestamp definitions and approaches as part of a larger project to chart the history of a theory.

Jenkins's video address presented an interest in a more comparative approach to transmedia broadened out beyond the dominant dyad of Japan and the United States to look at structures in other nations such as India and South Korea, for example, that can help further develop our understanding of these processes, in each case looking for what "is particular for each national location" in the mobilization of media across the network and what different forms fandom takes. Hartzheim addresses the absence of an industry point of view on transmedia theories in his latest edited collection and has since acknowledged (in a follow up email) that the limitations in the book were due to the case studies being America-centric.[28] At the transmedia workshop, Hartzheim developed this point by arguing that the academic publishing culture tends to have East Asian scholars being published in East Asian Studies journals and Western scholars in generalist film or cultural studies journals, which leads to an unfortunate siloing of theories.

A methodological issue felt throughout the panel was a consideration of the appropriateness of the methods used by academics to access the complex landscape of transmediality in North America and the media mix in Japan. Particularly pertinent to this is the level of access Anglophone scholars have over the Japanese cultural context. There is not only the issue of access to crucial scholarly writings and industrial deep texts, few of which are translated, but also the level of access we might have to a notoriously secretive industry. Industrial info (such as Caldwell's industry-embedded deep texts) has been accessed with varying degrees of success in the Hollywood context, since here there is at least an ability to access a trade press in the form of publications like *Variety*. However, Hartzheim argued that Japanese corporations seem to be far more secretive and controlling of these insider discourses. Scholars who do not speak Japanese therefore face a double block when it comes to researching the media mix: the linguistic barrier and the barrier of industrial control over industrial and financial data.

Steinberg also noted that we tend to focus on the big examples, but there may be some benefit in exploring the activities of smaller companies, which are often forced to innovate in order to compete. For instance, Bruno's workshop presentation on the neglected medium of visual novel games reveals a specific and vital sector of pop cultural production that compresses physical venues and virtual spaces in intriguing ways. Such a genre needs to be analyzed precisely because it differs so much from the cultural powerhouses like Studio Ghibli and can therefore offer us a new perspective. There are, however, some industrial approaches to Ghibli such as Rayna Denison's recent book.[29] Overall, the panel advocated a need for balanced, granular research into production cultures, the commercial growth of transmedia franchises, the understanding of the sites and conditions of distribution, and the practices and spread of intellectual property through fandoms.

Back to the Future: Thinking about the Workshop from 2023

In 2019, Henry Jenkins asked the panel: "To what degree has Japan followed the Hollywood model?" However, in 2023 (when this workshop report was written) it is also useful to flip this question and ask whether the Hollywood model, also uniquely threatened during the pandemic, is further pursuing the more flexible and divergent Japanese model of the media mix. After all, the above discussion has demonstrated the danger of holding Hollywood transmedia as the stable norm against which other systems of understanding media (like the media mix) are seen to be mere exceptions or, to borrow the terminology of transmedia, are seen to themselves be a kind of extension to the "American mothership" model. If the Japanese model of the media mix suggests a kind of extreme openness that the more traditionally hierarchical Hollywood system might find threatening, then it almost certainly presents a challenge to Western scholarly notions of transmedia as well. Ignoring the influence of the media mix on global culture (because there is much to suggest that the model is now influencing not simply Western media but, perhaps more crucially, the media of other Asian countries such as the recent Korean cultural wave) locks us into a theoretical cul-de-sac of parochial Western-centric notions of media ecology that do not do justice to the phenomenal changes that have been wrought in the last few years. This all moves us toward something closer to a cultural studies approach, or perhaps a kind of material led study of cultural and historical artifacts reminiscent of Michel Foucault's approach to discourses as they unfold in specific moments that leave traces in a myriad of cultural fragments.[30] With the need to consider the historical specificity of these terms in mind, we asked the panelists to provide a short update on their consideration of these topics to see if they had changed in recent years.

In 2022, Bowman and McLean sent follow-up emails to all the former workshop participants asking them to reflect on whether their previous position had changed. In each case we used a personalized question that related to their previous contribution. In her reply, Sugawa-Shimada reflected on her conceptualization of 2.5D fandom, which "depends on fans' deep commitment to the cultural content through [their] imagination and their interaction [with] other fans in their communities." She wrote that although the workshop addressed "regional specificities" in her ongoing work, she "wanted to try to shift a focus of discussions a little bit about how such types of multiuse of the content can function transnationally." With that in mind, she commented that "'embodied culture' has changed drastically due to . . . several global media platforms [emerging] after the COVID-19 pandemic." She noted that in Japan, users can access a wide array of media through cloud data services, such as DMM.com and eplus.jp. Within such technological paradigms, she notes the issue of "the language barrier has seemingly been solved thanks to online translation."

Even Tokyo's Akihabara, the ground zero of otaku fandom, saw its manga and video game stores close during the pandemic. This led Bruno, writing in his follow up email, to comment on how niche Japanese fan consumption had suffered with "the lack of a physical infrastructure . . . affecting the doujin scene, especially older content creators [where] adaptation has proven more difficult." Such changes have not been restricted to Japan, as the American context has changed drastically due to the pandemic. Jenkins noted a distinct shift in Marvel's adaptation strategy, which has turned "decisively in a transmedia direction." He elaborated:

[Previously] it definitely represented radical intertextuality between an ever-expanding number of film texts but it was primarily world-building within a single medium, hence the phrase cinematic universe . . . [and] there was little conscious integration between the comics and the films. . . . But with Disney's consolidation with 20th Century Fox unifying all of the Marvel characters under one owner and with the launch of Disney Plus as a streaming network, new possibilities have emerged and much fuller integration of film and television is taking place.

This suggests that the media mix model, which feeds so strongly into Jenkins' notion of transmediality, continues to exert an influence within Western media industries. The shift to digital platforms, accelerated by the pandemic, only serves to intensify these trends. "This is not the mothership model because there is no primary text," argues Jenkins, "only a series of interlocking media elements, some on film and some on television, which add to our overall understanding of the Marvel universe. This is much closer to the kind of equality among media that had been advocated by more independent media producers." Steinberg agreed, noting the example of Amazon Prime Video and how it "shows how an e-commerce giant and logistics company could deem streaming video to be a crucial commercial venture." He concluded: "While some of the specifics of the media mix paradigm change over time, I've lately found it to be increasingly helpful to explain how media works—not only in Japan, but elsewhere in the world too."

Despite this cultural slippage between America and Japan, Hartzheim argued that a growing sophistication in media and communication studies programs has developed an increased attention to media industries in Australia and Europe (in particular, the UK). However, this shift away from the parochial focus on Hollywood does not address the imbalance between English language media and non-Western media, which has been detrimentally impacted with a reduction in area studies more broadly. Hartzheim argued that there is a need for more comparative approaches to cross-fertilize perspectives and suggested the anthropological applications of critical media studies to Japanese texts, which tends to only be pursued by Western scholars such as Ian Condry[31] in anime and Mia Consalvo[32] in games.

Hartzheim also reflected on how his standpoint has changed since the workshop, writing: "I initially lamented this lack of 'industry' perspective covering the anime and manga industries," but "was quite mistaken in assuming there was no industry coverage." Hartzheim observed how industry coverage is actually mixed into consumer-orientated publications like *Animage* or *Newtype*. This practice makes sense with anime because the "line between consumers and producers has historically been blurred." He added that there is a growing online presence of industry-focused sites in Japanese and English that are "geared towards specific interests that blow the daily industry rags out of the water."

Hartzheim concluded that we need to understand the historical importance of anime texts and franchises compared to how they have been mythologized anecdotally or reported on by mass media outlets. "There is just so much of the past of the media mix that is still very much in its infancy in terms of being collated and analyzed in detail. My feeling is that our understanding of the history of certain anime will be very, very different in ten years' time once a lot more of this archival treasure trove is catalogued."

In this report on the workshop and its aftermaths, one of the important takeaways we see is that regardless of whether we are studying transmedia or the media mix, our approach should be more trans- or multidisciplinary. Fan studies and production studies, for instance, have important insights and can be pulled into transmedia studies more fully as a cultural (and sometimes transcultural) phenomenon. Just as Caldwell's work expands on the study of media artifacts to include industrial deep texts and rituals, fan studies famously sought to extend the text within the wider context of fan texts and practices, and self-theorizing. For a topical example of research in cultural rituals and self-theorizing in fan culture within transmedia networks, see James McLean's recent article in *Loading . . . .*[33] We would also be remiss in not acknowledging Matt Hills's work *Fan Cultures*.[34]

Our conclusion is that transmedia research should look to acknowledge production studies, fan studies and even, as argued above, game studies, as valuable synergetic additions to the domain of transmedia studies. However, the approach needs to be nuanced, as too much of a focus on fan cultures or production cultures could obscure the other, and therefore a balance is needed. The above workshop occurred at a crucial juncture in transmedia and media mix scholarship: a moment when the merger of media mix studies and game studies was being advocated for; a moment of both new scholarship on the media mix and a chance to reflect back on earlier scholarship; and a moment before the onset of the pandemic and changes in media circulation and consumption that accompanied it. Now we both look back and look forward, to new horizons of media mix and transmedia research with the lessons of the workshop in mind.

Dr. Dean Bowman is Associate Lecturer for Games Art and Design at Norwich University of the Arts and a scholar specializing in the fields of narratology, cultural studies, production studies, and game studies. He has a PhD from the University of East Anglia in which he analyzed innovative storytelling techniques in the indie games sector and has book chapters in *Rerolling Board Games* by McFarland Press, *Crank It Up! Jason Statham: Star* by Manchester University Press and *Gender in James Bond* by Emerald Press. He most recently co-authored with Dr. James McLean a special Issue of *Loading . . . The Canadian Game Studies Journal* on transmedia storytelling In the Kingdom Hearts Franchise. He has recently become obsessed with detective fiction, especially Agatha Christie and Sheishi Yokomizo, and is planning to write on the mechanics of detection in videogames.

Dr. James McLean is a lecturer and Programme Director for Media Production at Hull University. His research continues to explore the relationships forged from creative, industrial, and commercial media practices through the lens of transmedia franchises, adaptation, and fandoms. His PhD dissertation explored the uses, values, and meanings of genre within British factual television. James spent over a decade in the British media industry as a designer and storyboard artist, working on transmedia projects for franchises such as *Doctor Who, Star Wars,* and *High School Musical.* Recently James co-authored a special edition of the Games Studies journal *Loading . . .* with Dr. Dean Bowman on transmedia and the *Kingdom Hearts* franchise. His current research project explores storytelling as a form of advocacy for those with learning disabilities.

Notes

1. James McLean and Dean Bowman, "Charting the Kingdoms Between: Building Transmedia Universes and Transnational Audiences in the Kingdom Hearts Franchise," in *Loading . . .* 15, no. 25 (2022): 1–14, https://journals.sfu.ca/loading/index.php/loading/issue/view/31 (accessed September 22, 2022).
2. Sugawa-Shimada Akiko, "Emerging '2.5-Dimensional' Culture: Character-Oriented Cultural Practices and 'Community of Preferences' as a New Fandom in Japan and Beyond," *Mechademia* 12, no. 2 (2020): 124–39.
3. Henry Jenkins, Sam Ford, and Joshua Green, *Spreadable Media: Creating Value and Meaning in a Networked Culture* (New York: New York University Press, 2013).
4. McLean and Bowman, "Charting the Kingdoms Between."

5. Virginia Braun and Victoria Clarke, "Using Thematic Analysis in Psychology," *Qualitative Research in Psychology* 3, no. 2 (2006): 77–101.

6. John Thornton Caldwell, *Production Culture: Industrial Reflexivity and Critical Practice in Film and Television* (Durham: Duke University Press, 2008).

7. Henry Jenkins, *Convergence Culture: Where Old and New Media Collide*, 2nd ed. (New York: New York University Press, 2008).

8. Henry Jenkins, "Game Design as Narrative Architecture," in *First Person: New Media as Story, Performance and Game*, ed. Noah Wardrip-Fruin and Pat Harrigan (Cambridge, MA: MIT Press, 2004), 118–30.

9. Bryan Hikari Hartzheim, "Pretty Cure and the Magical Girl Media Mix," *Journal of Popular Culture* 49 no. 5 (2016): 1068.

10. Mark J. P. Wolf, *Building Imaginary Worlds: The Theory and History of Subcreation* (New York: Routledge, 2012).

11. Marc Steinberg, *Anime's Media Mix: Franchising Toys and Characters in Japan* (Minneapolis: University of Minnesota Press, 2012), 40.

12. Ōtsuka Eiji, "World and Variation: The Reproduction and Consumption of Narrative," trans. Marc Steinberg, *Mechademia* 5 (2010): 99–116.

13. Azuma Hiroki, *Otaku: Japan's Database Animals*, trans. Jonathan E. Abel and Kono Shion (Minneapolis: University of Minnesota Press, 2009).

14. Ōtsuka, "World and Variation," 108.

15. Ōtsuka, "World and Variation," 111.

16. Theresa M. Winge, *Costuming Cosplay: Dressing the Imagination* (London: Bloomsbury Visual Arts, 2019).

17. Sugawa-Shimada, "Emerging '2.5-Dimensional' Culture," 125.

18. Akiko Sugawa-Shimada and Sandra Annett, "Introduction," *Mechademia* 15, no. 2 (2023): 1–7. https://muse.jhu.edu/article/883162 (accessed April 4, 2023).

19. Jose Otero, "Nintendo Shuts Down Metroid 2 Fan Remake AM2R," *IGN*, August 8, 2016, https://www.ign.com/articles/2016/08/08/nintendo-shuts-down-metroid-2-fan-remake-am2r (accessed September 22, 2022).

20. Henry Jenkins, *Textual Poachers* (New York: Routledge, 1992).

21. Azuma, *Otaku*, 47–48.

22. McLean and Bowman, "Charting the Kingdoms Between."

23. Derek Johnson, *Media Franchising: Creative License and Collaboration in the Culture Industries* (New York: New York University Press, 2013), 6.

24. Janet Wasko, *Understanding Disney: The Manufacture of Fantasy* (Cambridge: Polity Press, 2001).

25. Caldwell, *Production Culture*, 26–27.

26. Sugawa-Shimada, "Emerging '2.5-Dimensional' Culture."

27. McLean and Bowman, "Charting the Kingdoms Between."

28. James Fleury, Bryan Hikari Hartzheim, Stephen Mamber, eds., *The Franchise Era: Managing Media in the Digital Economy*, Traditions in American Cinema Series (Edinburgh: Edinburgh University Press, 2019).

29. Rayna Denison, *Studio Ghibli: An Industrial History* (New York: Palgrave MacMillan, 2023)

30. Michel Foucault, "Nietzsche, Geneology, History," in *The Foucault Reader: An Introduction to Foucault's Thought,* ed. Paul Rabinow (London: Penguin Books, 1991), 76–100.

31. Ian Condry, *The Soul of Anime: Collaborative Creativity and Japan's Media Success Story* (Durham: Duke University Press, 2013).

32. Mia Consalvo, *Atari to Zelda: Japan's Videogames in Global Contexts* (Cambridge, MA: MIT Press, 2016).

33. James McLean, "Kingdom(s) Come: Character Remediations and Polyperspectivity of the Final Fantasy Franchise in Kingdom Hearts and Kingdom Hearts II," *Loading . . .* 15, no. 25 (2022): 58–75.

34. Matt Hills, *Fan Cultures* (London: Routledge, 2002).

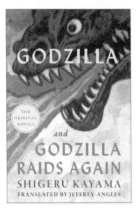

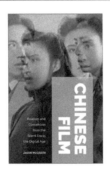